THE RECOLLECTIONS OF
ALEXIS DE TOCQUEVILLE

THE
RECOLLECTIONS OF
ALEXIS DE TOCQUEVILLE

Translated by Alexander Teixeira de Mattos
Edited by J. P. Mayer

Meridian Books
THE WORLD PUBLISHING COMPANY
CLEVELAND AND NEW YORK

To Jean de Tocqueville with profound gratitude.
Paris, 1939--London, 1947
The Editor

A MERIDIAN BOOK

Published by The World Publishing Company
2231 West 110th Street, Cleveland 2, Ohio
First Meridian printing October 1959.
Third printing January 1965.
Preface by J. P. Mayer copyright © 1959 by
The World Publishing Company.
Reprinted by arrangement with Columbia University Press
Library of Congress Catalog Card Number: 59-12916
Printed in the United States of America.   3WP165

CONTENTS

CONTENTS

PART THREE

CONTENTS

APPENDICES

BIBLIOGRAPHY

Apart from the books mentioned in the text and in the Introduction, the following studies may be of use to the reader.

Actes du congrès historique du centenaire de la révolution de 1848 (Paris, 1948).

Arnaud, René, *La Deuxième république et le second empire* (Paris, 1929).

Bastid, Paul, *Doctrines et institutions politiques de la seconde république* (Paris, 1945).

Bastid, Paul, *Les Institutions politiques de la monarchie parlementaire française: 1814-1848* (Paris, 1954).

Bastid, Paul, *Le Gouvernement d'Assemblée* (Paris, 1956).

Bernstein, S., "Marx in Paris: 1848," *Science and Society* (New York, 1939).

Bertaut, Jules, *1848 et la seconde république* (Paris, 1937).

Burckhardt, Carl J., *Bildnisse* (Frankfurt, 1958).

Burckhardt, Jacob, *Historische Fragmente* (Stuttgart, 1957).

Cassou, Jean, *Quarante-Huit* (Paris, 1939).

Curtis, E. Newtown, *The French Assembly of 1848 and American Constitutional Doctrines* (New York, 1918).

Dautry, Jean, *Histoire de la révolution de 1848 en France* (Paris, 1948).

Deslandres, Maurice, *Histoire constitutionnelle de la France de 1789 à 1870,* Vol. II (Paris, 1932).

Droz, Jacques, *Les Révolutions allemandes de 1848* (Paris, 1957).

Franz, E. G., *Das Amerikabild der deutschen Revolution von 1848-49* (Heidelberg, 1958).

Gargan, E. T., *Alexis de Tocqueville: The Critical Years 1848-1851* (Washington, 1955).

Genet, L.-Vidalenc J., *L'Epoque Contemporaine I: Restaurations et révolutions (1815-1871)* (Paris, 1953).

Lucas-Dubreton, J., *Louis Philippe* (Paris, 1938).

Mayer, J. P., *Prophet of the Mass Age: A Study of Alexis de Tocqueville* (New York, 1940).

Mayer, J. P., *Political Thought in France: From Sieyès to Sorel* (London, 1943).

McKay, Donald Cope, *The National Workshops: A Study in the French Revolution of 1848* (Cambridge [Mass.], 1933).

Namier, L. B., *1848: The Revolution of the Intellectuals* (London, 1944).

Pierson, G. W., *Tocqueville and Beaumont in America* (New York, 1938).

Pouthas, Charles-H., *Démocraties et capitalisme (1848-1860)* (Paris, 1941).

Quentin-Bauchart, Pierre, *La Crise sociale de 1848, les origines de la révolution du février* (Paris, 1920).

Robertson, Priscilla, *Revolutions of 1848* (Princeton, 1952).

Sée, Henri, *Evolution et révolutions* (Paris, 1929).

Stadler, P., *Geschichtsschreibung und historisches Denken in Frankreich: 1789-1871* (Zurich, 1958).

Stern, Alfred, *Geschichte Europas von 1848 bis 1871*, Vols. VI and VII (Stuttgart, 1911 and 1916).

Tocqueville, Alexis de, *Democracy in America* (New York, 1945).

Tocqueville, Alexis de, *The Old Régime and French Revolution* (New York, 1955).

Valentin, V., *Geschichte der deutschen Revolution: 1848-1849* (Berlin, 1930).

Woodward, E. L., *French Revolutions* (Oxford, 1934).

No other book on the 1848 period of European history has withstood the test of time as well as Tocqueville's *Recollections*. In this classic Tocqueville has synthesized a historical and sociological approach with a definitive normative view, and it is this synthesis that gives these pages their unique power and contemporary significance. It is only fitting that this new edition should appear during the centenary year of the great sociologist's death.

I have taken the opportunity to correct a few misprints and to add to the bibliography, which may help the reader to find his way through the many problems that *The Recollections* raise. The new entries in the bibliography indicate the scope and quality of the research undertaken since the previous edition was published ten years ago.

In the meantime my own work as editor of the French edition of Tocqueville's collected writings has progressed: eight volumes of the *Oeuvres Complètes* have now been published. Of these, two volumes, particularly the first volume of the English correspondence and the correspondence with Arthur de Gobineau, throw new light on the 1848 period. I have, however, seen no reason to change anything in my Introduction to the present work. It, too, seems to have withstood the test of the years.

J. P. MAYER

London, May 1959

INTRODUCTION

It is exactly fifty years since Alexis de Tocqueville's *Souvenirs* were published in English. For many years the book was almost unobtainable even on the second-hand book-market. Tocqueville's other works were more easily accessible. His *Democracy in America* was reprinted several times in the U.S.A., his *Ancien Régime and the Revolution* was also edited repeatedly.

Yet it appears that the slowly growing interest in Tocqueville's political and social philosophy, which has been discernible during the last ten years, would justify this new English edition of the *Souvenirs*, for this work is not less significant for an appreciation of Tocqueville's thought.

The *Souvenirs* were first published in France in 1893. An English translation appeared three years later. The translator was Alexander Teixeira de Mattos. His translation forms the basic text of the present edition, but his text has been carefully compared with the French edition and numerous alterations were thought necessary. Tocqueville—like Montesquieu—writes in a lawyer's style : sharp, concise and without ambiguity. Some of Tocqueville's sociological concepts must be seen in the light of his other works. From here they gain their systematic place in a great sociologist's view of the world. Perhaps we know more to-day about Tocqueville's significance as sociologist than de Mattos (and others) could have known fifty years ago. The mass age which the author of *Democracy in America* prophesied is to-day a full social reality.

But there is another reason for editing the *Souvenirs* again. M. Luc Monnier has edited a new French edition in Paris, published by Messrs. Gallimard in 1942. This edition gives a considerable number of new and important additions to the text of 1893. Unfortunately M.

Monnier has not clearly indicated which texts are new
ones. Consequently, we have compared the texts of 1893
and 1942 and marked all additions [   ] in order to enable the student to form an appreciation of the importance and meaning of the addenda. The first French
editor, Alexis de Tocqueville's grand-nephew, the Comte
de Tocqueville, had omitted these texts in his edition of
1893, following his great-uncle's testamentary instructions. In addition to M. Monnier's text, which will have
to be incorporated into the new French edition of
Tocqueville's *Oeuvres Complètes*, which is in preparation
under my direction, I have added an English translation
of Alexis de Tocqueville's last great speech as Minister of
Foreign Affairs in October 1849. Thus I thought I might
compensate the reader to some extent for the lack of an
account of the " Roman Question " which is unfortunately so marked in the *Souvenirs*. So much for our text.

Tocqueville's *Recollections* should not be regarded
as a work on the history of the 1848 Revolution. He
deliberately writes political *Mémoires*, nothing else.
Simpson's severe judgment in *Louis Napoleon and the Recovery of France* (p. 387) is wholly beside the point. The
first three paragraphs of the *Souvenirs* make Tocqueville's
autobiographical intention quite plain. In another passage (p. 86 sq.) he compares his own intention with
regard to the writing of his *Recollections* with Cardinal de
Retz's Memoirs. Evidently Tocqueville's *Souvenirs* apply
to politics or political affairs what Pascal's *Pensées* or
Montaigne's *Essais* had previously achieved in the realm
of philosophy. Tocqueville writes in their tradition.

The reader of the *Recollections* would do well, before
he begins their study, to familiarise himself with a
reliable history of the French Revolution of 1848. He
might, for instance, profitably read Seignobos' *La
Révolution de 1848—Le Second Empire* (1848–1859), published as the sixth volume of Lavisse's *Histoire de France*

contemporaine ; or if he chooses to look more to the Right, he might consult Pierre de la Gorce's *Histoire de la Seconde République* and the same author's *Histoire du Second Empire*. These works (and many others) provide us with the historical background of the *Souvenirs*.

Tocqueville writes as a sociologist or political scientist. He observes events, ideas or men, he observes himself, his own actions and attempts to analyse them in the perspective of French and European politics. He does not act like most of our contemporary politicians in the vacuum of the day. He knows that to-day is the result of very many yesterdays, and that past and present make the future. Tocqueville's power of historical and sociological analysis is unsurpassed. His prediction of the 1848 Revolution, a few weeks before its beginning, is too well-known to be quoted here. There are other equally perennial passages.

Perhaps I should illustrate only how Tocqueville viewed the *one* revolutionary process which began in 1789 and which to this very hour—we are writing in 1946—is still not complete :

" It does not come within the scope of these Recollections that I should seek for the causes which gave a socialistic character to the Revolution of February, and I will content myself with saying that the discovery of this new facet of the French Revolution was not of a nature to cause such great surprise as it did. Had it not long been perceived that the people had continually been improving and raising its condition, that its importance, its education, its desires, its power had been constantly increasing ? Its prosperity had also grown greater, but less rapidly, and was approaching the limit which it hardly ever passes in old societies, where there are many men and but few places. How should the poor and humble and yet powerful classes not have dreamt of issuing from their poverty and inferiority by means of their power, especially in an epoch when our view into another world has become dimmer, and the miseries of this world become more visible and seem more intolerable ? They had been working to this end for the last sixty years. . . . This natural restlessness in the minds of the people, this inevitable perturbation of its thoughts and its desires, these needs, these instincts of the crowd formed in a certain sense the fabric upon which the political innovators embroidered so many monstrous and grotesque figures. Their work may be regarded as ludicrous, but the material on which they worked is the most serious that it is possible for philosophers and statesmen to contemplate.

" Will Socialism remain buried in the disdain with which the Socialists of 1848 are so justly covered ? I put the question without making any reply. I do not doubt that the laws concerning the constitution of our modern society will in the long run undergo modification : they have already done so in many of their principal parts. But will they ever be destroyed and replaced by others ? It seems to me impracticable. I say no more, because— the more I study the former condition of the world and see the world of our own day in greater detail, the more I consider the prodigious variety to be met not only in laws, but in the principles of law, and the different forms even now taken and retained, whatever one may say, by the rights of property on this earth—the more I am tempted to believe that what we call necessary institutions are often no more than institutions to which we have grown accustomed, and that in matters of social constitution the field of possibilities is much more extensive than men living in their various societies are ready to imagine. . . ." (p. 80.)

There are probably not many passages in Tocqueville's work where he comes nearer to Karl Marx's teachings. Yet in my opinion the *Souvenirs* are infinitely superior to Marx's *Eighteenth Brumaire* or even more so to the *Class Struggles in France*. Marx wrote with the understandable impatience of the social revolutionary, whereas Tocqueville writes, favoured by his aristocratic, conservative instincts, with a fairer appreciation of the inherent brakes within his contemporary society. All the same, both thinkers have stated the fundamental problem which our generation and the next will have to solve.

Both Marx and Tocqueville regarded the Revolution of 1848 as a phase in *one* revolutionary process, but while Marx abused and ridiculed the revolutionaries of 1848 for having failed to establish a socialist society, Tocqueville did not measure his own time with norms which were not its own. Not that he did not see those *new* norms towards which French (and indeed European) society was moving, but he did not think that they could be realised then.

Tocqueville's understanding of the structure of the historic process was perhaps subtler than that of Marx :

" For my part," we read in the *Recollections* (p. 64), " I detest these absolutist systems which represent all the events of history as depending upon great first causes linked by the chain of fatality, and which, as it were, suppress men from the history of the human race . . . . Antecedent facts, the nature of institutions, the cast of minds and the state of morals are the materials of which are composed those impromptus which astonish and alarm us." Tocqueville was a realistic sociologist, Marx in comparison with him an Utopian. Yet there can be no doubt that the Utopian of 1848 exerted a greater influence on later generations than the uncomfortable loneliness of the great Frenchman.

Tocqueville stood for the maintenance of what he

thought to be the structure of the French society of his time. His traditions, his training as a lawyer and judge, in short his political philosophy which he had formulated in the three volumes of the *Democracy in America* had led him to these conclusions :

" I did not believe then, any more than I do now, that the republican form of government is the best suited to the needs of France. What I mean when I say the republican form of government, is the elective Executive power. With a people among whom habit, tradition, custom have assured so great a place to the Executive Power, its instability will always be, in periods of excitement, a cause of revolution, and in peaceful times, a cause of great uneasiness. Moreover, I have always considered the Republic an ill-balanced form of government, which always promised more, but gave less liberty than the Constitutional Monarchy. And yet I sincerely wished to maintain the Republic ; and although there were, so to speak, no Republicans in France, I did not look upon the maintenance of it as absolutely impossible." (*Recollections*, p. 223.)

With such convictions he accepted the high office of Minister of Foreign Affairs. His directives and policies are clearly indicated in the remarkable new addition to the old text of the *Recollections* (p. 269 sqq.) to which there is probably no parallel in French political literature since Richelieu's *Testament politique*. Nor should we forget to draw particular attention to Appendix 5, Tocqueville's speech on the Roman Question, which, according to his Chef du Cabinet, Arthur de Gobineau, is " incontestablement le meilleur (discours), le plus ferme et le plus net qu'il ait encore prononcé". (Cf. R. Pierre Marcel, *Essai politique sur Alexis de Tocqueville*, Paris 1910, p. 426.) We have taken this speech from the *Moniteur* of October 18th, 1849.

Tocqueville's account of the deliberations of the Committee on the Constitution of which he was a member is of special interest to the student of politics. (Again his account is not that of the historian. Cf. H. Michel, *Note sur la Constitution de* 1848 in *La Révolution de* 1848, vol. 1, pp. 41–56.) For here we see Tocqueville's political sociology at work. He formulates the laws of the historic state structure of France with brilliant clarity : " In France there is only one thing which we can't set up : that is, a free government ; and only one institution we can't destroy : that is, centralisation." (p. 189.) In these sentences the fundamental tenets of his *Ancien Régime and the Revolution* are proclaimed.

He relates with distress his and his friends' defeat on the question, whether the Second Republic ought to have a dual Chamber-System or not. Tocqueville was in favour of the dual system, though " public opinion had pronounced strongly in favour of a single Chamber, not only in Paris but in nearly every department". (p. 193.) Perhaps it is comforting to know that public opinion in France almost a hundred years later was less stubborn. The Constitution of the Fourth Republic will probably have the dual Chamber-System for which Tocqueville struggled in vain.

He is also not in doubt about the danger of having the President of the Republic elected directly by the people : " . . . we had retained the spirit of the Monarchy, while losing the taste for it. Under these conditions, what could a President elected by the people be other than a pretender to the Crown ? " Louis Napoleon's plebiscitary dictatorship was the answer to Tocqueville's question.

In summing up the work of the Committee on the Constitution, Tocqueville believes that " the only part of our work which was at all well thought out . . . , was that which related to justice". The Committee maintained the irremovability of the judges. Here, the example of the British Constitution manifests itself and it is not without satisfaction that Tocqueville writes :

" What we did in these matters is far in advance of all that had been attempted in the same direction for sixty years. It is probably the only part of the Constitution of 1848 which will survive." (*Recollections*, p. 202.)

Again Tocqueville thinks in the perspective of the *one* revolution of which the '48 period was only a phase.

His judgments on his contemporaries are not always just. He is severe, if not unfair, to Louis Blanc and Blanqui. Perhaps he has himself given us an explanation of this part of his character in the extraordinary example of self-analysis (p. 89 sq.) of which only a few lines need be quoted :

" This extreme distrust in my strength, in some way the proof of myself in the thought of others, did it originate in true modesty ? I rather believe it came from a great pride which is as restless and disquieted as the mind itself."

Indeed neither in Blanc nor in Blanqui could Tocqueville find the confirmation of his own thoughts.

The Revolution of 1848 and its surprising and terrifying results—Napoleon III's plebiscitary dictatorship— marks a watershed in European political thought. The French Republic, based on universal franchise, produced its dialectical contradiction. The best minds in Europe took notice of this event. Donoso Cortés, the great Spanish Catholic political philosopher, prophesied to the liberal bourgeoisie which he despised : " behind the sophists the hangman will appear ; "[1] Bismarck sent the

[1] Donoso Cortés, *Ensayo sobre el Catolicismo, el Liberalismo y el Socialismo*, Madrid 1851.

young German lawyer Constantin Frantz to Paris, where
he duly fabricated the first " coherent " philosophy of
the plebiscitary principle ;[1] Bagehot[2] demonstrated his
later brilliance by his early reports form the Paris of
1851 ; Jacob Burckhardt, the great Swiss historian,
writing and teaching in Basle, whence he could contemplate the policies of three European powers, summed up
the '48 period in his *Reflections on History* :

" At the same time, the events of 1848 had given the
ruling classes a deeper insight into the people. Louis
Napoleon had risked universal suffrage for the elections,
and others followed his lead. The conservative strain in
the rural populations had been recognised, though no
attempt had been made to assess precisely how far it
might be extended from the elections to everything and
everybody. . . . With all business swelling into big business, the views of the business man took the following
line : on the one hand, the State should be no more than
the protective guarantor of his interests and of his type
of intelligence, henceforth assumed to be the main purpose of the world. Indeed, it was his desire that his type
of intelligence should obtain possession of the State by
means of constitutional adjustments. On the other hand,
there prevailed a profound distrust of constitutional
liberty in practice, since it was more likely to be used by
destructive forces." (London, 1943, p. 165.)

Alexander Herzen fled from France to London to
write his equally sceptical and disillusioned memoirs on
the break-down of the revolutionary hopes.[3] Yet in spite
of his melancholic scepticism with regard to European

[1] Cf. my edition, Potsdam 1933.
[2] Cf. Walter Bagehot, *Literary Studies*, Vol. III., pp. 1 sqq.
[3] Cf. *The Memoirs of Alexander Herzen*, 6 vols., London 1924. *See*
particularly vol. IV., pp. 167 sqq.

politics, Herzen believed firmly in the political future of the Russian people.

Moreover, there was Proudhon[1] who transmitted the conviction that the 1848–1851 period was a watershed in European political thought to Georges Sorel, who became the involuntary teacher of Fascism. Similarly, through Marx's *Eighteenth Brumaire* (and his other historical writings), the powerful dynamics of the '48 period made the deepest impression on Lenin. But it was rather the *myth* of the Revolution, not its history, which was present in Lenin's mind during the Russian revolutionary struggles in 1917. Evidently in Lenin's *State and Revolution*, the classic study of revolutionary Marxism, the simplified and more virulent form of Marxist interpretation prevails. When Lenin formulated the theoretical foundations of the Soviet State in Switzerland, he thought the knowledge of reading and writing, and of a little arithmetic was enough to qualify the proletarian revolutionary for the task of State administration. When the Russian State machinery was conquered, he soon learned a different lesson.

Perhaps it is significant to remember that Marx himself to some extent corrected the simplified and, as it were, mythical picture he had drawn of the '48 period. When he re-edited *The Eighteenth Brumaire* in 1869 as a political refugee in London, he had lived long enough in England to understand the slow and *evolutionary* progress towards universal franchise. The following sentences were omitted from the second edition :

" ... in those momentous days the French nation

[1] Proudhon's *La Révolution sociale démontrée par le Coup d'Etat du Deux Décembre* (*Œuvres Complètes de P. J. Proudhon, Nouvelle Edition*, Paris. 1936) may serve as an illuminating corrective to Tocqueville's *Recollections*. Cf. particularly the suggestive introduction by MM. Molléans and Duveau. See also the important book by Édouard Dolléans: *Proudhon*, Paris, 1948.

committed a deadly crime against democracy, which, on its knees, now utters the daily prayer : ' Holy Universal Suffrage, pray for us ! ' Naturally enough, the believers in universal suffrage will not renounce their faith in a wonder-working power which has performed such great miracles on their behalf, which has transformed the second Bonaparte into a Napoleon, Saul into Paul, and Simon into Peter. The folk-spirit speaks to them through the ballot boxes as the god of the prophet Ezekiel spoke to the dry bones : ' Haec dicit dominus deus ossibus suis : Ecce ego intromittam in vos Spiritum et vivetis.' ''[1]

I have always wondered whether Lenin and his pupils have asked themselves, *why* Marx in 1869 adhered to a more objective interpretation of the sociological significance of universal franchise ?

In this respect, too, Tocqueville was the greater realist, for we read in the *Recollections* :

" . . . the universal franchise had shaken the country from top to bottom without bringing to light a single new man worthy of coming to the front. I have always held that, whatever method be followed in a general election, the great majority of the exceptional men, whom the nation possesses, definitely succeed in getting elected. The system of election adopted exercises a great influence only upon the class of ordinary individuals in the Assembly, who form the groundwork of every political body. These belong to very different orders and are of very diverse natures, according to the system upon which the election has been conducted. Nothing confirmed me in this belief more than did the sight of the Constituent Assembly. Almost all the men who played the first part in it were already known to me, but the bulk of the rest resembled nothing that I had seen before. . . ." (p. 114)

[1] Cf. my edition, Berlin 1932, pp. 10 sq.

Here Tocqueville's subtle mind penetrates through the *forms* of electoral mechanisms and lays bare the substance of the organisational structure of politics. Yet ultimately, myths, not realism, are the driving forces in history.

Thus as long as Europeans choose to and are allowed to think freely the *Souvenirs* remain the document of a man who, though ready to compromise as a politician, nevertheless fully anticipated as a sociologist the trends of future societies whose principal difficulty was to be the synthesis of equality and freedom.

Tocqueville's fearless and independent mind drove him into a " morose isolation ", an attitude with which we sympathise and which indeed we share.

To-day the problems of the French Revolution of 1848 are no longer French, nor European, but world problems. What in 1849 were party trends in France, are to-day national policies of Soviet Russia, U.S.A., and Great Britain. The final outcome of a perhaps possible constructive conciliation of these trends is still in the balance; may it draw strength from the wealth of the French political mind which has always been the laboratory of the Revolution whose course *still* continues.

London, June 1946   J. P. MAYER

PREFACE

ALEXIS DE TOCQUEVILLE made his entrance into political life in 1839. At the outbreak of the Revolution of
February he was in the prime of his age and in the
maturity of his talent. He threw himself into the struggle,
resolving to devote himself to the interests of the country
and of society, and he was one of the first among those
whole-hearted, single-minded men who endeavoured to
keep the Republic within a wise and moderate course by
steering clear of the two-fold perils of Caesarism on the
one hand and revolution on the other. A dangerous and
thankless enterprise, of which the difficulties were never
hidden from a mind so clear-sighted as his, and of which
he soon foresaw the ephemeral duration.

After the fall of his short-lived ministry, which had
been filled with so many cares and such violent agitation, thinking himself removed for a time (it was to be
for ever) from the conduct of public affairs, he went first
to Normandy and then to Sorrento, on the Bay of
Naples, in search of the peace and repose of which he
stood in need. The intellect, however, but rarely shows
itself the docile slave of the will, and his, to which idleness was a cause of real suffering, immediately set about
to seek an object worthy of its attention. This was soon
found in the great drama of the French Revolution,
which attracted him irresistibly, and which was destined
to form the subject-matter of his most perfect work.

It was at this time, while Alexis de Tocqueville was
also preoccupied by the daily increasing gravity of the

political situation at home, that he wrote the Recollections now first published. These consisted of mere notes jotted down at intervals on odds and ends of paper ; and it was not until the close of his life that, yielding to the persuasions of his intimates, he gave a reluctant consent to their publication. He took a certain pleasure in thus retracing and, as it were, re-enacting the events in which he had taken part, the character of which seemed the more transient, and the more important to establish definitely, inasmuch as other events came crowding on, precipitating the crisis and altering the aspect of affairs. Thus those travellers who, steering their adventurous course through a series of dangerous reefs, alight upon a wild and rugged island, where they disembark and live for some days, and when about to depart for ever from its shores, throw back upon it a long and melancholy gaze before it sinks from their eyes in the immensity of the waves. Already the Assembly had lost its independence : the reign of constitutional liberty, under which France had lived for thirty-three years, was giving way ; and, in the words of the famous phrase, " The Empire was a fact".

We are to-day well able to judge the period described in these Recollections, a period which seems still further removed from us by the revolutions, the wars, and even the misfortunes which the country has since undergone, and which now only appears to us in that subdued light which throws the principal outlines into especial relief, while permitting the more observant and penetrating eye to discover also the secondary features. Living close enough to those times to receive evidence from the lips of survivors, and not so close but that all passion has become appeased and all rancour extinguished, we should be in a position to lack neither light nor impartiality. As witness, for instance, the impression retained by us of the figure of Ledru-Rollin, which nevertheless terrified our fathers. We live in a generation which has beheld Raoul, Rigault and Delescluze at work. The theories of Louis Blanc and Considérant arouse no feeling of astonishment in these days, when their ideas have become current coin, and when the majority of politicians feel called upon to adopt the badge of some socialism or other, whether we call it Christian, State, or revolutionary socialism. Cormenin, Marrast and Lamartine belong to history as much as do Sieyès, Pétion or Mirabeau ; and we are able to judge as freely of the men and the events of 1848 as of those of 1830 or 1789.

Alexis de Tocqueville had the rare merit of being able to forestall this verdict of posterity ; and if we endeavour to discover the secret of this prescience, of the loftiness of sight with which he was so specially gifted, we shall find that, belonging to no party, he remained above all parties ; that, depending upon no leader, he kept his hands free ; and that, possessed of no vulgar ambition, he reserved his energies for the noble aim which he had in view—the triumph of liberty and of the dignity of man.

Interest will doubtless be taken in the account contained in these Recollections of the revolutionary period, written by one of the best-informed of its witnesses, and in the ebbs and flows of the short-lived ministry which was conducted with so much talent and integrity. But what will be especially welcome are the broad views taken by this great mind of our collective history ; his profound reflections upon the future of the country and of society ; the firm and conscientious opinions which he expresses upon his contemporaries ; and the portraits drawn by a master hand, always striking and always alive. When reading this private record, which has been neither revised nor corrected by its author, we seem to approach more closely to the sentiments, the desires, the aspirations, I was almost saying the dreams of this rare

PREFACE

mind, this great heart so ardently pursuing the chimera
of absolute good that nothing in men or institutions
could succeed in satisfying it.

Years passed, and the Empire foundered amid terrible
disaster. Alexis de Tocqueville was no more ; and we
may say that this proved at that time an irreparable loss
to his country. Who knows, what part he might have
been called upon to play, what influence he could have
brought to bear to unmask the guilty intrigues and baffle
the mean ambitions under whose load, after the lapse of
more than twenty years, we are still staggering ? Enlightened by his harsh experience of 1848, would he have
once again tried the experiment, which can never be
more than an eternal stop-gap, of governing the Republic with the support of the Monarchists ? Or rather, persuaded as he was that " the republican form of government is not the best suited to the needs of France", that
this " government without checks always promises more,
but gives less, liberty than a Constitutional Monarchy",
would he not have appealed to the latter to protect the
liberty so dear to him ? One thing is certain, that he
would never have " subordinated to the necessity of
maintaining his position that of remaining true to
himself".

We have thought that the present generation, which
so rarely has the opportunity of beholding a man of
character, would take pleasure in becoming acquainted
with this great and stately figure ; in spending some
short moments in those lofty regions, in which it may
learn a powerful lesson and find an example of public
life in its noblest form, ever faithful to its early aspirations, ever filled with two great ideas : the cult of honour
and the passion of liberty.

COMTE DE TOCQUEVILLE (1893).

PART ONE

Written in July, 1850, at Tocqueville

REMOVED for a time from the scene of public life, and
not able to pursue a continued share in any career of my
precarious health,[1] I am constrained, in the midst of
my solitude to turn my thoughts... myself awhile
to reflect upon contemporary events, in which I have
taken part or acted as a witness. ... It seems to me
that the best use I can make of my leisure is to retrace
these events, to portray the men who took part in them
under my eyes, and in this way to seize and engrave, if I
can, upon my memory the confused features which compose the disturbed physiognomy... my times.

In taking this resolve I have... another reason to which
I shall be no less faithful: these recollections will be a
relaxation of my mind rather than a work of literature. I
write them for myself alone. They shall be a mirror in
which I will amuse myself in contemplating my contemporaries and myself; not a picture painted for the
public. My best friends shall not see them, for I wish to
retain the liberty of describing them and myself. I shall depict
myself without flattery. I wish to arrive directly at the
secret motives which have caused them, me, and others
to act; and, when discovered, to reveal them here. In a
word, I wish the expression of my recollections to be a
sincere one, and to achieve this it is essential that it
should remain entirely secret.

My intention is, that my recollections shall not go
further back than the Revolution of 1848, nor extend
to a later date than the goal of October, 1849, when I

[1] The bracketed passages are not contained in the English Edition
of *The Recollections* of 1896, nor in the French Edition of 1893. (M)

CHAPTER I

*Origin and Character of these Recollections—General Aspects
of the Period preceding the Revolution of 1848—First
Symptoms of the Revolution.*

REMOVED for a time from one scene of public life, [and
not able to pursue a continued study on account of my
precarious health,][1] I am constrained, in the midst of
my solitude, to turn my thoughts upon myself, or rather
to reflect upon contemporary events in which I have
taken part or acted as a witness. Thus it seems to me
that the best use I can make of my leisure is to retrace
these events, to portray the men who took part in them
under my eyes, and in this way to seize and engrave, if I
can, upon my memory the confused features which compose the disturbed physiognomy of my time.

In taking this resolve I have taken another, to which
I shall be no less faithful : these recollections shall be a
relaxation of my mind rather than a work of literature. I
write them for myself alone. They shall be a mirror in
which I will amuse myself in contemplating my contemporaries and myself ; not a picture painted for the
public. My best friends shall not see them, for I wish to
retain the liberty of depicting them as I shall depict
myself, without flattery. I wish to arrive sincerely at the
secret motives which have caused them, me, and others
to act ; and, when discovered, to reveal them here. In a
word, I wish the expression of my recollections to be a
sincere one, and to achieve this, it is essential that it
should remain entirely secret.

My intention is that my recollections shall not go
further back than the Revolution of 1848, nor extend
to a later date than the 30th of October, 1849, when I

[1] The bracketed passages are not contained in the English Edition
of *The Recollections* of 1896, nor in the French Edition of 1893. (M).

resigned my office. It is only within these limits that the events which I propose to relate have any greatness, or that my position has enabled me to observe them well.

My life was passed, although in a rather secluded way, in the midst of the closing years of the Monarchy of July. Yet it would be no easy task for me to recall distinctly the events of a period so little removed from the present, and nevertheless leaving so confused a trace in my memory. The thread of my recollections is lost amid the labyrinth of petty incidents, of petty ideas, of petty passions, of personal views and contradictory projects in which the life of public men was at that time spent. The general aspect of this period remains vivid in my mind ; for I often regarded it with a curiosity mingled with dread, and I clearly discerned the special features by which it was characterized.

Our history from 1789 to 1830, viewed from a distance and as a whole, affords as it were the picture of a struggle to the death between the Ancien Régime, its traditions, memories, hopes, and men, as represented by the aristocracy, and the New France led by the Middle Class. The year 1830 closed the first period of our revolutions, or rather of our revolution : for there is but one, which has remained always the same in the face of varying fortunes, of which our fathers witnessed the beginning, and of which we, in all probability, shall not live to see the end. In 1830 the triumph of the middle class had been definite and so thorough that all political power, every franchise, every prerogative, and the whole government was confined and, as it were, heaped up within the narrow limits of this one class, to the statutory exclusion of all beneath them and the actual exclusion of all above. Not only did it thus rule society, but it may be said to have formed it. It entrenched itself in every vacant place, prodigiously augmented the number of places and accustomed itself to live almost as much upon the Treasury as upon its own industry.

No sooner had the Revolution of 1830 become an accomplished fact, than there ensued a great lull in political passion, a sort of general subsidence, accompanied by a rapid increase in public wealth. The particular spirit of the middle class became the general spirit of the government ; it ruled the latter's foreign policy as well as affairs at home : an active, industrious spirit, often dishonourable, generally orderly, occasionally reckless through vanity or egoism, but timid by temperament, moderate in all things except in its love of ease and comfort, and last but not least mediocre. It was a spirit which, mingled with that of the people or of the aristocracy, can do wonders ; but which, by itself, will never produce more than a government shorn of both virtue and greatness. Master of everything in a manner that no aristocracy has ever been or may ever hope to be, the middle class, when called upon to assume the government, took it up as an industrial enterprise ; it entrenched itself behind its power, and before long, in their egoism, each of its members thought much more of his private business than of public affairs ; of his personal enjoyment than of the greatness of the nation.

Posterity, which sees none but the more dazzling crimes, and which loses sight, in general, of mere vices, will never, perhaps, know to what extent the government of that day, towards its close, assumed the ways of an industrial enterprise, which conducts all its transactions with a view to the profits accruing to the shareholders. These vices were due to the natural instincts of the dominant class, to its absolute power, and also to the character of the time. King Louis-Philippe had contributed much to their growth. [He was the accident which made the malady mortal.] This prince was a singular medley of qualities, and one would have to have known him

3

longer and more nearly than I did to be able to portray him in detail. [But his main traits were easily seen even when one was far away or one was only passing by.

Though he came from one of the noblest families in Europe, he concealed all hereditary pride deeply in his soul ; nevertheless he certainly believed that there was no other human being like him. All the same he had most of the qualities and defects which belong more particularly to the subaltern orders of society. He had regular habits and wanted those around him to have them too. He was orderly in his conduct, simple in his habits, his tastes were tempered ; he was a born friend of the law, an enemy of all excesses, sober in his ways except in his desires. He was human without being sentimental, greedy and soft. He had no flaming passions, no ruinous weaknesses, no striking vices, and only one kingly virtue : courage. He was extremely polite, but without choice or greatness, a politeness of a merchant rather than of a Prince. He hardly appreciated literature or art, but he passionately loved industry. His memory was prodigious and capable of keeping the minutest detail. His conversation was prolix, diffuse, original and trivial, anecdotal, full of small facts, of salt and meaning ; it gave all satisfaction which one may find in intellectual pleasures when delicacy and elevation are absent. His mind was distinguished, but withdrawn and embarrassed for his soul was neither high nor profound. He was enlightened, subtle, flexible ; as he was only open to that which was useful, he was full of profound disdain for the truth, and he did so little believe in virtue that his sight was darkened. Thus he did not see the beauty which truth and decency show, he did not even understand any more their usefulness which they so often have. He had a profound knowledge of human beings, but he knew them only through their vices. He was unbeliever in religious matters as the eighteenth century and sceptical in politics

4

as the nineteenth ; having no belief himself, he did not believe in the belief of others. He was, as it were, naturally fond of power and of dishonest, mediocre, facile, and plain courtiers to be really born for the throne. His ambition only, limited by prudence, never satisfied, nor did it ever carry him away ; it always kept him near to the ground.

There have been several princes who resemble this portrait, but the special case of Louis-Philippe was his analogy or rather kind of parentship and consanguinity which bound his faults to those of his time ; this made him for his contemporaries and particularly for the class which held the power such an attractive, singularly dangerous and corruptive prince. Chief of the bourgeoisie—he pushed them towards their natural bent which they had only too much inclination to follow. They married their vices, and this family union first made each of them strong, singly, then accomplished the demoralization of the other, and finished by making them both perish.]

Nevertheless, although I was never one of his Council, I have frequently had occasion to come into contact with him. The last time that I spoke to him was shortly before the catastrophe of February. I was then director of the Académie Française, and I had to bring to the King's notice some matter or other which concerned that body. After treating the question which had brought me, I was about to retire, when the King detained me, took a chair, motioned me to another, and said, affably :

" Since you are here, Monsieur de Tocqueville, let us talk ; I want to hear you talk about America."

I knew him well enough to know that this meant : I shall talk about America myself. And he did actually talk of it at great length and very searchingly : it was not possible for me, nor did I desire, to get in a word, for he really interested me. He described places as though he

5

saw them before him ; he recalled the distinguished men whom he had met forty years ago as though he had seen them the day before ; he mentioned their names in full, Christian name and surname, gave their ages at the time, related their histories, their genealogies, their descendance, with marvellous exactness and with infinite, though in no way tedious, detail. From America he returned, without taking breath, to Europe, talked of all our foreign and domestic affairs with incredible unconstraint—for I had no title to his confidence—spoke very badly of the Emperor of Russia, whom he called " Monsieur Nicolas," casually alluded to Lord Palmerston as a buffoon, and ended by holding forth at length on the Spanish marriages, which had just taken place, and the annoyances to which they subjected him on the side of England.

" The Queen is very angry with me", he said, " and displays great irritation, but after all," he added, " all this outcry won't keep me from *driving my own cart*." Although this phrase dated back to the Ancien Régime, I felt inclined to doubt whether Louis XIV ever made use of it on accepting the Spanish Succession. I believe, moreover, to borrow his own language, that the Spanish marriage helped not a little to upset his cart.

After three-quarters of an hour, the King rose, thanked me for the pleasure my conversation had given him (I had not spoken four words), and dismissed me, feeling evidently as delighted as one generally is with a man before whom one thinks one has spoken well. This was my last audience of the King.

Louis-Philippe improvised all the replies which he made, even upon the most critical occasions, to the great State bodies ; he was as fluent then as in his private conversation, although not so happy or epigrammatic. [Ordinarily it was a deluge of commonplaces, delivered with false and exaggerated gestures, a great effort to

6

appear moved, vigorously beating his breast.] He would suddenly become obscure, for the reason that he boldly plunged headlong into long sentences, of which he was not able to estimate the extent nor perceive the end beforehand and from which he finally emerged struggling and by force, shattering the sentence, and not completing the thought. [Generally speaking, his style on such solemn occasions reminded one of the sentimental jargon of the end of the eighteenth century, a facile redundancy singularly incorrect : Jean-Jacques with a touch of a kitchenmaid of the nineteenth century. This reminds me that one day, I found myself very conspicuous and very much in the foreground during a visit the Chamber of Deputies paid to the Tuileries, when I almost broke into laughter and caused a scandal, because Rémusat, my colleague of the Académie Française and of the Chamber, maliciously whispered this beautiful sentence into my ear in a grave and melancholic tone : "At this moment the good citizen must be agreeably moved, but the academician suffers."]

In this political world thus constituted and conducted, what was most wanting, particularly towards the end, was political life itself. It could neither come into being nor be maintained within the legal circle which the Constitution had traced for it : the old aristocracy was vanquished, the people excluded. As all business was discussed among members of one class, in the interest and in the spirit of that class, there was no battlefield for contending parties to meet upon. This singular homogeneity of position, of interests, and consequently of views, reigning in what M. Guizot had once called the legal country, deprived the parliamentary debates of all originality, of all reality, and therefore of all genuine passion. I have spent ten years of my life in the company of truly great minds, who were in a constant state of agitation without succeeding in heating themselves, and who spent all their perspicacity in vain endeavours to find subjects upon which they could seriously disagree.

On the other hand, the preponderating influence which King Louis-Philippe had acquired in public affairs, which never permitted the politicians to stray very far from that Prince's ideas, lest they should at the same time be removed from power, reduced the different colours of parties to the merest shades, and debates to the splitting of straws. I doubt whether any parliament (not excepting the Constituent Assembly, I mean the true one, that of 1789) ever contained more varied and brilliant talents than did ours during the closing years of the Monarchy of July. Nevertheless, I am able to declare that these great orators were bored to death at listening to one another, and, what was worse, the whole country was bored with listening to them. France grew unconsciously accustomed to look upon the debates in the Chambers as exercises of the intellect rather than as serious discussions, and upon all the differences between the various parliamentary parties—the majority, the left centre, or the dynastic opposition—as domestic quarrels between children of one family trying to trick one another. A few glaring instances of corruption, discovered by accident, led the country to presuppose a number of hidden cases, and convinced it that the whole of the governing class was corrupt ; whence it conceived for the latter a silent contempt, which was generally taken for confiding and contented submission.

The country was at that time divided into two unequal parts, or rather zones : in the upper, which alone was intended to contain the whole of the nation's political life, there reigned nothing but languor, impotence, stagnation, and boredom ; in the lower, on the contrary, political life began to make itself manifest by means of

8

feverish and irregular signs, of which the attentive observer was easily able to seize the meaning.

I was one of these observers ; and although I was far from imagining that the catastrophe was so near at hand and fated to be so terrible, I felt a distrust springing up and insensibly growing in my mind, and the idea taking root more and more that we were making strides towards a fresh revolution. This denoted a great change in my thoughts : since the general appeasement and flatness that followed the Revolution of July had led me to believe for a long time that I was destined to spend my life amid an enervated and peaceful society. Indeed, anyone who had only examined the inside of the governmental fabric would have had the same conviction. Everything there seemed combined to produce with the machinery of liberty a preponderance of Royal power which verged upon despotism ; and, in fact, this result was produced almost without effort by the regular and tranquil movement of the machine. King Louis-Philippe was persuaded that, so long as he did not himself lay hand upon that fine instrument, and allowed it to work according to rule, he was safe from all peril. His only occupation was to keep it in order, and to make it work according to his own views, forgetful of society, upon which this ingenious piece of mechanism rested ; he resembled the man who refused to believe that his house was on fire, because he had the key to it in his pocket. I could neither have the same interests nor the same cares, and this permitted me to see through the mechanism of institutions and the agglomeration of petty every-day facts, and to observe the state of morals and opinions in the country. There I clearly saw the appearance of several of the portents that usually denote the approach of revolutions and I began to believe that in 1830 I had taken for the end of the play what was nothing more than the end of an act.

A short unpublished document which I composed at the time, and a speech which I delivered early in 1848, will bear witness to these pre-occupations of my mind.

Several of my friends in Parliament met together in October 1847, to decide upon the policy to be adopted during the next session. It was agreed that we should issue a programme in the form of a manifesto, and the task of drawing it up was deputed to me. Later, the idea of this publication was abandoned, but I had already written the document. I have discovered it among my papers, and I give the following extracts.[1] After commenting on the symptoms of languor in Parliament, I continued : " . . . The time will come when the country will find itself once again divided between two great parties. The French Revolution which abolished all privileges and destroyed all exclusive rights, has allowed one to remain, that of property. Let not the proprietors deceive themselves as to the strength of their position, nor think that the rights of property form an insurmountable barrier because they have not as yet been surmounted ; for our times are unlike any others. When the rights of property were merely the origin and commencement of a number of other rights, they were easily defended, or rather, they were never attacked ; they then formed the surrounding wall of society, of which all other rights were the outposts ; no blows reached them ; no serious attempt was ever made to touch them. But to-day, when the rights of property are nothing more than the last remnants of an overthrown aristocratic world ; when they alone are left intact, isolated privileges amid the universal levelling of society ; when they are no longer protected behind a number of still more controvertible and odious rights, the case is altered, and

[1] This document has been published under the title *De la classe Moyenne et du peuple* in Vol. IX of *Œuvres Complètes*. (M).

they alone are left daily to resist the direct and unceasing shock of democratic opinion.

" . . . Before long, the political struggle will be restricted to those who have and those who have not ; property will form the great field of battle ; and the principal political questions will turn upon the more or less important modifications to be introduced into the right of property. We shall then have once more among us great public agitations and great political parties.

" How is it that these premonitory symptoms escape the general view ? Can anyone believe that it is by accident, through some passing whim of the human mind, that we see appearing on every side these curious doctrines, bearing different titles, but all characterized in their essence by their denial of the rights of property, and all tending, at least, to diminish and weaken the exercise of these rights ? Who can fail here to recognize the final symptom of the old democratic disease of the time, whose crisis would seem to be at hand ? "

I was still more urgent and explicit in the speech which I delivered in the Chamber of Deputies on the 29th of January 1848, and which appeared in the *Moniteur* of the 30th.

The principal passages may be quoted here :

" . . . I am told that there is no danger because there are no riots ; I am told that, because there is no visible disorder on the surface of society, there is no revolution at hand.

" Gentlemen, permit me to say that I believe you are mistaken. True, there is no actual disorder ; but it has entered deeply into men's minds. See what is preparing itself amongst the working classes, who, I grant, are at present quiet. No doubt they are not disturbed by political passions, properly so-called, to the same extent that they have been ; but can you not see that their passions, instead of political, have become social ? Do you not see that they are gradually forming opinions and ideas which are destined not only to upset this or that law, ministry, or even form of government, but society itself, until it totters upon the foundations on which it rests to-day? Do you not listen to what they say to themselves each day? Do you not hear them repeating unceasingly that all that is above them is incapable and unworthy of governing them; that the distribution of goods prevalent until now throughout the world is unjust; that property rests on a foundation which is not an equitable one? And do you not realize that when such opinions take root, when they spread in an almost universal manner, when they sink deeply into the masses, they are bound to bring with them sooner or later, I know not when or how, a most formidable revolution?

" This gentlemen, is my profound conviction : I believe that we are at this moment sleeping on a volcano. I am profoundly convinced of it. . . .

" . . . I was saying just now that this evil would sooner or later, I know not how or whence it will come, bring with it a most serious revolution : be assured that that is so.

" When I come to investigate what, at different times, in different periods, among different peoples, has been the effective cause that has brought about the downfall of the governing classes, I perceive this or that event, man, or accidental or superficial cause ; but, believe me, the real reason, the effective reason which causes men to lose political power, is that they have become unworthy to retain it.

" Think, gentlemen, of the old Monarchy : it was stronger than you are, stronger in its origin ; it was able to lean more than you do upon ancient customs, ancient habits, ancient beliefs ; it was stronger than you are, and yet it has fallen to dust. And why did it fall? Do you think it was by particular mischance? Do you think it was by the act of some man, by the deficit, the oath in the Tennis Court, La Fayette, Mirabeau ? No, gentlemen ; there was another reason : the class that was then the governing class had become, through its indifference, its selfishness and its vices, incapable and unworthy of governing the country.

" That was the true reason.

" Well, gentlemen, if it is right to have this patriotic prejudice at all times, how much more is it not right to have it in our own ? Do you not feel, by some intuitive instinct which is not capable of analysis, but which is undeniable, that the earth is quaking once again in Europe? Do you not feel—what shall I say ?—as it were a gale of revolution in the air ? This gale, no one knows whence it springs, whence it blows, nor, believe me, whom it will carry with it ; and it is in such times as these that you remain calm before the degradation of public morality— for the expression is not too strong.

" I speak here without bitterness ; I am even addressing you without any party spirit ; I am attacking men against whom I feel no vindictiveness. But I am obliged to communicate to my country my firm and profound conviction. Well then, my firm and profound conviction is this : that public morality is being degraded, and that the degradation of public morality will shortly, very shortly perhaps, bring down upon you new revolutions. Is the life of kings held by stronger threads ? Are these more difficult to snap than those of other men ? Can you say to-day that you are certain of to-morrow ? Do you know what may happen in France a year hence, or even a month or a day hence ? You do not know ; but what you must know is that the tempest is looming on the horizon, that it is coming towards us. Will you allow it to take you by surprise ?

" Gentlemen, I implore you not to do so. I do not ask you, I implore you. I would gladly throw myself on my knees before you, so strongly do I believe in the reality and the seriousness of the danger, so convinced am I that my warnings are no empty rhetoric. Yes, the danger is great. Allay it while there is yet time; correct the evil by efficacious remedies, by attacking it, not in its symptoms but in itself.

" Legislative changes have been spoken of. I am greatly disposed to think that these changes are not only very useful, but necessary ; thus, I believe in the need of electoral reform, in the urgency of parliamentary reform; but I am not, gentlemen, so mad as not to know that no laws can affect the destinies of nations. No, it is not the mechanism of laws that produces great events, gentlemen, but the inner spirit of the government. Keep the laws as they are, if you wish. I think you would be very wrong to do so ; but keep them. Keep the men, too, if it gives you any pleasure. I raise no objection so far as I am concerned. But, in God's name, change the spirit of the government ; for, I repeat, that spirit will lead you to the abyss."[1]

These gloomy predictions were received with ironical cheers from the majority. The Opposition applauded loudly, but more from party feeling than from conviction. The truth is that no one as yet believed seriously in the danger which I was prophesying, although we were so near the catastrophe. The inveterate habit contracted by all the politicians, during this long parliamentary comedy, of over-colouring the expression of their opinion and grossly exaggerating their thoughts had deprived them of all power of appreciating what was real and true. For several years the majority had every day been declaring that the Opposition was imperilling society ; and the Opposition repeated incessantly that the

[1] This speech was delivered in the debate on the Address in reply to the Speech from the Throne as Tocqueville indicates. It is reprinted in full in Œuvres Complètes, Vol. IX, pp. 520 sqq. (M.)

Ministers were ruining the Monarchy. These statements had been made so constantly on both sides, without either side greatly believing in them, that they ended by not believing in them at all, at the very moment when the event was about to justify both of them. Even my own friends thought that I had overshot the mark, and that my facts were a little blurred by rhetoric.

I remember that, when I stepped from the tribune, Dufaure took me on one side, and said, with that sort of parliamentary intuition which is his only note of genius : " You have succeeded, but you would have succeeded much more if you had not gone so far beyond the feeling of the Assembly and tried to frighten us." And now that I am face to face with myself, searching in my memory to discover whether I was actually so much alarmed as I seemed, the answer is no, and I readily recognize that the event justified me more promptly and more completely than I foresaw (a thing which may sometimes have happened to other political prophets, better authorized to predict than I was). No, I did not expect such a revolution as we were destined to have ; and who could have expected it ? I did, I believe, perceive more clearly than the others the general causes which were making for the event ; but I did not observe the accidents which were to precipitate it. Meantime the days which still separated us from the catastrophe passed rapidly by.

CHAPTER II

The Banquets—Sense of Security entertained by the Government—Anxiety of the Leaders of the Opposition— Arraignment of Ministers.

I REFUSED to take part in the affair of the banquets. I had both serious and petty reasons for abstaining. What I call petty reasons I am quite willing to describe as bad reasons, although they were consistent with honour, and would have been unexceptionable in a private matter. They were the irritation and disgust aroused in me by the character and the tactics of the leaders of this enter-prize. Nevertheless, I confess that the private prejudice which we entertain with regard to individuals is a bad guide in politics.

A close alliance had at that time been effected between M. Thiers and M. Barrot, and a real fusion formed be-tween the two sections of the Opposition, which, in our parliamentary jargon, we called the Left Centre and the Left. Almost all the stubborn and intractable spirits which were found in the latter party had successively been softened, unbent, subjugated, made supple, by the promises of jobs wasted by M. Thiers. I believe that even M. Barrot had for the first time allowed himself not exactly to be won over, but surprised, by arguments of this kind. At any rate, the most complete intimacy reigned between the two great leaders of the Opposition, whatever was the cause of it, and M. Barrot, who likes to mingle a little simplicity with his weaknesses as well as with his virtues, exerted himself to his utmost to secure the triumph of his ally, even at his own expense. M. Thiers had allowed him to involve himself in this matter of the banquets; I even think that he had instigated Barrot in that direction without consenting to involve himself. He was willing to accept the results, but not the responsibilities of that dangerous agitation. Wherefore, surrounded by his personal friends, he stayed mute and motionless in Paris, while Barrot travelled all over the country for three months, making long speeches in every town he stopped at, and resembling in my opinion, those beaters who make a great noise in order to bring the game within easy reach of the sportsman's gun. Personally, I felt no inclination to take part in the sport. But the principal and more serious reason which restrained me was this : and I expounded it pretty often to those who wanted to drag me to those political meetings :

" For the first time for eighteen years," I used to tell them, " you are proposing to appeal to the people, and to seek support outside the middle class. If you fail in rousing the people (and I think this will be the most probable result), you will become still more odious than you already are in the eyes of the Government and of the middle class, who in its majority supports the Government. In this way you will strengthen the Administration which you desire to upset ; while if, on the contrary, you succeed in rousing the people, you are no more able than I am to foresee whither an agitation of this kind will lead you."

In the measure that the campaign of the banquets was prolonged, the latter hypothesis became, contrary to my expectation, the more probable. A certain anxiety began to oppress the leaders themselves ; an indefinite anxiety, passing vaguely through their minds. I was told by Beaumont, who was at that time one of the first among them, that the excitement occasioned in the country by the banquets surpassed not only the hopes, but the wishes of those who had started it. The latter were labouring to allay rather than increase it. Their intention was that there should be no banquet in Paris, and that there should be none held anywhere after the assembling of the Chambers. The fact is that they were only seeking a way out of the mischievous road which they had entered upon. And it was undoubtedly in spite of them that this final banquet was resolved on ; they were constrained to take part in it, drawn into it ; their vanity was compromised. The Government by its defiance, goaded the Opposition into adopting this dangerous measure, thinking thus to drive it to destruction. The Opposition let itself be caught in a spirit of bravado, lest it should be suspected of retreating ; and thus irritating each other, spurring one another on, they dragged each other towards the common abyss, which neither of them as yet perceived.

I remember that two days before the Revolution of February, at the Turkish Ambassador's ball, I met Duvergier de Hauranne. I felt for him both friendship and esteem ; although he possessed very nearly all the failings that arise from party spirit, he at least joined to them the sort of disinterestedness and sincerity which one meets with in genuine passions, two rare advantages in our day, when the only genuine passion is that of self. I said with the familiarity warranted by our relations :

" Courage, my friend ; you are playing a dangerous game." He replied gravely, but with no sign of fear : " Believe me, all will end well ; besides, one must risk something. There is no free government that had not to go through a similar experience."

This reply perfectly describes this determined but somewhat narrow character ; narrow, I say, although with plenty of brain, but with a brain which, while seeing clearly and in detail all that is on the horizon, is incapable of conceiving that the horizon may change ; scholarly, disinterested, ardent, vindictive, sprung from that learned and sectarian race which guides itself in politics by imitation of others and by historical recollection, and which restricts its thought to one sole idea, at which it warms, in which it blinds itself.

For the rest, the Government were even less uneasy

than the leaders of the Opposition. A few days before the above conversation. I had had another with Duchâtel, the Minister of the Interior. I was on good terms with this minister, although for the last eight years I had been very boldly (even too boldly, I confess, in the case of its foreign policy) attacking the Cabinet of which he was one of the principal members. I am not sure that this fault did not even make me find favour in his eyes, for I believe that at the bottom of his heart he had a sneaking fondness for those who attacked his colleague at the Foreign Office, M. Guizot. A battle which M. Duchâtel and I had fought some years before in favour of the penitentiary system had brought us together and given rise to a certain intimacy between us. This man was very unlike the one I mentioned above : he was as heavy in his person and his manners as the other was meagre, angular and sometimes trenchant and bitter. He was as remarkable for his scepticism as the other for his ardent convictions, for flabby indifference as the former for feverish activity ; he possessed a very supple, very quick, very subtle mind enclosed in a massive body ; he understood business admirably while pretending to be above it ; he was thoroughly acquainted with the evil passions of his party, and always knew how to turn them to advantage. He was free from all rancour and prejudice, cordial in his address, easy of approach, obliging, whenever his own interests were not compromised, and bore a kindly contempt for his fellow-creatures. [A man whom one could neither esteem nor hate.]

I was about to say that, some days before the catastrophe, I drew M. Duchâtel into a corner of the conference room, and observed to him that the Government and the Opposition seemed to be striving in concert to drive things to an extremity calculated by damaging everybody ; and I asked him if he saw no honest way of escape from a regrettable position, some honourable transaction which would permit everyone to draw back. I added that my friends and I would be happy to have such a way pointed out to us, and that we would make every exertion to persuade our colleagues in the Opposition to accept it. He listened attentively to my remarks, and assured me that he understood my meaning though I saw clearly that he did not enter into it for a moment.

" Things have reached such a pitch," he said, " that the expedient which I sought was no longer to be found. The Government was in the right, and could not yield. If the Opposition persisted in its course, the result might be a combat in the streets, but this combat had long been foreseen, and if the Government was animated with the evil passions with which it was credited, it would desire this fighting rather than dread it, being sure to triumph in the end."

He went on in his complaisant fashion to tell me in detail of all the military precautions that had been taken, the extent of the resources, the number of the troops, and the quantity of ammunition. I took my leave, satisfied that the Government, without exactly striving to promote an outbreak, was far from dreading one, and that the Ministry, in its certainty of ultimate victory, saw in the threatening catastrophe possibly its last means of rallying its scattered supporters and of finally reducing its adversaries to powerlessness. I confess that I thought as he did ; his air of unfeigned assurance had proved contagious.

The only really uneasy people in Paris at that moment were the Radical chiefs and the men who were sufficiently in touch with the people and the revolutionary party to know what was taking place in that quarter. I have reason to believe that most of these looked with dread upon the events which were ready to burst forth, whether because they kept up the tradition of their former passions rather than these passions themselves, or because they had become accustomed to a state of things in which they had taken up their position after so many times cursing it ; or again, because they were doubtful of success ; or rather because, being in a position to study and become well acquainted with their allies, they were frightened at the last moment of the victory which they expected to gain through their aid. On the very day before the outbreak, Madame de Lamartine betrayed extraordinary anxiety when calling upon Madame de Tocqueville, and gave such unmistakable signs of a mind heated and almost deranged by ominous thoughts that the latter became alarmed, and told me of it the same evening.

It is not one of the least bizarre characteristics of this singular revolution that the incident which led to it was brought about and almost longed for by the men whom it eventually precipitated from power, and that it was only foreseen and feared by those who were to triumph by its means.

Here let me for a moment resume the chain of history, so that I may the more easily attach to it the thread of my personal recollections.

It will be remembered that, at the opening of the session of 1848, King Louis-Philippe, in his speech from the Throne, had described the authors of the banquets as men excited by blind or hostile passions. This was bringing Royalty into direct conflict with more than one hundred members of the Chamber. This insult, which added anger to all the ambitious passions which were already disturbing the hearts of the majority of these men, ended by making them lose their reason. A violent debate was expected, but did not take place at once. The earlier discussions on the Address were calm : the majority and the Opposition both restrained themselves at the beginning, like two men who feel that they have lost their tempers, and who fear lest while in their condition, they should perpetrate some folly in word or deed.

But the storm of passion broke out at last, and continued with unaccustomed violence. The extraordinary heat of these debates was already redolent of civil war for those who knew how to scent revolutions from afar.

The spokesman of the moderate section of the Opposition was led, in the heat of debate, to assert that the right of assembling at the banquets was one of our most undeniable and essential rights ;[1] that to question it, was equivalent to trampling liberty itself underfoot and to violating the Charter, and that those who did so unconsciously made an appeal, not to discussion, but to arms.

On his side M. Duchâtel, who ordinarily was very dexterous in debate, displayed in this circumstance a consummate want of tact.[2] He absolutely denied the right of assembling, and yet would not say clearly that the Government had made up its mind to prohibit thenceforth any manifestations of the kind. On the contrary, he seemed to invite the Opposition to try the experiment once more, so that the question might be brought before the Courts. His colleague, M. Hébert, the Minister of Justice, was still more tactless, but this was his habit. I have always observed that lawyers never make statesmen ; but I have never met anyone who was less of a statesman than M. Hébert. He remained the

[1] See the speech of M. Duvergier de Hauranne, 7th February, 1848. (Note of the Editor of the 1893 edition.)

[2] The Minister replied to M. Léon de Mandeville. He quoted the laws of 1790 and 1791, which empowered the authorities to oppose any public meetings which seemed to threaten public peace, and he declared that the Government would be failing in its duty if it were to give way before manifestations of any description. At the end of his speech he again brought in the phrase "blind or hostile passions" and endeavoured to justify it. (Note of the Editor of the 1893 edition.)

Public Prosecutor down to the marrow of his bones ; he had all the mental and physical characteristics of that office. You must imagine a little wizened, sorry face, shrunk at the temples, with a pointed forehead, nose and chin, cold, bright eyes, and thin, in-drawn lips. Add to this a long quill generally held across the mouth, and looking at a distance like a cat's bristling whiskers, and you have a portrait of a man, than whom I have never seen anyone more resembling a carnivorous animal. At the same time, he was neither stupid nor even ill-natured ; but he was by nature hot-headed and un-yielding ; he always overshot his goal, for want of know-ing when to turn aside or stop still ; and he fell into violence without intending it, and from sheer want of discrimination. It showed how little importance M. Guizot attached to conciliation, that under the circum-stances he sent a speaker of this stamp to the tribune ;[1] his language while there, was so outrageous and so provok-ing, that Barrot, quite beside himself and almost without knowing what he was doing, exclaimed, in a voice half stifled with rage, that the ministers of Charles X, that Polignac and Peyronnet, had never dared to talk like that. I remember that I shuddered involuntarily in my seat when I heard this naturally moderate man exas-perated into recalling, for the first time, the terrible memories of the Revolution of 1830, holding it up in some sort as an example, and unconsciously suggesting the idea of repeating it.

We know that the result of this heated discussion was a sort of challenge to mortal combat exchanged between the Government and the Opposition, the scene of the duel to be the law-courts. It was tacitly agreed that the challenged party should meet at one final banquet ; that

[1] Replying to M. Odilon Barrot, M. Hébert maintained that, since the right of public meeting was not laid down in the Charter, it did not exist. (Note of the Editor of the 1893 edition.)

the authorities, without interfering to prevent the meeting, should prosecute its organizers, and that the courts should pronounce judgment.

The debates on the Address were closed, if I remember rightly, on the 12th of February, and it is really from this moment that the revolutionary movement burst out. The Constitutional Opposition, which had for many months been constantly pushed on by the Radical party, was from this time forward led and directed not so much by the members of that party who occupied seats in the Chamber of Deputies (the greater number of these had become lukewarm and, as it were, enervated in the Parliamentary atmosphere), as by the younger, bolder, and more irresponsible men who wrote for the demagogic press. This change was especially apparent in two principal facts which had an overwhelming influence upon events—the programme of the banquet and the arraignment of Ministers.

On the 20th of February, there appeared in almost all the Opposition newspapers, by way of programme of the approaching banquet, what was really a proclamation, convoking the schools and inviting the National Guard itself to attend the ceremony as a body. It read like a decree emanating from the Provisional Government which was to be set up three days later. The Cabinet, which had already been blamed by many of its followers for tacitly authorizing the banquet, considered that it was justified in retracing its steps. It officially announced that it forbade the banquet, and that it would prevent it by force.

It was this declaration of the Government which provided the field for the battle. I am in a position to state, although it sounds hardly credible, that the programme which thus suddenly turned the banquet into an insurrection was resolved upon, drawn up and published without the participation or the knowledge of the members of Parliament who considered themselves to be still leading the movement which they had called into existence. The programme was the hurried work of a nocturnal gathering of journalists and Radicals, and the leaders of the Dynastic Opposition heard of it at the same time as the public, by reading it in the papers in the morning.

And see by what counter-strokes human affairs are pushed on ! M. Odilon Barrot, who disapproved of the programme as much as anyone, dared not disclaim it for fear of offending the men, who, till then, had seemed to be moving with him ; and then, when the Government, alarmed by the publication of this document, prohibited the banquet, M. Barrot, finding himself brought face to face with civil war, drew back. He himself gave up this dangerous demonstration ; but at the same time that he was making this concession to the men of moderation, he granted to the extremists the impeachment of Ministers. He accused the latter of violating the Constitution by prohibiting the banquet, and thus furnished an excuse to those who were about to take up arms in the name of the violated Constitution.

Thus the principal leaders of the Radical Party, who thought that a revolution would be premature, and who did not yet desire it, had considered themselves obliged, in order to differentiate themselves from their allies in the Dynastic Opposition, to make very revolutionary speeches and fan the flame of insurrectionary passion. On the other hand, the Dynastic Opposition, which had had enough of the banquets, had been forced to persevere in this bad course so as not to present an appearance of retreating before the defiance of the Government. And finally the mass of the Conservatives, who believed in the necessity of great concessions and were ready to make them, were driven by the violence of their adversaries and the passions of some of their chiefs to deny even the right of meeting in private banquets and to refuse the country any hopes of reform.

One must have lived long amid political parties, and in the very whirlwind in which they move, to understand to what extent men mutually push each other away from their respective plans, and how the destinies of this world proceed as the result, but often as the contrary result, of the intentions that produce them, similarly to the kite which flies by the antagonistic action of the wind and the cord.

CHAPTER III

Troubles of the 22nd of February—The Sitting of the 23rd—The New Ministry—Opinions of M. Dufaure and M. de Beaumont.

I DID not perceive anything on the 22nd of February calculated to give rise to serious apprehensions. There was a crowd in the streets, but it seemed to be composed rather of sight-seers and fault-finders than of the seditiously inclined : the soldier and the townsman chaffed each other when they met, and I heard more jokes than cries uttered by the crowd. I know that it is not safe to trust one's self to these appearances. It is the street boys of Paris who generally commence insurrections, and as a rule they do so light-heartedly, like schoolboys breaking up for the holidays.

When I came to the Chamber, I found an apparent listlessness reigning there, beneath which one could perceive the inner seething of a thousand restrained passions. It was the only place in Paris in which, since the early morning, I had not heard discussed aloud what was then absorbing all France. They were languidly discussing a bill for the creation of a bank at Bordeaux ; but in reality no one, except the man talking on the tribune and the man who was to reply to him, showed any interest in the matter. M Duchâtel told me that all was going well. He said this with an air of combined confidence and nervousness which struck me as suspicious. I noticed that he twisted his neck and shoulders (a common trick with him) much more frequently and violently than usual ; and I remember that this little observation gave me more food for reflection than all the rest.

I learnt that, as a matter of fact, there had been serious troubles in many parts of the town which I had not visited ; a certain number of men had been killed or wounded. People were no longer accustomed to this sort of incident, as they had been some years before and as they became still more a few months later; and the excitement was great. I happened to be invited to dine that evening at the house of one of my fellow-members of Parliament and of the Opposition, M. Paulmier, the deputy for Calvados. I had some difficulty in getting there through the troops which guarded the surrounding streets. I found my host's house in great disorder. Madame Paulmier, who was expecting her *accouchement* and who had been frightened by a skirmish that had taken place beneath her windows, had gone to bed. The dinner was magnificent, but the table was deserted; out of twenty guests invited, only five presented themselves; the others were kept back either by material impediments or by the preoccupations of the day. We sat down with a very thoughtful air amid all this abundance. Among the guests was M. Sallandrouze, the inheritor of the great business house of that name, which had made a large fortune by its manufacture of textile fabrics. He was one of those young Conservatives, richer in money than in honours, who, from time to time, made a show of opposition, or rather, of captious criticism, mainly, I think, to give themselves a certain importance. In the course of the last debate on the Address, M. Sallandrouze had moved an amendment[1] which would have compromised the Cabinet, had it been adopted. At the time

[1] M. Sallandrouze de Lamornaix' amendment proposed to modify the expression "blind and hostile passions", by adding the words: "Amid these various demonstrations, your Government will know how to recognize the real and lawful desires of the country; it will, we trust, take the initiative by introducing certain wise and moderate reforms called for by public opinion, among which we must place first parliamentary reform. In a Constitutional Monarchy, the union of the great powers of the State removes all danger from a progressive policy, and allows every moral and material interest of the country to be satisfied." (Note of the Editor of the 1893 edition.)

when this incident was most occupying attention, M. Sallandrouze one evening went to the reception at the Tuileries, hoping that this time, at least, he would not remain unrecognized in the crowd. And, in fact, no sooner had King Louis-Philippe seen him than he came up to him with a very assiduous air, and solemnly took him aside and began to talk to him eagerly, and with a great display of interest, about the branch of manufacture to which the young deputy owed his fortune. The latter, at first, felt no astonishment, thinking that the King, who was known to be clever at managing men's minds, had selected this little private road in order to lead round to affairs of State. But he was mistaken ; for, after a quarter of an hour, the King changed not the conversation but the person addressed, and left our friend standing very confused amid his carpets and woollen stuffs. M. Sallandrouze had not yet got over this trick, played upon him, but he was beginning to feel very much afraid that he would be revenged too well. He told us that M. Émile Girardin had said to him the day before, " In two days the Monarchy of July will have ceased to exist". This seemed to all of us a piece of journalistic hyperbole, and perhaps it was ; but the events that followed turned it into an oracle.

On the next day, the 23rd of February, I learnt, on waking, that the excitement in Paris, so far from becoming calmer, was increasing. I went early to the Chamber ; silence reigned around the Assembly ; battalions of infantry occupied and closed the approaches, while troops of Cuirassiers were drawn up along the walls of the Palace. Inside, men's feelings were excited without their quite knowing the reason.

The sitting had been opened at the ordinary time ; but the Assembly had not had the courage to go through the same parliamentary comedy as on the day before, and had suspended its labours ; it sat receiving reports from the different quarters of the town, awaiting events and counting the hours, in a state of feverish idleness. At a certain moment, a loud sound of trumpets was heard outside. It appeared that the Cuirassiers guarding the Palace were amusing themselves, in order to pass the time, by sounding flourishes on their instruments. The gay, triumphant tones of the trumpets contrasted in so melancholy a fashion with the thoughts by which all our minds were secretly disturbed, that a message was hurriedly sent out to stop this offensive and indiscreet performance, which caused such painful reflections to all of us.

At last, it was determined to speak aloud of what all had been discussing in whispers for several hours. A Paris deputy, M. Vavin, began to question the Cabinet upon the state of the city. At three o'clock M. Guizot appeared at the door of the House. He entered with his firmest step and his loftiest bearing, silently crossed the gangway, ascended the tribune, throwing his head almost back from his shoulders for fear of seeming to lower it, and stated in two words that the King had called upon M. Molé to form a new ministry. Never did I see such a piece of clap-trap.

The Opposition kept their seats, most of them uttering cries of victory and satisfied revenge ; the leaders alone sat silent, busy in communing with themselves upon the use they would make of their triumph, and careful not to insult a majority of which they might soon be called upon to make use. As to the majority, they seemed thunderstruck by this so unexpected blow, moved to and fro like a mass that sways from side to side, uncertain as to which side it shall fall on, and then descended noisily into the semi-circle. A few surrounded the ministers to ask them for explanations or to pay them their last respects, but the greater number clamoured against them with noisy and insulting shouts. " To throw up office, to abandon your political friends under such circumstances," they said, " is a piece of gross cowardice " ; while others exclaimed that the members ought to proceed to the Tuileries in a body, and force the King to re-consider his fatal resolve.

This despair will arouse no astonishment when it is remembered that the greater number of these men felt themselves attacked not only in their political opinions, but in the most sensitive part of their private interest. The fall of the Government compromised the entire fortune of one, the daughter's dowry of another, the son's career of a third. It was by this that they were almost all held. Most of them had not only bettered themselves by means of their votes, but one may say that they had lived on them. They still lived on them, and hoped to continue to live on them ; for, the Ministry having lasted eight years, they had accustomed themselves to think that it would last for ever ; they had grown attached to it with the honest, peaceful feeling of affection which one entertains for one's fields. From my seat, I watched this swaying crowd ; I saw surprise, anger, fear and avarice mingle their various expressions upon those bewildered countenances ; and I drew an involuntary comparison between all these legislators and a pack of hounds which with their jaws half filled, see the quarry withdrawn from them.

I grant, however, that, so far as many of the Opposition were concerned, it only wanted that they should be put to a similar test in order to make the same display. If many of the Conservatives only defended the Ministry with a view to keeping their places and emoluments, I am bound to say that many of the Opposition seemed to me only to attack it in order to reap the plunder in their turn. The truth—the deplorable truth—is that a taste for holding office and a desire to live on the public money is not with us a disease restricted to either party, but the great, chronic ailment of the whole nation ; the result of the democratic constitution of our society and of the excessive centralization of our Government ; the secret malady which has undermined all former governments, and which will undermine all governments to come.

At last the uproar ceased, as the nature of what had happened became better known : we learnt that it had been brought about by the insurrectionary inclinations of a battalion of the Fifth Legion and the representations made direct to the King by several officers of that section of the Guard.

As soon as he was informed of what was going on, King Louis-Philippe, who was less prone to change his opinions, but more ready to change his line of conduct than any man I ever saw, had immediately made up his mind ; and after eight years of complacency, the Ministry was dismissed by him in two minutes and without ceremony.

The Chamber rose without delay, each member thinking only of the change of government, and forgetting about the revolution.

I went out with M. Dufaure, and soon perceived that he was not only preoccupied but constrained. I at once saw that he felt himself in the critical and complicated position of a leader of the Opposition, who was about to become a minister, and who, after experiencing the use his friends could be to him, was beginning to think of the difficulties which their pretensions might well cause him.

M. Dufaure had a somewhat cunning mind, which readily admitted such thoughts as these, and he also possessed a sort of natural rusticity which, combined with great integrity, but rarely permitted him to conceal them. He was, moreover, the most sincere and by far the most respectable of all those who at that moment had a

chance of becoming ministers. He believed that political
power was at last within his grasp, and his ambition
betrayed such a passion that he was the more eager inasmuch as it was discreet and suppressed. M. Molé in his
place would have felt much greater egoism and still more
ingratitude, but he would have been only all the more
openhearted and amiable.

I soon left him, and went to M. de Beaumont's. There
I found every heart rejoicing. I was far from sharing this
joy, and finding myself among people with whom I could
talk freely, I gave my reasons. " The National Guard of
Paris," I said, " has upset a Cabinet ; therefore it is
during its good pleasure only that the new Ministers will
remain at the head of affairs. You are glad that the
Government is upset ; but do you not see that it is
authority itself which is overthrown ? " This sombre view
of the political situation was not much to Beaumont's
taste ; he was carried away by rancour and ambition.
" You always take a gloomy view of everything," he said.
" Let us first rejoice at the victory : we can lament over
the results later."

Madame de Beaumont, who was present at the conversation, seemed herself to share her husband's elation,
and nothing ever so thoroughly proved to me the irresistible power of party feeling. For, by nature, neither hatred
nor self-interest had a place in the heart of this distinguished and attractive woman, one of the most truly
and consistently virtuous that I have met in my life, and
one who best knew to make virtue both touching and
lovable. To the nobility of heart of the La Fayette's she
added a mind that was witty, refined, kindly and just.

I, nevertheless, sustained my theory against both, him
and her, arguing that upon the whole the incident was a
regrettable one, or rather that we should see more in it
than a mere incident, a great event which was destined
to change the whole aspect of affairs. It was very easy

to philosophise thus, since I did not share the illusions of my friend Dufaure.

The impulse given to the political machine seemed to me to be too violent to permit of the reins of government falling into the hands of the intermediate party to which I belonged, and I foresaw that they would soon fall to those who were almost as obnoxious to me as the men from whose hands they had slipped.

I went dining with another of my friends, M. Lanjuinais, of whom I shall have to speak often in future. The company was fairly numerous, and embraced many shades of political opinion. Many of the guests rejoiced at the day's work, while others expressed alarm ; but all thought that the insurrectionary movement would stop of its own accord, to break out again later on another occasion and in another form. All the rumours that reached us from the town seemed to confirm this belief ; cries of war were replaced by cries of joy. Portalis, who became Attorney-General of Paris a few days later, was among us : not the son, but the nephew of the Chief President of the Court of Appeal. This Portalis had neither his uncle's rare intelligence, nor his exemplary character, nor his solemn dullness. His coarse, violent, perverse mind had quite naturally entered into all the false ideas and extreme opinions of our times. Although he was in relation with most of those who are regarded as the authors and leaders of the Revolution of 1848, I can conscientiously declare that he did not that night expect the revolution any more than we did. I am convinced that, even at that supreme moment, the same might have been said of the greater number of his friends. It would be a waste of time to try to discover what secret conspiracies brought about events of this kind. Revolutions accomplished by means of popular risings are generally longed for beforehand rather than premeditated. Those who boast of having contrived them have done no more than turn them to account. They spring spontaneously into being from a general malady of men's minds, brought suddenly to the critical stage by some fortuitous and unforeseen circumstance. As to the so-called originators or leaders of these revolutions, they originate and lead nothing ; their only merit is identical with that of the adventurers who have discovered most of the unknown countries. They simply have the courage to go straight before them as long as the wind impels them.

I took my leave early, and went straight home to bed. Although I lived close to the Foreign Office, I did not hear the firing which so greatly influenced our destinies, and I fell asleep without realizing that I had seen the last day of the Monarchy of July.

CHAPTER IV

The 24th of February—The Ministers' Plan of Resistance— The National Guard—General Bedeau.

THE next morning was the 24th of February. On leaving my bed-room, I met the cook, who had been out ; the good woman was quite beside herself, and poured out a sorrowing rigmarole, of which I failed to understand a word, except that the Government was massacring the poor people. I went downstairs at once, and had no sooner set foot in the street than I breathed for the first time the atmosphere of revolutions. The roadway was empty ; the shops were not open ; there were no carriages nor pedestrians to be seen ; none of the ordinary hawkers' cries were heard ; neighbours stood talking in little groups at their doors, with subdued voices with a frightened air ; every face seemed distorted with fear or anger. I met a National Guard hurrying along, gun in hand, with a tragic gait ; I accosted him, but could learn nothing from him, save that the Government was massacring the people (to which he added that the National Guard would know how to put that right). It was the same old refrain : it is easily understood that this explanation explained nothing. I was too well acquainted with the vices of the Government of July not to know that cruelty was not one of them. I considered it one of the most corrupt, but also one of the least bloodthirsty, that had ever existed, and I only repeat this observation in order to show the sort of rumour that assists the progress of revolutions.

I hastened to M. de Beaumont, who lived in the next street. There I learnt that the King had sent for him during the night. The same reply was given to my en-quiry at M. de Rémusat's, where I went next. M. de Corcelles, whom I met in the street, gave me his account

36

of what was happening, but in a very confused manner ; for in a city in a state of revolution, as on a battle-field, each one readily regards the incidents of which he himself is a witness as the events of the day. He told me of the firing on the Boulevard des Capucines, and of the rapid development of the insurrection of which this act of unnecessary violence was the cause or the pretext ; of M. Molé's refusal to take office under these circumstances ; and lastly, of the summons to the Palace of Messrs. Thiers, Barrot and their friends, who were definitely charged with the formation of a cabinet, facts too well known to permit of my lingering over them. I asked M. de Corcelles how the ministers proposed to set about appeasing people's minds.

" M. de Rémusat," said he, " is my authority for saying that the plan adopted is to withdraw all the troops and to flood Paris with National Guards." These were his own words. I have always observed that in politics people were often ruined through possessing too good a memory.

The men who were now charged to put an end to the Revolution of 1848 were exactly the same who had made the Revolution of 1830. They remembered that at that time the resistance of the army had failed to stop them, and that on the other hand the presence of the National Guard, so imprudently dissolved by Charles X, might have embarrassed them greatly and prevented them from succeeding. They took the opposite steps to those adopted by the Government of the Elder Branch, and arrived at the same result. So true is it that, if humanity be always the same, the course of history is always different, that the past is not able to teach us much concerning the present, and that those old pictures, when forced into new frames, never have a good effect.

After chatting for a little while on the dangerous position of affairs, M. de Corcelles and I went to fetch M.

Lanjuinais, and all three of us went together to M. Dufaure, who lived in the Rue Le Peletier. The boulevard, which we followed to get there, presented a strange spectacle. There was hardly a soul to be seen, although it was nearly nine o'clock in the morning, and one heard not the slightest sound of a human voice ; but all the little sentry-boxes which stand along this endless avenue seemed to move about and totter upon their base, and from time to time one of them would fall with a crash, while the great trees along the curb came tumbling down into the roadway as though of their own accord. These acts of destruction were the work of isolated individuals, who went about their business silently, regularly, and hurriedly, preparing in this way the materials for the barricades which others were to erect. Nothing ever seemed to me more to resemble the carrying on of an industry, and, as a matter of fact, for the greater number of these men it was nothing less. The instinct of disorder had given them the taste for it, and their experience of so many former insurrections the practice. I do not know that during the whole course of the day I was so keenly struck as in passing through this solitude in which one saw, so to speak, the worst passions of mankind at play, without the good ones appearing. I would rather have met in the same place a furious crowd ; and I remember that, calling Lanjuinais' attention to those tottering edifices and falling trees, I gave vent to the phrase which had long been on my lips, and said : " Believe me, this time it is no longer a riot : it is a revolution".

M. Dufaure told us all that concerned himself in the occurrences of the preceding evening and of the night. M. Molé had at first applied to him to assist him to form the new Cabinet ; but the increasing gravity of the situation had soon made them both understand that the moment for their intervention had passed. M. Molé told the King so about midnight, and the King sent him to fetch M. Thiers, who refused to accept office unless he was given M. Barrot for a colleague. Beyond this point, M. Dufaure knew no more than we did. We separated without having succeeded in deciding upon our line of action, and without coming to any resolution beyond that of proceeding to the Chamber as soon as it opened.

M. Dufaure did not come, and I never precisely learnt why. It was certainly not from fear, for I have since seen him very calm and very firm under much more dangerous circumstances. I believe that he grew alarmed for his family, and desired to take them to a place of safety outside Paris. His private and his public virtues, both of which were very great, did not keep step : the first were always ahead of the second, and we shall see signs of this on more than one subsequent occasion. Nor, for that matter, would I care to lay this to his account as a serious charge. Virtues of any kind are too rare to entitle us to vex those who possess them about their character or their degree.

The time which we had spent with M. Dufaure had sufficed to enable the rioters to erect a large number of barricades along the road by which we had come ; they were putting the finishing touches to them as we passed on our way back. These barricades were cunningly constructed by a small number of men, who worked very diligently : not like guilty men hurried by the dread of being taken in the act, but like good workmen anxious to get their task done well and expeditiously. The public watched them quietly, without expressing disapproval or offering assistance. I did not discover any signs of that sort of general seething which I had witnessed in 1830, and which made me at the time compare the whole city to a huge boiling caldron. This time the public was not overthrowing the Government ; it was allowing it to fall.

We met on the boulevard a column of infantry falling

back upon the Madeleine. No one addressed a word to it, and yet its retreat resembled a rout. The ranks were broken, the soldiers marched in disorder, with hanging heads and an air that was both downcast and frightened. Whenever one of them became separated for a mere instant from the main body, he was at once surrounded, seized, embraced, disarmed and sent back : all this was the work of a moment.

Crossing the Place du Havre, I met for the first time a battalion of that National Guard with which Paris was to be flooded. These men marched with a look of astonishment and an uncertain step, surrounded by street boys shouting, " Reform for ever ! " to whom they replied with the same cry, but in a smothered and somewhat constrained voice. This battalion belonged to my neighbourhood, and most of those who composed it knew me by sight, although I knew hardly any of them. They surrounded me and greedily pressed me for news ; I told them that we had obtained all we wanted, that the ministry was changed, that all the abuses complained of were to be reformed, and that the only danger we now ran was lest people should go too far, and that it was for them to prevent it. I soon saw that this view did not appeal to them.

" That's all very well, sir," said they, " the Government has got itself into this scrape through its own fault, let it get out of it as best it can."

It was of small use my representing to them that it was much less a question for the Government at present than for themselves :

" If Paris is delivered to anarchy," I said, " and all the Kingdom is in confusion, do you think that none but the King will suffer ? "

It was of no avail, and all I could obtain in reply was this astonishing absurdity : it was the Government's fault, let the Government run the danger ; we don't want to get killed for people who have managed their business so badly. And yet this was that middle class which had been pampered for eighteen years : the current of public opinion had ended by dragging it along, and was driving it against those who had flattered it until it had become corrupt.

This was the occasion of a reflection which has often since presented itself to my mind ; in France a government always does wrong to rely solely for support upon the exclusive interests and selfish passions of one class. This can only succeed with nations more self-interested and less vain than ours : with us, when a government established upon this basis becomes unpopular, it follows that the members of the very class for whose sake it has lost its popularity prefer the pleasure of traducing it with all the world to the privileges which it assures them. The old French aristocracy, which was more enlightened than our modern middle class and possessed much greater *esprit de corps*, had already given the same example ; it had ended by thinking it a mark of distinction to run down its own privileges, and by thundering against the abuses upon which it existed. That is why I think that, upon the whole, the safest method of government for us to adopt, in order to endure, is that of governing well, of governing in the interest of everybody. I am bound to confess, however, that, even when one follows this course, it is not very certain that one will endure for long.

I soon set out to go to the Chamber, although the time fixed for the opening of the sitting had not yet come: it was, I believe, about eleven o'clock. I found the Place Louis XV still clear of people, but occupied by several regiments of cavalry. When I saw all these troops drawn up in such good order, I began to think that they had only deserted the streets in order to mass themselves around the Tuileries and defend themselves there. At the foot of the obelisk were grouped the staff, among whom, as I drew nearer, I recognized Bedeau, whose unlucky star had quite recently brought him back from Africa, in time to bury the Monarchy. I had spent a few days with him, the year before, at Constantine, and there had sprung up between us a sort of intimacy which has since continued. As soon as Bedeau caught sight of me, he sprang from his horse, came up to me, and grasped my hand in a way that clearly betrayed his excitement. His conversation gave yet stronger evidence of this, and I was not surprised, for I have always observed that the men who lose their heads most easily, and who generally show themselves weakest on days of revolution, are soldiers ; accustomed as they are to have an organized force facing them and an obedient force in their hands, they readily become confused before the uproarious shouts of a crowd and in presence of the hesitation and the occasional connivance of their own men. Unquestionably, Bedeau was confused, and everybody knows what were the results of this confusion : how the Chamber was invaded by a handful of men within pistol-shot of the squadrons protecting it, and how, in consequence, the fall of the Monarchy was proclaimed and the Provisional Government elected. The part played by Bedeau on this fatal day was, unfortunately for himself, of so preponderating a character that I propose to stop a moment in order to analyze this man and his motives for acting as he did. We have been sufficiently intimate both before and after this event to enable me to speak with knowledge. It is true that he received the order not to fight ; but why did he obey so extraordinary an order, which circumstances had rendered so impracticable ?

Bedeau was assuredly not timid by nature, nor even, properly speaking, undecided ; for, when he had once made up his mind, you saw him making for his goal with great firmness, coolness and courage ; but his mind was the most methodical, the least self-reliant, the least adventurous, and the least adapted for unpremeditated action that can well be imagined. He was accustomed to consider the action which he was about to undertake in all its aspects before setting to work, taking the worst aspects first, and losing much precious time in diluting a single thought in a multitude of words. For the rest, he was a just man, moderate, liberal-minded, as humane as though he had not waged war in Africa for eighteen years, modest, moral, even refined, and religious : the kind of honest, virtuous man who is very rarely to be met with in military circles, or, to speak plainly, elsewhere. It was assuredly not from want of courage that he did certain acts which seemed to point to this defect, for he was brave beyond measure ; still less was treachery his motive : although he may not have been attached to the Orleans Family, he was as little capable of betraying those Princes as their best friends could have been, and much less so than their creatures eventually were. His misfortune was that he was drawn into events which were greater than himself, and that he had only merit where genius was needed, and especially the genius to grapple with revolutions, which consists principally in regulating one's actions according to events, and in knowing how to disobey at the right time. The remembrance of February poisoned General Bedeau's life, and left a cruel wound deep down in his soul, a wound whose agony betrayed itself unceasingly by endless recitals and explanations of the events of that period.

While he was engaged in telling me of his perplexities, and in endeavouring to prove that the duty of the Opposition was to come down to the streets in a body and calm the popular excitement with their speeches, a crowd of people glided in between the trees of the Champs-Elysées and came down the main avenue towards the Place Louis XV. Bedeau perceived these men, dragged me towards them on foot until he was more than a hundred paces from his cavalry, and began to harangue them, for he was more disposed to speech-making than any military man I have ever known.

While he was holding forth in this way, I observed that the circle of his listeners was gradually extending itself around us, and would soon close us in ; and through the first rank of sightseers I clearly caught sight of men of riotous aspect moving about, while I heard dull murmurs in the depths of the crowd of these dangerous words, " It's Bugeaud." I leant towards the general and whispered in his ear :

" I have more experience than you of the ways of the populace ; take my word, get back to your horse at once, for if you stay here, you will be killed or taken prisoner before five minutes are over."

He took my word for it, and it was well he did. A few moments later, these same men whom he had under-taken to convert murdered the occupants of the guard-house in the Rue des Champs-Élysées; I myself had some difficulty in forcing my way through them. One of them, a short, thick-set man, who seemed to belong to the lower class of workmen, asked me where I was going.

I replied, " To the Chamber," adding, to show that I was a member of the Opposition, " Reform for ever ! You know the Guizot Ministry has been dismissed ? "

" Yes, sir, I know," replied the man, jeeringly, and pointing to the Tuileries, " but we want more than that."

CHAPTER V

The Sitting of the Chamber—Madame la Duchesse D'Orléans—The Provisional Government.

I ENTERED the Chamber; the sitting had not yet commenced. The deputies were wandering about the lobbies like men distraught, living on rumours, and quite without information. It was not so much an assembly as a mob, for nobody was leading it.

The leaders of both parties were absent: the ex-ministers had fled, the new ones had not appeared. Members cried loudly for the sitting to open impelled rather by a vague desire for action than by any definite intention; the President refused: he was accustomed to do nothing without instructions, and since there was no one left to instruct him, he was unable to make up his mind. I was begged to go and find him, and persuade him to take the chair, and I did so. I found this excellent man—for so he was, in spite of the fact that he often indulged in well-meaning pieces of trickery, in little pious frauds, in petty villainies, in all the venial sins which a faint heart and a wavering mind are able to suggest to an honest nature—I found him, as I have said, walking to and fro in his room, a prey to the greatest excitement. M. Sauzet possessed good but not striking features; he had the dignity of a parish beadle, a big fat body, with very short arms. At times when he was restless and perplexed—and he almost always was so— he used to wave his little arms convulsively, and move them about like a swimmer. His demeanour during our conversation was of the strangest: he walked about, stopped still, sat down with one foot underneath his clumsy frame, as he used to do in moments of great excitement, stood up again, sat down anew, and came to no decision. It was very unfortunate for the House of

45

Orleans that it had an honest man of this kind to preside over the Chamber on a day like this : an audacious rogue would have served its turn better.

M. Sauzet gave me many reasons for not opening the sitting, but one which he did not give me convinced me that he was right. Seeing him so helpless and so incapable of adopting any resolution, I considered that he would only confuse men's minds the more he tried to regulate them. I therefore left him, and thinking it more important to find protectors for the Chamber than to open its deliberations, I went out, intending to proceed to the Ministry of the Interior and ask for help.

As I crossed the Place du Palais-Bourbon with this object, I saw a very mixed crowd accompanying two men, whom I soon recognized as Barrot and Beaumont, with loud cheers. Both of them wore their hats crushed down over their eyes ; their clothes were covered with dust, their cheeks looked hollow, their eyes weary : never were two men in triumph so suggestive of men about to be hanged. I ran up to Beaumont, and asked him what was happening. He whispered that the King had abdicated in his presence, and had taken to flight ; that Lamoricière had apparently been killed when he went out to announce the abdication to the rioters (in fact, an aide-de-camp had come back to say that he had seen him at a distance fall from his horse), that everything was going wrong, and finally, that he and Barrot were now on their way to the Ministry of the Interior in order to take possession of it, and to try and establish somewhere a centre of authority and resistance.

" And the Chamber ! " I said. " Have you taken any precautions for the defence of the Chamber ? "

Beaumont received this observation with ill-humour as though I had been speaking of my own house. " Who is thinking of the Chamber ? " he replied brusquely.

" What good or what harm can it do at the present juncture ? "

I thought, and rightly, that he was wrong to speak like this. The Chamber, it is true, was at that moment in a curious state of powerlessness, its majority despised and its minority left behind by public opinion. But M. de Beaumont forgot that it is just in times of revolution that the very least instruments of the law, and much more its outer symbols, which recall the idea of the law to the minds of the people, assume the greatest importance ; for it is especially in the midst of this universal anarchy and turmoil that the need is felt of some simulacrum of authority and tradition in order to save the remnants of a half-destroyed constitution or to complete its over-throw. Had the deputies been able to proclaim the Regency, the latter might have ended by triumphing, in spite of the unpopularity of the deputies ; and, on the other hand, it is an undoubted fact that the Provisional Government owed much to the chance which caused it to come into being between the four walls which had so long sheltered the representatives of the nation.

I followed my friends to the Ministry of the Interior, where they were going. The crowd which accompanied us entered, or rather swept in, tumultuously, and even penetrated with us as far as the room which M. Duchâtel had just quitted. Barrot tried to free himself and dismiss the mob, but was unable to succeed.

These people, who held two very different sets of opinions, as I was then enabled to observe, some being Republicans and others Constitutionalists, began vehemently to discuss with us and among themselves the measures which were to be taken ; and as we were all squeezed together in a very small space, the heat, dust, confusion, and uproar soon became unbearable. Barrot, who always launched out into long, pompous phrases at the most critical moments, and who preserved an air of dignity, and even of mystery, in the most ludicrous circumstances, was holding forth at his best *in angustiis*. His voice occasionally rose above the tumult, but never succeeded in quelling it. In despair and disgust at so violent and ludicrous a scene, I left this place, where they were exchanging almost as many cuffs as arguments, and returned to the Chamber.

I reached the entrance to the building without suspecting what was happening inside, when I saw people come running up, crying that Madame la Duchesse d'Orléans, the Comte de Paris and the Duc de Nemours had just arrived. At this news, I flew up the stairs of the Palace, four at a time, and rushed into the House.

I saw the three members of the Royal Family whom I have named, at the foot of the tribune, facing the House. The Duchesse d'Orléans was seated, dressed in mourning, calm and pale ; I could see that she was greatly excited, but her excitement seemed to be that of courageous natures, more prone to turn to heroism than fright.

The Comte de Paris displayed the carelessness of his age and the precocious impassiveness of princes. Standing by their side was the Duc de Nemours, tightly clad in his uniform—cold, stiff, and erect. He was, to my mind, the only man who ran any real danger that day ; and during the whole time that I saw him exposed to it, I constantly observed in him the same firm and silent courage. [A courage more fit to discourage and weaken his friends than to impress his adversaries ; a courage which could hardly help him to die decently when the moment came.]

Around these unhappy Princes pressed the National Guards who had come with them, some deputies, and a small number of the crowd. The galleries were empty and closed, with the exception of the press gallery, into which an unarmed but clamorous crowd had forced its way. I was more struck by the cries that issued at intervals from there than by all else that occurred during the sitting.

Fifty years had passed since the last scene of this kind. Since the time of the Convention, the galleries had been silent, and the silence of the galleries had become part of our parliamentary customs. However, if the Chamber at this moment already felt embarrassed in its actions, it was not as yet in any way constrained ; the deputies were in considerable numbers, though the party leaders were still absent. I heard enquiries on every side for M. Thiers and M. Barrot ; I did not know what had become of M. Thiers, but I knew only too well what M. Barrot was doing. I hurriedly sent one of our friends to tell him of what was happening, and he came running up with all speed. I can answer for that man that his soul never knew fear.

After for a moment watching this extraordinary sitting, I had hastened to take my usual seat on the upper benches of the Left Centre : it has always been my contention that at critical moments one should not only be present in the assembly of which one is a member, but occupy the place where one is generally to be found.

A sort of confused and turbulent discussion had been opened : I heard M. Lacrosse, who since became my colleague in office, cry amid the uproar :

" M. Dupin wishes to speak ! "

" No, no ! "

"No," replied M. Dupin, "I made no such request."

" No matter," came from every side, " speak, speak, speak ! "

Thus urged, M. Dupin ascended the tribune, and proposed in two words that they should return to the law of 1842, and proclaim the Duchesse d'Orléans Regent. This was received with applause in the Assembly, exclamations in the gallery, and murmurs in the lobbies. The lobbies, which at first were pretty clear, began to grow crowded in an alarming manner. The people did not yet come into the Chamber in streams, but entered little by little, one by one ; each moment there appeared a new face ; the Chamber grew flooded as it were by drops. Most of the newcomers belonged to the lowest classes ; many of them were armed.

I witnessed this growing invasion from a distance, and I felt the danger momentarily increase with it. I cast my eyes round the Chamber in search of the man best able to resist the torrent ; I saw only Lamartine, who had the necessary position and the requisite capacity to make the attempt ; I remembered that in 1842 he was the only one who proposed the regency of the Duchesse d'Orléans. On the other hand, his recent speeches, and especially his recent writings, had obtained for him the favour of the people. His talent, moreover, was of a kind that appeals to the popular taste. I was not aware that, half an hour before, he had been extolling the Republic to an assemblage of journalists and deputies in one of the offices of the Chamber. I saw him standing by his bench. I elbowed my way to him, and, when I reached him :

" We shall be lost," I whispered, hurriedly : " you alone can make yourself heard at this supreme moment ; go to the tribune and speak."

I can see him still, as I write these lines, so struck was I with his appearance. I see his long, straight, slender figure, his eye turned towards the semi-circle, his fixed and vacant gaze absorbed in inward contemplation rather than in observing what was passing around him. When he heard me speak, he did not turn towards me, but only stretched out his arm towards the place where the Princes stood, and, replying to his own thought rather than to mine, said :

" I shall not speak as long as that woman and that child remain where they are."

I said no more ; I had heard enough. Returning to my bench, I passed by the Right Centre, near where Lanjuinais and Billault were sitting, and asked, " Can you suggest nothing that we could do ? " They mournfully shook their heads, and I continued on my way.

Meantime, the crowd had accumulated to such an extent in the semi-circle, that the Princes ran the risk of being crushed or suffocated at any moment.

The President made vain efforts to clear the House ; failing in his endeavours, he begged the Duchesse d'Orléans to withdraw. The courageous Princess refused, whereupon her friends, with great difficulty, extricated her from the throng, and made her climb to the top bench of the Left Centre, where she sat down with her son and the Duc de Nemours.

Marie and Crémieux had just, amid the silence of the deputies and the acclamations of the people, proposed the establishment of a provisional government, when Barrot at last appeared. He was out of breath, but not alarmed. Climbing the stairs of the tribune :

" Our duty lies before us," he said ; " the Crown of July rests on the head of a child and a woman."

The Chamber, recovering its courage, plucked up heart to burst into acclamations, and the people in their turn were silent. The Duchesse d'Orléans rose from her seat, seemed to wish to speak, hesitated, listened to timid counsels, and sat down again : the last glimmer of her fortune had gone out. Barrot finished his speech without renewing the impression of his opening words ; nevertheless, the Chamber had gathered strength, and the crowd wavered.

At that moment, the crowd filling the semi-circle was driven back, by a stream from outside, towards the centre benches, which were already almost deserted ; it burst and spread over the benches. Of the few deputies who still occupied them, some slipped away and left the

House, while others retreated from bench to bench, like victims surprised by the tide, who retreat from rock to rock always pursued by the rising waters. All this commotion was produced by two troops of men, for the most part armed, which marched through the two lobbies, each with officers of the National Guards and flags at their head. The two officers who carried the flags, of whom one, a swaggering individual, was, as I heard later, a half-pay colonel called Dumoulin, ascended the tribune with a theatrical air, waved their standards, and with much skipping about and great melodramatic gestures, bawled out some revolutionary balderdash or other. The President declared the sitting suspended, and proceeded to put on his hat, as is customary; but, since he had the knack of making himself ridiculous in the most tragic situations, in his precipitation he seized the hat of a secretary instead of his own, and pulled it down over his eyes and ears.

Sittings of this sort, as may be believed, are not easily suspended, and the President's attempts only succeeded in adding to the disorder.

Thenceforth there was nothing but one continuous uproar, broken by occasional moments of silence. The speakers appeared in the tribune in groups; Crémieux, Ledru-Rollin, and Lamartine sprang into it at the same time. Ledru-Rollin drove Crémieux out, and himself held on with his two great hands, while Lamartine, without leaving or struggling waited for his colleague to finish speaking. Ledru-Rollin began incoherently, interrupted every instant by the impatience of his own friends. " Finish ! finish ! " cried Berryer, more experienced than he, and warier in his dynastic ill-will than was the other in his republican passion. Ledru-Rollin ended by demanding the appointment of a provisional government and descended the stair.

Then Lamartine stepped forward and obtained silence. He commenced with a splendid eulogium on the courage of the Duchesse d'Orléans, and the people themselves, sensible, as always, to generous sentiments wrapped up in fine phrases, applauded. The deputies breathed again. " Wait," said I to my neighbours, " this is only the exordium." And in fact, before long, Lamartine tacked round and proceeded straight in the same direction as Ledru-Rollin.

Until then, as I said, all the galleries except the one reserved for the press had remained empty and closed ; but while Lamartine was speaking, loud blows were heard at the door of one of them, and yielding to the strain, the door burst into atoms. In a moment the gallery was invaded by an armed mob of men, who noisily filled it and soon afterwards all the others. A man of the lower orders, placing one foot on the cornice, pointed his gun at the President and the speaker ; others seemed to level theirs at the assembly. The Duchesse d'Orléans and her son were hurried out of the Chamber by some devoted friends and into the corridor behind the Chair. The President muttered a few words to the effect that the sitting was adjourned, and stepped, or rather slid, off the platform on which the chair was placed. I saw him passing before my eyes like a shapeless mass : never would I have believed that fear could have inspired with such speed, or rather, suddenly reduced to a sort of fluidity, so huge a body. All who had remained of the Conservative members then dispersed, and the populace sprawled over the centre benches, crying, " Let us take the place of the corrupt crew ! "

During all the turbulent scenes which I have just described, I remained motionless in my seat, very attentive, but not greatly excited ; and now, when I ask myself why I felt no keener emotion in presence of an event bound to exercise so great an influence upon the destinies of France and upon my own, I find that the form assumed by this great occurrence did much to diminish the impression it made upon me.

In the course of the Revolution of February, I was present at two or three scenes which possessed the elements of grandeur (I shall have occasion to describe them in their turn) ; but this scene lacked them entirely, for the reason that there was nothing genuine in it. We French, especially in Paris, are prone to introduce our literary or theatrical reminiscences into our most serious demonstrations ; this often gives rise to the belief that the sentiments we express are not genuine, whereas they are only clumsily adorned. In this case the imitation was so evident that the terrible originality of the facts remained concealed beneath it. It was a time when every imagination was besmeared with the crude colours with which Lamartine had been daubing his *Girondins*. The men of the first Revolution were living in every mind, their deeds and words present to every memory. All that I saw that day bore the visible impress of those recollections ; it seemed to me throughout as though they were engaged in acting the French Revolution, rather than continuing it.

Despite the presence of drawn swords, bayonets and muskets, I was unable to persuade myself for a single instant not only that I was in danger of death, but that anybody was, and I honestly believe that no one really was. Bloodthirsty hatreds only showed themselves later : they had not yet had the time to spring up ; the special spirit which was to characterize the Revolution of February did not yet manifest itself. Meantime, men were fruitlessly endeavouring to warm themselves at the fire of our fathers' passions, imitating their gestures and attitudes as they had seen them represented on the stage, but unable to imitate their enthusiasm or to be inflamed with their fury. It was the tradition of violent deeds that was being imitated by cold hearts which understood not the spirit of it. Although I clearly saw that the catastrophe of the piece would be a terrible one, I was never able to take the actors very seriously, and the whole seemed to me like a bad tragedy performed by provincial actors.

I confess that what moved me most that day was the sight of that woman and child, who were made to bear the whole weight of faults that they had not committed. I frequently looked with compassion towards that foreign Princess, thrown into the midst of our civil discords ; and when she had fled, the remembrance of the sweet, sad, firm glances which I had seen her cast upon the Assembly during that long agony came back so vividly to my memory, I felt so touched with pity when I thought of the perils attending her flight that, suddenly springing from my seat, I rushed in the direction which my knowledge of the building led me to believe that she and her son would have taken to seek a place of safety. In a moment I made my way through the crowd, crossed the floor, passed out through the cloak-room, and reached the private staircase which leads from the entrance in the Rue de Bourgogne to the upper floor of the Palace. A messenger whom I questioned as I ran past him told me that I was on the track of the Royal party ; and, indeed, I heard several persons hurriedly mounting the upper portion of the stairs, I therefore continued my pursuit, and reached a landing ; the steps which preceded me had just ceased. Finding a closed door in front of me, I knocked at it, but it was not opened. [There I stood then, not ashamed, but rather astonished to find myself there ; for after all I had no reason to attach myself in such a way to the fortunes of this family. They had never shown me kindness or even confidence. I had seen their elevation to the throne with regret, and, if I faithfully helped to keep them there, it was only public interest, not affection for them that prompted my action. This

55

family had one attraction for me : that which the great unfortunates exert.] If princes were like God, who reads our hearts and accepts the intention for the deed, assuredly these would be pleased with me for what I wished to do that day ; but they will never know, for no one saw me and I told no one.

I returned to the Chamber and resumed my seat. Almost all the members had left ; the benches were occupied by men of the populace. Lamartine was still in the tribune between the two banners, continuing to address the crowd, or rather conversing with them ; for there seemed to be almost as many orators as listeners. The confusion was at its height. In a moment of semi-silence, Lamartine began to read out a list containing the names of the different people proposed by I don't know whom to take share in the Provisional Government that had just been decreed, nobody knows how. Most of these names were accepted with acclamations, some rejected with groans, others received with jest, for in scenes in which the people take part, as in the plays of Shakespeare, burlesque often rubs shoulders with tragedy, and wretched jokes sometimes come to the relief of the ardour of revolution. When Garnier-Pagés' name was proposed, I heard a voice cry, "You've made a mistake, Lamartine ; it's the dead one that's the good one " ; Garnier-Pagés having had a celebrated brother, to whom he bore no resemblance except in name.

M. de Lamartine, I think, was beginning to grow greatly embarrassed at his position ; for in a rebellion, as in a novel, the most difficult part to invent is the end. When, therefore, someone took it into his head to cry, " To the Hôtel de Ville " Larmartine echoed, " Yes to the Hôtel de Ville, " and went out forthwith taking half the crowd with him ; the others remained with Ledru-Rollin, who, in order, I suppose, to retain a leading part for himself, felt called upon in his turn to go through the same mock election, after which he too set out for the Hôtel de Ville. There the same electoral display was gone through once more ; in connection with which I cannot refrain from repeating an anecdote which I was told, a few months later, by M. Marrast. It interrupts the thread of my story a little, but it gives a marvellous picture of two men who were both at that moment playing a great part, and shows the difference, if not in their opinions, at least in their education and habits of thought.

"A list of candidates for the Provisional Government," said Marrast, "had hurriedly been drawn up. It had to be read out to the people, and I handed it to Lamartine, asking him to read it aloud from the top of the steps. 'I can't,' replied Lamartine, after looking at it ; 'my name is on it.' I then passed it on to Crémieux, who, after reading it, said, 'You're making fun of me : you're asking me to read out to the people a list which has not got my name on it !'"

When I saw Ledru-Rollin leave the House, where remained behind none but the sheer dregs of the insurrection, I saw that there was nothing more to be done there. I accordingly went away, but as I did not care to find myself in the middle of the mob marching towards the Hôtel de Ville, I took the opposite direction, and began to go down those steep steps, like cellar stairs, which lead to the inner yard of the Palace. I then saw coming towards me a column of armed National Guards, ascending the same staircase at a run, with set bayonets. In front of them were two men in civilian dress, who seemed to be leading them, shouting at the top of their voices, " Long live the Duchesse d'Orléans and the Regency ! " In one I recognized General Oudinot and in the other Andryane, who was imprisoned in the Spielberg, and who wrote his Memoirs in imitation of those of Silvio Pellico. I saw no one else, and nothing could prove more clearly how difficult it is for the public ever to learn the truth of events happening amid the tumult of a revolution. I know that a letter exists, written by Marshal Bugeaud, in which he relates that he succeeded in getting together a few companies of the Tenth Legion, inspired them in favour of the Duchesse d'Orléans, and led them at the double through the yard of the Palais Bourbon and to the door of the Chamber, which he found empty. The story is true, but for the presence of the marshal, whom I should most certainly have seen had he been there ; but there was no one I repeat, except General Oudinot and M. Andryane. The latter seeing me standing still and saying nothing, took me, sharply by the arm, exclaiming :

" Monsieur, you must join us, to help to free Madame la Duchesse d'Orléans and save the Monarchy."

"Monsieur", I replied, " your intention is good, but you are too late : the Duchesse d'Orléans has disappeared, and the Chamber has risen."

Now, where was the spirited defender of the Monarchy that evening ? The incident is worthy of being told and noted among the many incidents of versatility with which the history of revolutions abounds.

M. Andryane was in the office of M. Ledru-Rollin, officiating in the name of the Republic as general secretary to the Ministry of the Interior.

To return to the column which he was leading : I joined it, although I had no longer any hope of success for its efforts. Mechanically obeying the impulse communicated to it, it proceeded as far as the doors of the Chamber. There the men who composed it learnt what had taken place ; they turned about for a moment, and then dispersed in every direction. Half an hour earlier, this handful of National Guards might (as on the ensuing 15th of May) have changed the fortunes of France. I allowed this new crowd to pass by me, and then, alone and very pensive, I resumed my road home, not without casting a last look on the Chamber, now silent and deserted, in which, during nine years, I had listened to the sound of so many eloquent and futile words.

M. Billault, who had left the Chamber a few minutes before me by the entrance in the Rue de Bourgogne, told me that he met M. Barrot in this street.

"He was walking", he said, " at a rapid rate, without perceiving that he was hatless, and that his grey hair, which he generally carefully brushed back along his temples, was falling on either side and fluttering in disorder over his shoulders ; he seemed beside himself."

This man had made heroic efforts all day long to maintain the Monarchy on the declivity down which he himself had pushed it, and he remained as though crushed beneath its fall. I learned from Beaumont, who had not left him during any part of the day, that in the morning M. Barrot faced and mounted twenty barricades, walking up to each unarmed, meeting sometimes with insults, often with shots, and always ending by overcoming with his words those who guarded them. His words, in fact, were all-powerful with the multitude. He had all that was wanted to act upon them at a given moment : a strong voice, an inflated eloquence, and a fearless heart.

While M. Barrot, in disorder, was leaving the Chamber, M. Thiers, still more distraught, wandered round Paris, not daring to venture home. He was seen for an instant at the Assembly before the arrival of the Duchesse d'Orléans, but disappeared at once, giving the signal for the retreat of many others. The next morning, I learnt the details of his flight through M. Talabot, who had assisted in it. I was connected with M. Talabot by fairly intimate party ties, and M. Thiers, I believe, by former business relations. M. Talabot was a man full of mental vigour and resolution, very fit for an emergency of that kind. He told me as follows—I believe I have neither omitted nor added anything :

" It seems," he said, " that M. Thiers, when crossing the Place Louis XV, had been insulted and threatened by some of the populace. He was greatly excited and upset when I saw him enter the House ; he came up to me, led me aside, and told me that he would be murdered by the mob if I did not assist him to escape. I took him by the arm and begged him to go with me and fear nothing. M. Thiers wished to avoid the Pont Louis XVI, for fear of meeting the crowd. We went to the Pont des Invalides, but when we got there, he thought he saw a gathering on the other side of the river, and again refused to cross. We then made for the Pont d'Iéna, which was free, and crossed it without any difficulty. When we reached the other side, M. Thiers discovered some street-boys, shouting, on the foundations of what was to have been the palace of the King of Rome, and forthwith turned down the Rue d'Auteuil and made for the Bois de Boulogne. There we had the good luck to find a cabman, who consented to drive us along the outer boulevards to the neighbourhood of the Barriére de Clichy, through which we were able to reach his house. During the whole journey," added M. Talabot, " and especially at the start, M. Thiers seemed almost out of his senses, gesticulating, sobbing, uttering incoherent phrases. The catastrophe he had just beheld, the future of his country, his own personal danger, all contributed to form a chaos amid which his thoughts struggled and strayed unceasingly."

[Thus, of the four men who had contributed most to bring about the events of February 27th—Louis Philippe, M. Guizot, M. Thiers and M. Barrot—the two former were exiles at the end of this very day, and the two latter were almost demented.]

PART TWO

Everything contained in this note-book (Chapters I. to XI. inclusive) was written in stray moments at Sorrento, in November and December 1850, *and January, February and March* 1851.

CHAPTER I

*My Explanation of the 24th of February and My
Thoughts as to its Effects upon the Future.*

AND so the Monarchy of July was fallen, fallen without
a struggle, and before rather than beneath the blows of
the victors, who were as astonished at their triumph as
were the vanquished at their defeat. I have often, since
the Revolution of February, heard M. Guizot and even
M. Molé and M. Thiers declare that this event should
only be attributed to a surprise and regarded as a mere
accident, a bold and lucky stroke and nothing more. I
have always felt tempted to answer them in the words
which Molière's Misanthrope uses to Oronte :

> Pour en juger ainsi, vous avez vos raisons ;

for these three men had conducted the affairs of France,
under the guidance of King Louis-Philippe, during
eighteen years, and it was difficult for them to admit that
it was the King's bad government which had prepared
the catastrophe which hurled him from the Throne.

As for me, I have not the same motives of belief for
forming an opinion, and I could hardly persuade myself
to be of theirs. I am not prepared to say that accidents
played no part in the Revolution of February : on the
contrary, they played a great one ; but they were not
the only thing.

I have come across men of letters, who have written
history without taking part in public affairs, and politicians, who have only concerned themselves with
producing events without thinking of describing them.
I have observed that the first are always inclined to find
general causes, whereas the others, living in the midst of
disconnected daily facts, are prone to imagine that every-

thing is attributable to particular incidents, and that the wires which they pull are the same that move the world. It is to be presumed that both are equally deceived.

For my part, I detest these absolute systems, which represent all the events of history as depending upon great first causes linked by the chain of fatality, and which, as it were, suppress men from the history of the human race. They seem narrow, to my mind, under their pretence of broadness, and false beneath their air of mathematical exactness. I believe (*pace* the writers who have invented these sublime theories in order to feed their vanity and facilitate their work) that many important historical facts can only be explained by accidental circumstances, and that many others remain totally inexplicable. Moreover, chance, or rather that tangle of secondary causes which we call chance, for want of the knowledge how to unravel it, plays a great part in all that happens on the world's stage ; although I firmly believe that chance does nothing that has not been prepared beforehand. Antecedent facts, the nature of institutions, the cast of minds and the state of morals are the materials of which are composed those impromptus which astonish and alarm us.

The Revolution of February, in common with all other great events of this class, sprang from general causes, impregnated, if I am permitted the expression, by accidents ; and it would be as superficial a judgment to ascribe it necessarily to the former or exclusively to the latter.

The industrial revolution which, during the past thirty years, had turned Paris into the principal manufacturing city of France and attracted within its walls an entire new population of workmen (to whom the works of the fortifications had added another population of labourers at present deprived of work), [together with the excess in material pleasures fostered by the government itself], tended more and more to inflame this multitude. Add to this the democratic disease of envy, which was silently permeating it ; the economical and political theories which were beginning to make their way and which strove to prove that human misery was the work of laws and not of Providence, and that poverty could be suppressed by changing the conditions of society ; the contempt into which the governing class, and especially the men who led it, had fallen, a contempt so general and so profound that it paralysed the resistance even of those who were most interested in maintaining the power that was being overthrown ; the centralization which reduced the whole revolutionary movement to the overmastering of Paris and the seizing of the machinery of government ; and lastly, the mobility of all this, institutions, ideas, men and customs, in a fluctuating state of society which had, in less than sixty years, undergone the shock of seven great revolutions, without numbering a multitude of smaller, secondary upheavals. These were the general causes without which the Revolution of February would have been impossible. The principal accidents which led to it were the passions of the dynastic Opposition, which brought about a riot in proposing a reform ; the suppression of this riot, first over-violent and then abandoned ; the sudden disappearance of the old Ministry, unexpectedly snapping the threads of power, which the new ministers, in their confusion, were unable either to seize upon or to reunite ; the mistakes and disorder of mind of these ministers, so powerless to reestablish that which they had been strong enough to overthrow ; the vacillation of the generals ; the absence of the only princes who possessed either personal energy or popularity ; and above all, the senile imbecility of King Louis-Philippe, his weakness, which no one could have foreseen, and which still remains almost incredible, after the event has proved it.

I have sometimes asked myself what could have produced this sudden and unprecedented depression in the King's mind. Louis-Philippe had spent his life in the midst of revolutions, and certainly lacked neither experience, courage, nor readiness of mind, although these qualities all failed him so completely on that day. In my opinion, his weakness was due to his excessive surprise ; he was overwhelmed with consternation before he had grasped the meaning of things. The Revolution of February was *unforeseen* by all, but by him more than any other ; he had been prepared for it by no warning from the outside, for since many years his mind had withdrawn into that sort of haughty solitude into which in the end the intellect almost always settles down of princes who have long lived happily, and who, mistaking luck for genius, refuse to listen to anything, because they think that there is nothing left for them to learn from anybody. Besides, Louis-Philippe had been deceived, as I have already said that his ministers were, by the misleading light cast by antecedent facts upon present times. One might draw a strange picture of all the errors which have thus been begotten, one by the other, without resembling each other. We see Charles I driven to tyranny and violence at the sight of the progress which the spirit of opposition had made in England during the gentle reign of his father ; Louis XVI determined to suffer everything because Charles I had perished by refusing to endure anything ; Charles X provoking the Revolution, because he had with his own eyes beheld the weakness of Louis XVI ; and lastly, Louis-Philippe, who had more perspicacity than any of them, imagining that, in order to remain on the Throne, all he had to do was to observe the letter of the law while violating its spirit, and that, provided he himself kept within the bounds of the Charter, the nation would never exceed them. To warp the spirit of the Constitution without changing the letter ; to set the vices of the country in opposition to each other ; gently to drown revolutionary passion in the love of material enjoyment ; such was the idea of his whole life. Little by little, it had become, not his leading, but his sole idea. He had wrapped himself in it, he had lived in it ; and when he suddenly saw that it was a false idea, he became like a man who is awakened in the night by an earthquake, and who, feeling his house crumbling in the darkness, and the very ground seeming to yawn beneath his feet, remains distracted amid this unforeseen and universal ruin.

I am arguing very much at my ease to-day concerning the causes that brought about the events of the 24th of February ; but on the afternoon of that day I had many other things in my head : I was thinking of the events themselves, and sought less for what had produced them than for what was to follow.

I returned slowly home. I explained in a few words to Madame de Tocqueville what I had seen, and sat down in a corner to think. I cannot remember ever feeling my soul so full of sadness. It was the second revolution I had seen accomplish itself, before my eyes, within seventeen years!

On the 30th of July, 1830, at daybreak, I had met the carriages of King Charles X on the outer boulevards of Versailles, with damaged escutcheons, proceeding at a foot pace, in Indian file, like a funeral, and I was unable to restrain my tears at the sight. This time my impressions were of another kind, but even keener. Both revolutions had afflicted me ; but how much more bitter were the impressions caused by the last! I had until the end felt a remnant of hereditary affection for Charles X ; but that King fell for having violated rights that were dear to me, and I had every hope that my country's freedom would be revived rather than extinguished by his fall. But now this freedom seemed dead ; the Princes who were fleeing were nothing to me, but I felt that the cause I had at heart was lost.

I had spent the best days of my youth amid a society which seemed to increase in greatness and prosperity as it increased in liberty ; I had conceived the idea of a balanced, regulated liberty, held in check by religion, custom and law ; the attractions of this liberty had touched me ; it had become the passion of my life ; I felt that I could never be consoled for its loss, and that I must renounce all hope of its recovery.

I had gained too much experience of men to be able to content myself with empty words ; I knew that, if one great revolution is able to establish liberty in a country, a number of succeeding revolutions make all regular liberty impossible for very many years.

I could not yet know what would issue from this last revolution, but I was already convinced that it could give birth to nothing that would satisfy me ; and I foresaw that, whatever might be the lot reserved for our posterity, our own fate was to drag on our lives miserably amid alternate reactions of licence and oppression.

I began to pass in review the history of our last sixty years, and I smiled bitterly when I thought of the illusions formed at the conclusion of each period in this long revolution ; the theories on which these illusions had been fed ; the sapient dreams of our historians, and all the ingenious and deceptive systems by the aid of which it had been endeavoured to explain a present which was still incorrectly seen, and a future which was not seen at all.

The Constitutional Monarchy had succeeded the Ancien Régime ; the Republic, the Monarchy ; the Empire, the Republic ; the Restoration, the Empire ; and then came the Monarchy of July. After each of these successive changes it was said that the French Revolution having accomplished what was presumptuously called its work, was finished ; this had been said and it had been believed. Alas ! I myself had hoped it under the Restoration, and again after the fall of the Government of the Restoration ; and here is the French Revolution beginning over again, for it is still the same one. As we go on, its end seems farther off and shrouded in greater darkness. Shall we ever—as we are assured by other prophets, perhaps as delusive as their predecessors—shall we ever attain a more complete and more far-reaching social transformation than our fathers foresaw and desired, and than we ourselves are able to foresee ; or are we not destined simply to end in a condition of inter-mittent anarchy, the well-known chronic and incurable complaint of old peoples ? As for me, I am unable to say ; I do not know when this long voyage will be ended ; I am weary of seeing the shore in each successive mirage, and I often ask myself whether the *terra firma* we are seeking does really exist, and whether we are not doomed to rove upon the seas for ever !

I spent the rest of the day with Ampère, who was my colleague at the Institute, and one of my best friends. He came to discover what had become of me in the affray, and to ask himself to dinner. I wished at first to relieve myself by making him share my vexation ; but I soon perceived that his impression was not the same as mine, and that he looked differently upon the revolution which was in progress. Ampère was a man of intelligence and, better still, a man full of heart, gentle in manner, and reliable. His good nature caused him to be liked ; and he was popular because of his versatile, witty, amusing, good-humoured conversation, in which he made many remarks that were at once entertaining and agreeable to hear, but too shallow to remember. Unfor-tunately, he was inclined to carry the *esprit* of the salons into literature and the *esprit* of literature into politics. What I call literary *esprit* in politics consists in seeking for what is novel and ingenious rather than for what is true ; in preferring the showy to the useful ; in showing one's self very sensible to the playing and elocution of the actors, without regard to the results of the play ; and, lastly, in judging by impressions rather than reasons. I need not say that this eccentricity exists among others besides Academicians. To tell the truth, the whole nation is a little inclined that way, and the French public very often takes a man-of-letters' view of politics. Ampère held the fallen Government in great contempt, and its last actions [in favour of the Swiss Catholics][1] had irritated him greatly. [The hate in which he held the latter, and particularly their French friends, was the only feeling of hatred I ever met in him. He had a deadly fear of bores, but bigotry he detested from the bottom of his heart. It is true that bigots had hurt him rather cruelly and clumsily, for he was not naturally their adversary, and nothing proves better their blind intolerance than to have inflamed against them a man who was such a good Christian as Ampère. I would not say a good Christian by belief, but by intention, by taste, and, if I may so put it, by temperament. Thus Ampère easily consoled himself for the fall of a government which had served him so ill.] Moreover, he had witnessed many instances of courage, disinterestedness, and even generosity among the insurgents ; and he had been bitten by the popular excitement.

I saw that he not only did not enter into my view, but that he was disposed to take quite an opposite one. Seeing this, I was suddenly impelled to turn against Ampère all the feelings of indignation, grief and anger that had been accumulating in my heart since the morning ; and

[1] The Seven Roman Catholic Swiss Cantons had formed an armed Separate League which received arms and money from Piedmont, France and Austrian Italy. Cf. *The Cambridge Modern History*, vol. XI, pp. 240 sqq. (M.)

I spoke to him with a violence of language which I have often since recalled with a certain shame, and which none but a friendship so sincere as his could have excused. I remember saying to him, *inter alia* :

" You understand nothing of what is happening ; you are judging like a poet or a Paris cockney. You call this the triumph of liberty, when it is its final defeat. I tell you that the people which you so artlessly admire has just succeeded in proving that it is unfit and unworthy to live a life of freedom. Show me what experience has taught it ! Where are the new virtues it has gained, the old vices it has laid aside ? No, I tell you, it is always the same, as impatient, as thoughtless, as contemptuous of law and order, as easily led and as cowardly in the presence of danger as its fathers were before it. Time has altered it in no way, and has left it as frivolous in serious matters as it used to be in trifles."

After much vociferation we both ended by appealing to the future, that enlightened and upright judge who always, alas ! arrives too late.

CHAPTER II

*Paris on the Morrow of the 24th of February and the
Next Days—The Socialistic Character of the New
Revolution.*

THE night passed without accidents, although not until
the morning did the streets cease to resound with cries
and gun-shots ; but these were sounds of triumph, not
of combat. As soon as it was light, I went out to observe
the appearance of the town, and to discover what had
become of my two young nephews, who were being
educated at the Little Seminary, [an educational institution which does little to prepare its pupils for life in a
revolutionary period such as this, and where, moreover,
they are not safe when the time has come]. The Little
Seminary was in the Rue de Madame, at the back of the
Luxembourg, so that I had to cross a great part of the
town to reach it.

I found the streets quiet, and even half deserted, as
they usually are in Paris on a Sunday morning, when
the rich are still asleep and the poor are resting. From
time to time, along the walls one met the victors of the
preceding day ; but they were filled with wine rather
than political ardour, and were, for the most part, making for their homes without taking heed of the passers-by.
A few shops were open, and one caught sight of the
frightened, but still more astonished, shopkeepers, who
reminded one of spectators witnessing the end of a play
which they did not quite understand. What one saw most
of in the streets deserted by the people, was soldiers ;
some walking singly, others in little groups, all unarmed,
and crossing the city on their roads home. The defeat
these men had just sustained had left a very vivid and
lasting impression of shame and anger upon them. This
was noticed later, but was not apparent at the time : the

72

pleasure of finding themselves at liberty seemed to absorb every other feeling in these lads ; they walked with a careless air, with a light and easy gait.

The Little Seminary had not been attacked nor even insulted. My nephews, however, were not there ; they had been sent home the evening before to their maternal grandmother. Accordingly, I turned back, taking the Rue du Bac, to find out what had become of Lamoricière, who was then living in that street ; and it was only after recognizing me that the servants admitted that their master was at home, and consented to take me to him.

I found this singular person, whom I shall have occasion to mention more than once, stretched upon his bed, and reduced to a state of immobility very much opposed to his character or taste. His head was half broken open ; his arms pierced with bayonet-thrusts ; all his limbs bruised and powerless. [He was only able to move part of his arm and his right hand and, from time to time, to put a cigar in his mouth.] For the rest, he was the same as ever, with his bright intelligence and his indomitable heart. He told me of all that happened to him the day before, and of the thousand dangers which he had only escaped by miracle. I strongly advised him to rest until he was cured, and even long after, so as not uselessly to endanger his person and his reputation in the chaos about to ensue : good advice, undoubtedly, to give a man so enamoured of action and so accustomed to act that, after doing what is necessary and useful, he is always ready to undertake the injurious and dangerous, rather than do nothing ; but no more effective than all those counsels which go against nature.

I spent the whole afternoon in walking about Paris. Two things in particular struck me : the first was, I will not say the mainly, but the uniquely and exclusively popular character of the revolution that had just taken place ; the omnipotence it had given to the people properly so-called—that is to say, the classes who work with their hands—over all others. The second was the comparative absence of malignant passion, or, as a matter of fact, of any keen passion—an absence which at once made it clear that the lower orders had suddenly become masters of Paris.

Although the working classes had often played the leading part in the events of the First Revolution, they had never been the sole leaders and masters of the State, either *de facto* or *de jure* ; it is doubtful whether the Convention contained a single man of the people ; it was composed of *bourgeois* and men of letters. The war between the Mountain and the Girondists was conducted on both sides by members of the middle class, and the triumph of the former never brought power down into the hands of the people alone. The Revolution of July was effected by the people, but the middle class had stirred it up and led it, and secured the principal fruits of it. The Revolution of February, on the contrary, seemed to be made entirely outside the *bourgeoisie* and against it.

In this great concussion, the two parties of which the social body in France is mainly composed had, in a way, been thrown more completely asunder, and the mass of the people, which had stood alone, remained in sole possession of power. Nothing more novel had been known in our annals. Similar revolutions had taken place, it is true, in other countries and other days ; for the history of our own times, however new and unexpected it may seem, always belongs at bottom to the old history of humanity, and what we call new facts are most often nothing more than facts forgotten. Florence, in particular, towards the close of the middle ages, had presented on a small scale a spectacle analogous to ours ; the noble classes had first been succeeded by the burgher classes, and then one day the latter were in their turn expelled from the government, and a *gonfalonier* was seen marching barefoot at the head of the people, and thus leading the Republic. But in Florence this popular revolution was the result of transient and special causes, while with us it was brought about by causes very permanent and of a kind so general that, after stirring up France, it was to be expected that it would excite all the rest of Europe. This time it was not only a question of the triumph of a party ; the aim was to establish a social science, a philosophy, I might almost say a religion, fit to be learned and followed by all mankind. This was the really new portion of the old picture.

Throughout this day, I did not see in Paris a single one of the former agents of the public authority : not a soldier, not a gendarme, not a policeman ; the National Guard itself had disappeared. The people alone bore arms, guarded the public buildings, watched, gave orders, punished ; it was an extraordinary and terrible thing to see in the sole hands of those who possessed nothing, all this immense town, so full of riches, or rather this great nation : for, thanks to centralization, he who reigns in Paris governs France. Hence the terror of all the other classes was extreme ; I doubt whether at any period of the revolution it had been so great, and I should say that it was only to be compared to that which the civilized cities of the Roman Empire must have experienced when they suddenly found themselves in the power of the Goths and Vandals. As nothing like this had ever been seen before, many people expected acts of unexampled violence. For my part I did not once partake of these fears. What I saw led me to predict strange disturbances in the near future—singular crises. But I never believed that the rich would be pillaged ; I knew the men of the people in Paris too well not to know that their first movements in times of revolution are usually generous, and that they are best pleased to spend the days immediately following their triumph in boasting of their victory, laying down the law, and playing at being great men. During that time it generally happens that some government or other is set up, the police returns to its post, and the judge to his bench ; and when at last our great men consent to step down to the better known and more vulgar ground of petty and malicious human passion, they are no longer able to do so, and are reduced to live simply like honest men. Besides, we have spent so many years in insurrections that there has arisen among us a kind of morality peculiar to times of disorder, and a special code for days of rebellion. According to these exceptional laws, murder is tolerated and havoc permitted, but theft is strenuously forbidden ; although this, whatever one may say, does not prevent a good deal of robbery from occurring upon those days,' for the simple reason that society in a state of rebellion cannot be different from that at any other time, and it will always contain a number of rascals who as far as they are concerned, scorn the morality of the main body, and despise its point of honour when they are unobserved. What reassured me still more was the reflection that the victors had been as much surprised by success as their adversaries were by defeat : their passions had not had time to take fire and become intensified in the struggle ; the Government had fallen undefended by others, or even by itself. It had long been attacked, or at least keenly censured, by the very men who at heart most deeply regretted its fall.

For a year past the dynastic Opposition and the republican Opposition had been living in fallacious intimacy, acting in the same way from different motives. The misunderstanding which had facilitated the revolution tended to mitigate its after-effects. Now that the Monarchy had disappeared, the battle-field seemed empty ; the people no longer clearly saw what enemies remained for them to pursue and strike down ; the former objects of their anger, themselves, were no longer there ; the clergy had never been completely reconciled to the new dynasty, and witnessed its ruin without regret ; the old nobility were delighted at it, whatever the ultimate consequences might be : the first had suffered through the system of intolerance of the middle classes, the second through their pride : both either despised or feared their government.

For the first time in sixty years, the priests, the old aristocracy and the people met in a common sentiment—a feeling of revenge, it is true, and not of affection ; but even that is a great thing in politics, where a community of hatred is almost always the foundation of friendships. The real, the only vanquished, were the middle class ; but even this had little to fear. Its reign had been exclusive rather than oppressive ; corrupt, but not violent ; it was despised rather than hated. Moreover, the middle class never forms a compact body in the heart of the nation, a part very distinct from the whole ; it always participates a little with all the others, and in some places merges into them. This absence of homogeneity and of exact limits makes the government of the middle class weak and uncertain, but it also makes it intangible, and, as it were, invisible to those who desire to strike it when it is no longer governing.

From all these united causes proceeded that languor of the people which had struck me as much as its omnipotence, a languor which was the more discernible, in that it contrasted strangely with the turgid energy of the language used and the terrible recollections which it evoked. [The truth is that never was a greater change in the government, and even in the very condition of a nation, brought about by citizens who were themselves so little moved. The *History of the Revolution* by M. Thiers, *The Girondins* by M. Lamartine, as well as other works, particularly plays, which are less well known, had re-habilitated the period of the Terror and brought it to some extent into fashion.] The lukewarm passions of the time were made to speak in the bombastic periods of '93, and one heard cited at every moment the name and example of the illustrious ruffians whom no one possessed either the energy or even a sincere desire to resemble.

It was the Socialistic theories which I have already described as the philosophy of the Revolution of February that later kindled genuine passion, embittered jealousy, and ended by stirring up war between the classes. If the actions at the commencement were less disorderly than might have been feared, on the very morrow of the Revolution there was displayed an extra-ordinary agitation, an unequalled disorder, in the ideas of the people.

From the 25th of February onwards, a thousand strange systems came issuing pell-mell from the minds of innovators, and spread among the troubled minds of the crowd. Everything still remained standing except Royalty and Parliament ; yet it seemed as though the shock of the Revolution had reduced society itself to dust, and as though a competition had been opened for the new form that was to be given to the edifice about to be erected in its place. Everyone came forward with a plan of his own : this one printed it in the papers, that other on the placards with which the walls were soon covered, a third proclaimed his loud-mouthed in the open air. One aimed at destroying inequality of fortune, another inequality of education, a third undertook to do away with the oldest of all inequalities, that between man and woman. Specifics were offered against poverty, and remedies for the disease of work which has tortured humanity since the first days of its existence.

These theories were of very varied natures, often opposed and sometimes hostile to one another ; but all of them, aiming lower than the government and striving to reach society itself, on which government rests, adopted the common name of Socialism.

Socialism will always remain the essential character-istic and the most redoubtable remembrance of the Revolution of February. The Republic will only appear to the on-looker to have come upon the scene as a means not as an end.

It does not come within the scope of these Recollec-tions that I should seek for the causes which gave a socialistic character to the Revolution of February, and I will content myself with saying that the discovery of this new facet of the French Revolution was not of a nature to cause so great surprise as it did. Had it not long been perceived that the people had continually been improving and raising its condition, that its im-portance, its education, its desires, its power had been constantly increasing ? Its prosperity had also grown greater, but less rapidly, and was approaching the limit which it hardly ever passes in old societies, where there are many men and but few places. How should the poor and humbler and yet powerful classes not have dreamt of issuing from their poverty and inferiority by means of their power, especially in an epoch when our view into another world has become dimmer, and the miseries of this world become more visible and seem more intoler-able ? They had been working to this end for the last sixty years. The people had first endeavoured to help itself by changing every political institution, but after each change it found that its lot was in no way improved, or was only improving with a slowness quite incom-patible with the eagerness of its desire. Inevitably, it must sooner or later discover that that which held it fixed in its position was not the constitution of the government but the unalterable laws that constitute society itself; and it was natural that it should be brought to ask itself if it had not both the power and the right to alter those laws, as it had altered all the rest. And to speak more specially of property, which is, as it were, the foundation of our social order—all the privileges which covered it and which, so to speak, concealed the privilege of property having been destroyed, and the latter remaining the principal obstacle to equality among men, and appearing to be the only sign of inequality—was it not necessary, I will not say that it should be abolished in its turn, but at least that the thought of abolishing it should occur to the minds of those who did not enjoy it?

This natural restlessness in the minds of the people, this inevitable perturbation of its thoughts and its desires, these needs, these instincts of the crowd formed in a certain sense the fabric upon which the political innovators embroidered so many monstrous and grotesque figures. Their work may be regarded as ludicrous, but the material on which they worked is the most serious that it is possible for philosophers and statesmen to contemplate.

Will Socialism remain buried in the disdain with which the Socialists of 1848 are so justly covered? I put the question without making any reply. I do not doubt that the laws concerning the constitution of our modern society will in the long run undergo modification; they have already done so in many of their principal parts. But will they ever be destroyed and replaced by others? It seems to me to be impracticable. I say no more, because—the more I study the former condition of the world and see the world of our own day in greater detail, the more I consider the prodigious variety to be met with not only in laws, but in the principles of law, and the different forms even now taken and retained, whatever one may say, by the rights of property on this earth—the more I am tempted to believe that what we call necessary institutions are often no more than institutions to which we have grown accustomed, and that in matters of social constitution the field of possibilities is much more extensive than men living in their various societies are ready to imagine.

CHAPTER III

Uncertainty of the Members of the Old Parliament as to the Attitude they should Adopt—My Own Reflections on my Course of Action and my Resolves.

DURING the days immediately following upon the 24th of February, I neither went in search of nor fell in with any of the politicians from whom the events of that day had separated me. I felt no necessity nor, to tell the truth, any inclination to do so. I felt a sort of instinctive repugnance to remembering this wretched parliamentary world, in which I had spent ten years of my life, and in whose midst I had seen the Revolution sprouting up.

Moreover, at that time I saw the great vanity of any sort of political conversation or combination. However feeble the reasons may have been which first imparted the movement to the crowd, that movement had now become irresistible. I felt that we were all in the midst of one of those great floods of democracy in which the embankments, intended to resist individuals and even parties, only serve to drown those who build them, and in which, for a time, there is nothing to be done but to study the general character of the phenomenon. I therefore spent all my time in the streets with the victors, as though I had been a worshipper of fortune. True, I paid no homage to the new sovereign, and asked no favours of it. I did not even address it, but contented myself with listening to and observing it.

Nevertheless, after the lapse of some days, I resumed relations with the vanquished : I once more met ex-deputies, ex-peers, men of letters, men of business and finance, land-owners, all who in the language of the moment were commencing to be known as the idle. I found that the aspect of the Revolution was no less extraordinary when thus seen from above than it had seemed to me when, at the commencement, I viewed it from below. I encountered much fear, but as little genuine passion as I had seen in other quarters ; a curious feeling of resignation, no vestige of hope, and I should almost say no idea of ever returning to the Government which they had only just left. Although the Revolution of February was the shortest and the least bloody of all our revolutions, it had filled men's minds and hearts with the idea of its omnipotence to a much greater extent than any of its predecessors. I believe this was, to a great extent, due to the fact that these minds and hearts were void of political faith and ardour, and that, after so many disappointments and vain agitations, they retained nothing but a taste for comfort—a very tenacious and very exclusive, but also a very agreeable feeling, which easily accommodates itself to any form of government, provided it be allowed to satisfy itself.

I observed, therefore, an universal endeavour to make the best of the new state of things and to win over the new master. The great landlords were glad to remember that they had always been hostile to the middle class and always favoured the people. [The priests once more found the dogma of equality in the Gospels and assured us that they had always seen it there] ; the *bourgeois* themselves remembered with a certain pride that their fathers had been working men, and when they were unable, owing to the inevitable obscurity of their pedigrees, to trace back their descent to a labourer who had worked with his hands, they at least strove to discover a plebeian ancestor who had been the architect of his own fortune. They took as great pains to make a display of the latter as, not long before, they would have taken to conceal his existence : so true is it that human vanity, without changing its nature, can show itself under the most diverse aspects. It has an obverse and a reverse side, but it is always the same medal.

As there was no longer any genuine feeling left save that of fear, far from breaking with those of his relations who had thrown themselves into the Revolution, each strove to draw closer to them. The time had come to try and turn to account any scapegrace whom one had in one's family. If good luck would have it that one had a cousin, a brother, or a son who had become ruined by his disorderly life, one could be sure that he was in a fair way to succeed ; and if he had become known by the promulgation of some extravagant theory or other, he might hope to attain to any height. Most of the com-missaries and under-commissaries of the Government were men of this type. [Those bad men whom one avoid-ed mentioning, who, formerly, would have been put in the Bastille and who, in our days, would be sent as public functionaries to Algiers, suddenly came into the lime-light and became the support of their families.]

As to King Louis-Philippe, there was no more question of him than if he had belonged to the Merovingian Dynasty. Nothing struck me more than the absolute silence that had suddenly surrounded his name. I did not hear it pronounced a single time, so to speak, either by the people or by the upper class. Those of his former courtiers whom I saw did not speak of him, and I honestly believe they did not think of him. The Revo-lution had so completely turned their thoughts in another direction, that they had forgotten their Sover-eign. I may be told that this is the ordinary fate of fallen kings ; but what seems more worthy of remark, his enemies even had forgotten him : they no longer feared him enough to slander him, perhaps even to hate him, which is one of fortune's greatest, or at least rarest, insults.

I do not wish to write the history of the Revolution of 1848, I only wish to retrace my own actions, ideas, and impressions during the course of this revolution ; and I therefore pass over the events that took place during the weeks immediately following the 24th of February, and come to the period preceding the General Election.

The time had come to decide whether one cared merely to watch the progress of this singular revolution or to take part in events. I found the former party leaders divided among themselves ; and each of them, more-over, seemed divided also within himself, to judge by the incoherence of the language used and the vacillation of opinion. These politicians, who had almost all been trained to public business amid the regulated, restrained movement of constitutional liberty, and upon whom a great revolution had unexpectedly come, were like river oarsmen who should suddenly find themselves called upon to navigate their boat in mid-ocean. The knowledge they had acquired in their freshwater trips would be of more trouble than assistance to them in this greater adventure, and they would often display more confusion and un-certainty than the passengers themselves.

M. Thiers frequently expressed the opinion that they should go to the poll and get elected, and as frequently urged that it would be wiser to stand aside. I do not know whether his hesitation arose from his dread of the dangers that might follow upon the election or his fear lest he should not be elected. Rémusat, who always sees so clearly what might, and so dimly what should be done, set forth the good reasons that existed for staying at home, and the no less good reasons for going to the country. Duvergier was distracted. The Revolution had overthrown the system of the balance of power in which his mind had sat motionless during so many years, and he felt as though he were hung up in mid-air. As for the Duc de Broglie, he had not put his head out of his shell since the 24th of February, and in this attitude he await-ed the end of society, which in his opinion was close at hand. M. Molé alone, although he was by far the oldest of all the former parliamentary leaders, and possibly for that very reason, resolutely maintained the opinion that they should take part in public affairs and try to lead the Revolution : perhaps because his longer experience had taught him that in troubled times it is dangerous to play the looker-on ; perhaps because the hope of again having something to lead cheered him and hid from him the danger of the undertaking ; or perhaps because, after being so often bent in contrary directions, under so many different régimes, his mind had become firmer as well as more supple and more indifferent as to the kind of master it might serve. On my side, as may be imagined, I very attentively considered which was the best resolution to adopt.

I should like here to inquire into the reasons which determined my course of action, and having found them, to set them down without evasion : but how difficult it is to speak well of one's self ! I have observed that the greater part of those who have written their Memoirs have only well shown us their bad actions or their weaknesses when they happened to have taken them for deeds of prowess or fine instincts, a thing which often occurs. As in the case of the Cardinal de Retz, who, in order to be credited with what he considers the glory of being a good conspirator, confesses his schemes for assassinating Richelieu, and tells us of his hypocritical devotions and charities lest he should fail to be taken for a clever man. In such cases it is not the love of truth that guides the pen, but the warped mind which involuntarily betrays the vices of the heart.

And even when one wishes to be sincere, it is very rarely that one succeeds in the endeavour. The fault lies in the first place with the public, which likes to see one accuse, but will not suffer him to praise, himself; even one's friends are wont to describe as amiable candour all the harm, and as unbecoming vanity all the good, that

he says of himself ; so that at this rate sincerity becomes
a very thankless trade, by which one has everything to
lose and nothing to gain. But the difficulty, above all,
lies with the subject himself : he is too close to himself to
see well, and prone to lose himself amid the views,
interests, ideas, thoughts and inclinations that have
guided his actions. This net-work of little foot-paths,
which are little known even by those who use them,
prevent one from clearly discerning the main roads followed by the will before arriving at the most important
conclusions.

Nevertheless, I will try to discover myself amid this
labyrinth, for it is only right that I should take the same
liberties with myself which I have taken, and shall often
continue to take, with others.

Let me say, then, that when I came to search carefully
into the depths of my own heart, I discovered, with some
surprise, a certain sense of relief, a sort of gladness
mingled with all the griefs and fears to which the Revolution had given rise. I suffered from this terrible event
for my country, but clearly not for myself ; on the contrary, I seemed to breathe more freely than before the
catastrophe. I had always felt myself stifled in the atmosphere of the parliamentary world which had just been
destroyed : I had found it full of disappointments, both
where others and where I myself was concerned ; and to
commence with the latter, I was not long in discovering
that I did not possess the necessary qualifications to play
the brilliant rôle that I had imagined : both my qualities
and my defects were impediments. I had not the virtues
necessary to command respect, and I was too upright to
stoop to all the petty practices which were at that time
essential to a speedy success. And observe that this
uprightness was irremediable ; for it forms so integral a
part both of my temperament and my principles, that
without it I am never able to turn myself to any account.

Whenever I have, by ill-luck, been obliged to speak in defence of a bad cause, or to assist in bad measures, I have immediately found myself deprived of all talent and all ardour ; and I confess that nothing has consoled me more at the want of success with which my uprightness has often met, than the certainty I have always been in that I could never have made more than a very clumsy and mediocre rogue. [I wrongly believed that I would rediscover on the tribune of Parliament the success with which my book had met.[1] The experiences of the writer and of the orator do one another more harm than good. Nothing is less like a good speech than a good chapter. I soon observed and clearly understood that I was classified among the correct and clever speakers, sometimes profound, but always cold and consequently without power. I was never able to change in this respect. Surely I do not lack passions, but on the rostrum the passion of saying things well has always momentarily extinguished in me all the other passions.] I also ended by discovering that I was absolutely lacking in the art of grouping and leading a large number of men. I have always been incapable of dexterity, except in *tête-à-tête*, and embarrassed and dumb in the presence of a crowd ; I do not mean to say that at a given moment I am unable to say and do what will please it, but that is not enough : those great occasions are very rare in parliamentary warfare. The trick of the trade, in a party leader, is to be able to mix continually with his followers and even with his adversaries, to show himself, to move about daily, to play continually now to the boxes, now to the gallery, so as to reach the level of every intelligence, to discuss and argue without end, to say the same things a thousand times in different ways, and to be impassioned eternally in the face of the same objects. These are all things of which I am quite incapable. I find it troublesome to

[1] Tocqueville alludes here to *Democracy in America*. (M.)

discuss matters which interest me little, and painful to discuss those in which I am keenly concerned. Truth is for me so rare and precious a thing that, once found, I do not like to risk it on the hazard of a debate ; it is a light which I fear to extinguish by waving it to and fro. And as to consorting with men, I could not do so in any habitual and general fashion, because I never recognize more than a very few. Unless a person strikes me by something out of the common in his intellect or opinions, I, so to speak, do not see him. I have always taken it for granted that mediocrities, as well as men of merit, had a nose, a mouth, eyes ; but I have never, in their case, been able to fix the particular shape of these features in my memory. I am constantly inquiring the name of strangers whom I see every day, and as constantly forgetting them ; and yet I do not despise them, only I consort but little with them, treating them as constant quantities. I honour them, for the world is made up of them ; but they weary me profoundly.

What completed my disgust was the mediocrity and monotony of the parliamentary events of that period, as well as the triviality of the passions and the vulgar perversity of the men who pretended to cause or to guide them.

I have sometimes thought that, though the habits of different societies may differ, the morality of the politicians at the head of affairs is everywhere the same. What is very certain is that, in France, all the party leaders whom I have met in my time have, with few exceptions, appeared to me to be equally unworthy of holding office, some because of their lack of personal character or of real insight, most by their lack of any sort of virtue. [I have hardly seen in any one of them that disinterested attitude towards the well-being of men which it seemed I had discovered in myself—in spite of my faults and weaknesses.] I thus experienced as great a difficulty in joining with others as in being satisfied with myself, in obeying as in acting on my own initiative. [Thus I found myself living almost continuously in morose isolation. I was only seen from afar and was judged without evidence. Every day, I felt, I was endowed with imaginary qualities and faults. It was through that I showed an ability in conduct, a profundity in certain matters, a cunning ambition which I do not possess ; furthermore my dissatisfaction with myself, my weariness and reserve were taken for presumptuousness, a fault which makes more enemies than the most glaring vices. It was believed that I was sly and underhand because I kept silence. I was also thought to have a natural austerity and a revengeful and bitter temperament which are quite unlike me ; for I am indulgent to the point of weakness ; and I put aside so quickly the remembrance of injustices of which I could complain, that this forgetfulness of wrongs suffered resembles more the weakness of a soul incapable of retaining the memory of an affront than the virtuous effort to efface such memories.

This cruel misunderstanding not only made me suffer but lowered my abilities well below their natural level. There is no man for whom approval is more healthy than for myself, nor anyone who needs more than I do be helped by public confidence and respect to raise himself to those actions of which he is capable. This extreme distrust of my strength, in some way the proof of myself in the thought of others, did it originate in true modesty ? I rather believe it came from a great pride which is as restless and disquieted as the mind itself.]

But that which most tormented and depressed me during the nine years I had spent in business, and which to this day remains my most hideous memory of that time, is the incessant uncertainty in which I had to live as to the best daily course to adopt. I am inclined to think that my uncertainty of character arises rather from the clouds of my intelligence than from any weakness of heart, and that I never experienced either hesitation or difficulty in following the most rugged road, when once I clearly saw where it would lead me. But amid all these little dynastic parties, differing so little in aim, and resembling one another so much in the bad methods which they put into practice, which was the thoroughfare that led visibly to honour, or even to utility? Where lay truth? Where falsehood? On which side were the rogues? On which side the honest men? I was never, at that time, fully able to distinguish it, and I declare that even now I should not well be able to do so. Most party men allow themselves to be neither distressed nor unnerved by doubts of this kind; many even have never known them, or know them no longer. They are often accused of acting without conviction; but my experience has proved that this was much less frequently the case than one might think. Only they possess the precious and sometimes in politics, even necessary faculty of creating transient convictions for themselves, according to the passions and interests of the moment, and thus they succeed in committing, honourably enough, actions which in themselves are little to their credit. Unfortunately, I could never bring myself to illuminate my intelligence with these special and artificial lights, nor so readily to convince myself that my own advantage was one and the same with the general good.

It was this parliamentary world, in which I had suffered all the wretchedness that I have just described, which was broken up by the Revolution; it had mingled and confounded the old parties in one common ruin, deposed their leaders, and destroyed their traditions and discipline. There had issued from this, it was true, a disordered and confused state of society, but one in which ability became less necessary and less highly rated than

courage and disinterestedness ; in which personal character was more important than elocution or the art of
leadership ; but, above all, in which there was no field
left for uncertainty of mind : on this side lay the salva-
tion of the country ; on that, its destruction. There was
no longer any mistake possible as to the road to follow ;
we were to walk in broad daylight, supported and
encouraged by the crowd. The road seemed dangerous,
it is true, but my mind is so constructed that it is less
afraid of danger than of doubt. I felt, moreover, that I
was still in the prime of life, [that I had no children],
that I had few needs, and, above all, that I was able to
find at home the support, so rare and precious in times
of revolution, of a devoted wife, whom a firm and penetrating mind and a naturally lofty soul would easily
maintain at the level of every situation and above every
reverse.

I therefore determined to plunge boldly into the
arena, and in defence, not of any particular government,
but of the laws which constitute society itself, to risk my
fortune, my person, and my peace of mind. The first
thing was to secure my election, and I left speedily for
Normandy in order to put myself before the electors.

CHAPTER IV

My Candidature for the Department of La Manche—The Aspect of the Country—The General Election.

As everyone knows, the Department of La Manche is peopled almost exclusively by farmers. It contains few large towns, few manufacturers, and, with the exception of Cherbourg, no places in which workmen are gathered in large numbers. At first, the Revolution was hardly noticed there. The upper classes immediately bent beneath the blow, and the lower classes scarcely felt it. Generally speaking, agricultural populations are slower than others in perceiving, and more stubborn in retaining, political impressions ; they are the last to rise and the last to settle down again. The steward of my estate, himself half a peasant, describing what was taking place in the country immediately after the 24th of February, wrote :

" People here say that if Louis-Philippe has been sent away, it is a good thing, and that he deserved it. . . ."

This was to them the whole moral of the play. But when they heard tell of the disorder reigning in Paris, of the new taxes to be imposed, and of the general state of war that was to be feared ; when they saw commerce cease and money seem to sink down into the ground, and when, in particular, they learnt that the principle of property was being attacked, they did not fail to perceive that there was something more than Louis-Philippe in question.

Fear, which had first displayed itself in the upper circles of society, then descended into the depths of the people, and universal terror took possession of the whole country. This was the condition in which I found it when I arrived about the middle of March. I was at once struck by a spectacle that both astonished and charmed me. A certain demagogic agitation reigned, it is true, among the workmen in the towns ; but in the country all the landed proprietors, whatever their origin, antecedents, education or means, had come together, and seemed to form but one class : all former political hatred and rivalry of caste or fortune had disappeared from view. There was no more jealousy or pride displayed between the peasant and the squire, the nobleman and the commoner ; instead, I found mutual confidence, reciprocal friendliness, and regard. Property had become with all those who owned it, a sort of bond of fraternity. The wealthy were the elder, the less endowed the younger brothers ; but all considered themselves members of one family, having the same interest in defending the common inheritance. As the French Revolution had infinitely increased the number of land-owners, the whole population seemed to belong to that vast family. I had never seen anything like it, nor had anyone in France within the memory of man. Experience has shown that this union was not so close as it appeared, and that the former parties and the various classes had drawn closer rather than mingled together ; fear had acted upon them as a mechanical pressure might upon very hard bodies, which are compelled to adhere to one another so long as the pressure continues, but which separate as soon as it is relaxed.

As a matter of fact, from the first moment I saw no trace whatever of political opinions, properly so-called. One would have thought that the republican form of government had suddenly become not only the best, but the only one imaginable for France. Dynastic hopes and regrets were buried so profoundly in the souls of men that not even the place they had once occupied was visible. The Republic respected persons and property, and it was accepted as lawful. In the spectacle I have just described, I was most struck at witnessing the universal hatred, together with the universal terror, now for the first time inspired by Paris. In France, provincials have for Paris, and for the central power of which Paris is the seat, feelings analogous to those which the English entertain for their aristocracy, which they sometimes support with impatience and often regard with jealousy, but which at bottom they love, because they alway hope to turn its privileges to their private advantage. This time Paris and those who spoke in its name had so greatly abused their power and seemed to be giving so little heed to the rest of the country, that the idea of shaking off the yoke and of acting for themselves came to many who had never before conceived it : uncertain and timid desires, it is true, feeble and ephemeral passions from which I never believed that there was much to be either hoped or feared ; but these new feelings were then turning into electoral ardour. Everyone clamoured for the elections ; for to elect the enemies of the demagogues of Paris presented itself to public opinion less as the constitutional exercise of a right, than as the least dangerous method one could employ of making a stand against the tyrant.

I fixed my headquarters in the little town of Valognes, which was the natural centre of my influence ; and as soon as I had ascertained the condition of the country, I set about my candidature. I then saw what I have often observed under a thousand different circumstances, that nothing makes more for success than not to desire it too ardently. I very much wanted to get elected ; but in the difficult and critical condition of affairs then reigning, I easily reconciled myself to the idea of being rejected ; and from this placid anticipation of a rebuff I drew a tranquillity and clearness of mind, a respect for myself and a contempt for the follies of the time, that I should perhaps not have found in the same degree had I been swayed only by a longing to succeed.

The country began to fill with roving candidates, hawking their protestations of Republicanism from hustings to hustings. I refused to present myself before any other electoral body than that of the place where I lived.[1] Each small town had its club, and each club questioned the candidates regarding their opinions and actions, and subjected them to formulas. I refused to reply to any of these insolent interrogatories. These refusals, which might have seemed disdainful, appeared in the light of dignity and independence in the face of the new rulers, and I was more esteemed for my rebelliousness than the others for their obedience. I therefore contented myself with publishing an address and having it posted up throughout the department.

Most of the candidates had resumed the old customs of '92. When writing to people they called them " Citizens ", and signed themselves " fraternally yours ". I would never consent to adopt this revolutionary nonsense. I headed my address, "Gentlemen ", and ended by proudly declaring myself my electors' " very humble servant ".

" I do not come to solicit your suffrages", I said, " I come only to place myself at the orders of my country. I asked to be your representative when the times were easy and peaceful ; my honour forbids me to refuse to be so in a period full of agitation, which may become full of danger. [Thus, I do not ask for your votes, but I am ready to devote to you my fortune and my life.] That is the first thing I had to tell you."

I added that I had been faithful to the end to the oath I had taken to the Monarchy, but that the Republic, which had been brought about without my aid, should have my energetic support, and that I would not only accept but assist it. Then I went on :

[1] Cf. E. L'Hommedé *Un Département Français sous la Monarchie de Juillet. Le Conseil Général de la Manche et Alexis de Tocqueville*. Paris 1933. (M.)

"But of what Republic is it a question? There are some who, by a Republic, understand a dictatorship exercised in the name of liberty; who think that the Republic should not only change political institutions but the face of society itself. There are some who think that the Republic should needs be of an aggressive and propagandist kind. I am not a Republican after this fashion. If this were your manner of being Republicans, I could be of no use to you, for I should not be of your opinion; but if you understand the Republic as I understand it myself, you can rely upon me to devote myself heart and soul to the triumph of a cause which is mine as well as yours."

Men who show no fear in times of revolution are like princes with the army; they produce a great effect by very ordinary actions, because the peculiar position which they occupy naturally places them above the level of the crowd and brings them very much in view. My address was so successful that I myself was astonished at it; within a few days it made me the most popular man in the department of La Manche, and the object of universal attention. My old political adversaries, the agents of the old Government, the Conservatives themselves who had so vigorously opposed me, and whom the Republic had overthrown, came in crowds to assure me that they were ready not only to vote for me, but to follow my views in everything.

In the meantime, the first meeting of the electors of the Arrondissement of Valognes took place. I appeared together with the other candidates. A shed did duty for a hall; the chairman's platform was at the bottom, and at the side was a professorial pulpit which had been transformed into a tribune. The chairman, who himself was a professor at the College of Valognes, said to me with a loud voice and a magisterial air, but in a very respectful tone: " Citizen de Tocqueville, I will tell you the questions which are put to you, and to which you will have to reply "; to which I replied, carelessly, " Mr. Chairman, please put the questions ".

A parliamentary orator, whose name I will not mention, once said to me :

" Look here, my dear friend, there is only one way of speaking well from the tribune, and that is to be fully persuaded, as you get into it, that you are the most clever man in the world."

This had always appeared to me easier to say than to do in the presence of our great political assemblies. But I confess that here the maxim was easy enough to follow, and that I thought it a wonderfully good one. Nevertheless, I did not go so far as to convince myself that I was more clever than all the world; but I soon saw that I was the only one who was well acquainted with the facts they brought up, and even with the political language they wished to speak. It would be difficult to show one's self more maladroit and more ignorant than did my adversaries ; they overwhelmed me with questions which they thought very close, and which left me very free, while I on my side made replies which were sometimes not very brilliant, but which always to them appeared most conclusive. The ground on which they hoped, above all, to crush me was that of the banquets. I had refused, as I have already said, to take part in these dangerous demonstrations. My political friends had found fault with me for abandoning them in that matter, and many continued to bear me ill-will, although—or perhaps because—the Revolution had proved me to be right.

" Why did you part from the Opposition on the occasion of the banquets ? " I was asked.

I replied boldly :

" I could easily find a pretext, but I prefer to give you my real reason : I did not want the banquets because I did not want a revolution ; and I venture to say that hardly any of those who sat down to the banquets would have done so, had they foreseen, as I did, the events to which these would lead. The only difference I can see between you and myself is that I knew what you were doing while you did not know it yourselves." This bold profession of anti-revolutionary had been preceded by one of republican faith ; the sincerity of the one seemed to bear witness to that of the other ; the meeting laughed and applauded. My adversaries were scoffed at, and I came off triumphant. [I have found in the minutes the following answers and questions which I insert because they indicate clearly the preoccupations of the moment and the true state of my mind. Question : " If the mob decide to roar round the National Assembly, if an armed mob were to invade it, do you swear to stay at your post if necessary, and to die ? "—Answer : " My presence here is my answer. After nine years of incessant work and of useless effort to bring the government which has just fallen to more liberal and more honest ways, it would have been more to my taste to retire into privacy and to wait until the storm has passed. But my honour forbade me to do this. Yes, I believe as you do that perils threaten those who attempt to represent you faithfully, but with these perils there is glory, and it is because there are perils and there is glory that I am here."]

I had won the agricultural population of the department by my address ; I won the Cherbourg workmen by a speech. The latter had been assembled to the number of two thousand at a patriotic dinner. I received a very obliging and pressing invitation to attend, and I did.

When I arrived, the procession was ready to start for the banqueting hall, with, at its head, my old colleague Havin, who had come expressly from Saint-Lô to take the chair. It was the first time I had met him since the 24th of February. On that day, I saw him giving his arm to the Duchesse d'Orléans, and the next morning I heard that he was Commissary of the Republic in the department of La Manche. I was not surprised, for I knew him as one of those easily bewildered, ambitious men who had found themselves fixed for ten years in opposition, after thinking at first that they were in it only for a little. How many of these men have I not seen around me, tortured with their own virtue, and despairing because they saw themselves spending the best part of their lives in criticizing the faults of others without ever in some measure realizing by experience what were their own, and finding nothing to feed upon but the sight of public corruption! Most of them had contracted during this long abstinence so great an appetite for places, honours and money that it was easy to predict that at the first opportunity they would throw themselves upon power with a sort of gluttony, without taking time to choose either the moment or the morsel. Havin was the very type of these men. The Provisional Government had given him as his associate, and even as his chief, another of my former colleagues in the Chamber of Deputies, M. Vieillard, who has since become famous as a particular friend of Prince Louis Napoleon's. Vieillard was entitled to serve the Republic, since he had been one of the seven or eight republican deputies under the Monarchy. Moreover, he was one of the Republicans who had passed through the saloons of the Empire before attaining demagogism. In literature he was a bigoted classic ; a Voltairean in religious belief ; rather fatuous, very kind-hearted ; an honest man, and even an intelligent ; but a very fool in politics. Havin had made him his tool : whenever he wished to strike a blow at one of his own enemies, or to reward one of his own friends, he invariably put forward Vieillard, who allowed him to do as he pleased. In this manner Havin made his way sheltered beneath the honesty and republicanism of Vieillard, whom he always kept before him, as the miner does his gabion.

Havin scarcely seemed to recognize me ; he did not invite me to take a place in the procession. I modestly withdrew into the midst of the crowd ; and when we arrived at the banqueting-hall, I sat down at one of the lower tables. We soon got to the speeches : Vieillard delivered a very proper speech, which was well received. I, too, was very much inclined to speak, but my name was not down, and moreover I did not quite see how I was to begin. A word which one of the orators (for all the speakers called themselves orators) dropped to the memory of Colonel Briqueville gave me my opportunity. I asked for permission to speak, and the meeting consented. When I found myself perched in the tribune, or rather in that pulpit placed twenty feet above the crowd, I felt a little confused ; but I soon recovered myself, and delivered a little piece of oratorical fustian which I should find it impossible to recollect to-day. I only know that it contained a certain appositeness, besides the warmth which never fails to make itself apparent through the disorder of an improvised speech, a merit quite sufficient to succeed with a popular assembly, or even with an assembly of any sort ; for, it cannot be too often repeated, speeches are made to be listened to and not to be read, and the only good ones are those that move the audience.

The success of mine was marked and complete, and I confess it seemed very sweet to me to revenge myself in this way on the manner in which my former colleague had endeavoured to abuse what he considered the favours of fortune.

If I am not mistaken, it was between this time and the elections that I made my journey to Saint-Lô, as member of the Council General. The Council had been summoned to an extraordinary sitting. It was still composed as under the Monarchy : most of its members had shown themselves complaisant towards Louis-Philippe's ministers, and may be reckoned among those who had most contributed to bring that Prince's government into contempt in our country. The only thing I can recall of the Saint-Lô journey is the singular servility of these ex-Conservatives. Not only did they make no opposition to Havin, who had insulted them for the past ten years, but they became his most attentive courtiers. They praised him with their words, supported him with their votes, smiled upon him approvingly ; they even spoke well of him among themselves, for fear of indiscretion. I have often seen greater pictures of human baseness, but never any that was more perfect ; and I think it deserves, despite its pettiness, to be brought fully to light. I will, therefore, display it in the light of subsequent events, and I will add that some months later, when the turn of the popular tide had restored them to power, they at once set about pursuing this same Havin anew with unheard-of violence and even injustice. All their old hatred became visible amid the quaking of their terror, and it seemed to have become still greater at the remembrance of their temporary complaisance.

Meantime the general election was drawing near, and each day the aspect of the future became more sinister. All the news from Paris represented the capital as on the point of constantly falling into the hands of armed Socialists. It was doubted whether these latter would allow the electors to vote freely, or at least whether they would submit to the National Assembly. Already in every part of the country the officers of the National Guard were being made to swear that they would march against the Assembly if a conflict arose between that body and the people. The provinces were becoming more and more alarmed, but were also strengthening themselves at the sight of the danger.

I spent the few days preceding the contest at my poor, dear Tocqueville. It was the first time I had visited it since the Revolution : I was perhaps about to leave it for ever ! I was seized on my arrival with so great and uncommon a feeling of sadness that it has left in my memory traces which have remained marked and visible to this day amid all the vestiges of the events of that time. I was not expected. The empty rooms, in which there was none but my old dog to receive me, the undraped windows, the heaped-up dusty furniture, the extinct fires, the rundown clocks—all seemed to point to abandonment and to foretell ruin. This little isolated corner of the earth, lost, as it were, amid the fields and hedges of our Norman coppices, which had so often seemed to me the most charming of solitudes, now appeared to me, in the actual state of my thoughts, as a desolate desert ; but across the desolation of its present aspect I discovered, as though from the depth of a tomb, the sweetest and most attractive episodes of my life. I wonder how our imagination gives so much deeper colour and so much more attractiveness to things than they possess. I had just witnessed the fall of the Monarchy ; I have since been present at the most sanguinary scenes ; and nevertheless I declare that none of these spectacles produced in me so deep and painful an emotion as that which I experienced that day at the sight of the ancient abode of my forefathers, when I thought of the peaceful days and happy hours I had spent there without knowing their value—I say that it was then and there that I best understood all the bitterness of revolutions.

The local population had always been well disposed to me ; but this time I found them affectionate, and I was never received with more respect than now, when all the walls were placarded with the expression of degrading equality. We were all to go and vote together at the borough of Saint-Pierre, about one league away from our village. On the morning of the election, all the voters (that is to say, all the male population above the age of twenty) collected together in front of the church. All these men formed themselves in a double column, in alphabetical order. I took up my place in the situation denoted by my name, for I knew that in democratic times and countries one must be nominated to the head of the people, and not place one's self there. At the end of the long procession, in carts or on pack-horses, came the sick or infirm who wished to follow us; we left none behind save the women and children. We were one hundred and sixty-six all told. At the top of the hill which commands Tocqueville there came a halt; they wished me to speak. I climbed to the other side of a ditch; a circle was formed round me, and I spoke a few words such as the circumstances inspired. I reminded these worthy people of the gravity and importance of what they were about to do; I recommended them not to allow themselves to be accosted or turned aside by those who, on our arrival at the borough, might seek to deceive them, but to march on solidly and stay together, each in his place, until they had voted. " Let no one," I said, " go into a house to seek food or shelter (it was raining) before he has done his duty." They cried that they would do as I wished, and they did. All the votes were given at the same time, and I have reason to believe that they were almost all given to the same candidate.

After voting myself, I took my leave of them, and set out to return to Paris.

CHAPTER V

*The First Sitting of the Constituent Assembly—The
Appearance of this Assembly.*

I STOPPED at Valognes only long enough to bid good-bye to some of my friends. Many left me with tears in their eyes, for there was a belief current in the country that the representatives would be exposed to great danger in Paris. Several of these worthy people said to me, " If they attack the National Assembly, we will come and defend you ". I feel a certain remorse at having seen only vain words in this promise at the time ; for, as a matter of fact, they did all come, they and many more, as I shall show later.

It was only when I reached Paris that I learnt that I had received 110,704 votes out of a possible 120,000. Most of my new colleagues belonged to the old dynastic Opposition : two only had professed republican principles before the Revolution, and were what was called in the jargon of the day "Republicans of yesterday". The same was the case in most parts of France.

There have certainly been more wicked revolutionaries than those of 1848, but I doubt if there were ever any more stupid ; they neither knew how to make use of universal suffrage nor how to do without it. If they had held the elections immediately after the 24th of February, while the upper classes were still bewildered by the blow they had just received, and the people more amazed than discontented, they would perhaps have obtained an Assembly after their hearts ; if, on the other hand, they had boldly seized the dictatorship, they might have been able for some time to retain it. But they trusted themselves to the nation, and at the same time did all that was most likely to set the latter against them ; they threatened it while placing themselves in its power ;

they alarmed it by the recklessness of their proposals and the violence of their language, while inviting it to resistance by the feebleness of their actions ; they pretended to lay down the law to it at the very time that they were placing themselves at its disposal. Instead of opening out their ranks after the victory, they jealously closed them up, and seemed, in one word, to be striving to solve this insoluble problem, namely, how to govern through the majority and yet against its inclination.

Following the examples of the past without understanding them, they foolishly imagined that to summon the crowd to take part in political life was sufficient to attach it to their cause ; and that to popularize the Republic, it was enough to give the public rights without offering them any profits. They forgot that their predecessors, when they gave every peasant the vote, at the same time did away with tithes, abolished statute labour and the other seignorial privileges, and divided the property of the nobles among the peasants ; whereas they were not in a position to do anything of the kind. In establishing universal suffrage they thought they were summoning the people to the assistance of the Revolution : they were only giving them arms against it. Nevertheless, I am far from believing that it was impossible to arouse revolutionary passions, even in the country districts. In France, every agriculturist owns some portion of the soil, and most of them are more or less involved in debt ; it was not, therefore, the landlords that should have been attacked, but the creditors ; not the abolition promised of the rights of property, but the abolition of debts. The demagogues of 1848 did not think of this scheme ; they showed themselves much clumsier than their predecessors, but no less dishonest, for they were as violent and unjust in their desires as the others in their acts. Only, to commit violent and unjust acts, it is not enough for a government to have the will, or even the power ; the habits, ideas, and passions of the time must lend themselves to the committal of them.

As the party which held the reins of government saw its candidates rejected one after the other, it displayed great vexation and rage, complaining now sadly and now rudely of the electors, whom it treated as ignorant, ungrateful blockheads, and enemies of their own good ; it lost its temper with the whole nation ; and, its impatience exhausted by the latter's coldness, it seemed ready to say with Molière's Arnolfe, when he addresses Agnès :

" *Pourquoi ne m'aimer pas, madame l'impudente ?* "

One thing was not ridiculous, but really ominous and terrible ; and that was the appearance of Paris on my return. I found in the capital a hundred thousand armed workmen formed into regiments, out of work, dying of hunger, but with their minds crammed with vain theories and visionary hopes. I saw society cut into two ; those who possessed nothing, united in a common greed ; those who possessed something, united in a common terror. There were no bonds, no sympathy between these two great sections ; everywhere the idea of an inevitable and immediate struggle seemed at hand. Already the *bourgeois* and the *peuple* (for the old nicknames had been resumed) had come to blows, with varying fortunes, at Rouen, Limoges, Paris ; not a day passed but the owners of property were attacked or menaced in either their capital or income : they were asked to employ labour without selling the produce ; they were expected to remit the rents of their tenants when they themselves possessed no other means of living. They gave way as long as they could to this tyranny, and endeavoured at least to turn their weakness to account by publishing it. I remember reading in the papers of that time this advertisement, among others, which still strikes me as a model of vanity, poltroonery, and stupidity harmoniously mingled :

" Mr. Editor", it read, " I make use of your paper to inform my tenants that, desiring to put into practice in my relations with them the principles of fraternity that should guide all true democrats, I will hand to those of my tenants who apply for it a formal receipt for their next quarter's rent."

Meanwhile, a gloomy despair had overspread this bourgeoisie thus threatened and oppressed, and imperceptibly this despair was changing into courage. I had always believed that it was useless to hope to settle the movement of the Revolution of February peacefully and gradually, and that it could only be stopped suddenly, by a great battle fought in the streets of Paris. I had said this immediately after the 24th of February ; and what I now saw persuaded me that this battle was not only inevitable but imminent, and that it would be well to seize the first opportunity to deliver it.

The National Assembly met at last on the 4th of May ; it was doubtful until the last moment whether it would meet at all. I believe, in fact, that the more ardent of the demagogues were often tempted to do without it, but they dared not ; they remained crushed beneath the weight of their own dogma of the sovereignty of the people.

I should have before my eyes the picture which the Assembly presented at its opening ; but I find, on the contrary, that only a very confused recollection of it has lingered in my mind. It is a mistake to believe that events remain present in one's memory in proportion to their importance or their greatness alone ; rather is it certain little particularities which occur, and cause them

ALEXIS DE TOCQUEVILLE

to penetrate deep into the mind, and fix them there in a lasting manner. I only remember that we shouted, "Long live the Republic" fifteen times during the course of the sitting, trying who could out-shout the other. The history of the Assemblies is full of parallel incidents, and one constantly sees one party exaggerating its feelings in order to embarrass its opponents, while the latter feign to hold sentiments which they do not possess, in order to avoid the trap. Both sides, with a common effort, went either beyond, or in the contrary direction to, the truth. Nevertheless, I think the cry was sincere enough ; only it responded to diverse or even contrary thoughts. All at that time wished to preserve the Republic ; but some wished to use it for purposes of attack, others for purposes of defence. The newspapers spoke of the enthusiasm of the Assembly and of the public ; there was a great deal of noise, but no enthusiasm at all. Everyone was too greatly preoccupied with the immediate future to allow himself to be carried beyond that thought by sentiment of any kind. A decree of the Provisional Government laid down that the representatives should wear the costume of the Conventionals, and especially the white waistcoat with turn-down collar in which Robespierre was always represented on the stage. I thought at first that this fine idea originated with Louis Blanc or Ledru-Rollin ; but I learned later that it was due to the flowery and literary imagination of Armand Marrast. No one obeyed the decree, not even its author ; Caussidière was the only one to adopt the appointed disguise. This drew my attention to him ; for I did not know him by sight any more than most of those who were about to call themselves the Montagnards, always with the idea of keeping up the recollection of '93. I saw a very big and very heavy body, on which was placed a sugar-loaf head, sunk deep between the two shoulders, with a wicked, cunning eye, and an air of general good-nature spread over the rest of his face. In short, he was a mass of shapeless matter, in which worked a mind sufficiently subtle to know how to make the most of his coarseness and ignorance.

In the course of the two subsequent days, the members of the Provisional Government, one after the other, told us what they had done since the 24th of February. Each said a great deal of good of himself, and even a certain amount of good of his colleagues, although it would be difficult to meet a body of men who mutually hated one another more sincerely than these did. Independently of the political hatred and jealousy that divided them, they seemed still to feel towards each other that peculiar irritation common to travellers who have been compelled to live together upon the same ship during a long and stormy passage, without suiting or understanding one another. At this first sitting I met again almost all the members of Parliament among whom I had lived. With the exception of M. Thiers, who had been defeated ; of the Duc de Broglie, who had not stood, I believe ; and of Messrs. Guizot and Duchâtel, who had fled, all the famous orators and most of the better-known talkers of the political world were there ; but they found themselves, as it were, out of their element, they felt isolated and suspected, they both felt and inspired fear, two contraries often to be met with in the political world. As yet they possessed none of that influence which their talents and experience were soon to restore to them. All the remainder of the Assembly were as much novices as though we had issued fresh from the Ancien Régime ; for, thanks to our system of centralization, public life had always been confined within the limits of the Chambers, and those who were neither peers nor deputies scarcely knew what an Assembly was, nor how one should speak or behave in one. They were absolutely ignorant of its most ordinary, everyday habits and customs ; and they were inattentive at decisive moments, and listened eagerly to unimportant things. Thus, on the second day, they crowded round the tribune and insisted on perfect silence in order to hear read the minutes of the preceding sitting, imagining that this insignificant form was a most important piece of business. I am convinced that nine hundred English or American peasants, picked at random, would have better represented the appearance of a great political body.

Continuing to imitate the National Convention, the men who professed the most radical and the most revolutionary opinions had taken their seats on the highest benches ; they were very uncomfortable up there ; but it gave them the right to call themselves Montagnards, and as men always like to feed on pleasant imaginations, these very rashly flattered themselves that they bore a resemblance to the celebrated blackguards whose name they took.

The Montagnards soon divided themselves into two distinct bands : the Revolutionaries of the old school and the Socialists. Nevertheless, the two shades were not sharply defined. One passed from the one to the other by imperceptible tints : the Montagnards proper had almost all some socialistic ideas in their heads, and the Socialists quite approved of the revolutionary proceedings of the others. However, they differed sufficiently among themselves to prevent them from always marching in step, and it was this that saved us. The Socialists were the more dangerous, because they answered more nearly to the true character of the Revolution of February, and to the only passions which it had aroused ; but they were men of theory rather than action, and in order to upset Society at their pleasure they would have needed the practical energy and the science of insurrections which only their colleagues in any measure possessed.

From the seat I occupied it was easy for me to hear what was said on the benches of the Mountain, and especially to see what went on. This gave me the opportunity of studying pretty closely the men sitting in that part of the Chamber. It was for me like discovering a new world. We console ourselves for not knowing foreign countries, with the reflection that at least we know our own ; but we are wrong, for even in the latter there are always districts which we have not visited, and races which are new to us. I experienced this now. It was as though I saw these Montagnards for the first time, so greatly did their idioms and manners surprise me. They spoke a lingo which was not, properly speaking, the French of either the ignorant or the cultured classes, but which partook of the defects of both, for it abounded in coarse words and ambitious phrases. One heard issuing from the benches of the Mountain a ceaseless torrent of insulting or jocular comments ; and at the same time there was poured forth a host of quibbles and maxims ; in turns they assumed a very humorous or a very superb tone. It was evident that these people belonged neither to the tavern nor the drawing-room ; I think they must have polished their manners in the cafés, and fed their minds on no literature but that of the daily press. In any case, it was the first time since the commencement of the Revolution that this type made any display in one of our Assemblies ; until then it had only been represented by sporadic and unnoticed individuals, who were more occupied in concealing than in showing themselves.

The Constituent Assembly had two other peculiarities which struck me as quite as novel as this, although very different from it. It contained an infinitely greater number of landlords and even of noblemen than any of the Chambers elected in the days when it was a necessary condition, in order to be an elector or elected, that you should have money. And also there was a more numerous

ALEXIS DE TOCQUEVILLE

and more powerful religious party than even under the
Restoration ; I counted three bishops, several vicars-
general, and a Dominican monk, whereas Louis XVIII
and Charles X had never succeeded in securing the
election of more than one single abbé.

The abolition of all quit-rents, which made part of the
electors dependent upon the rich, and the danger
threatening property, which led the people to choose for
their representatives those who were most interested in
defending it, are the principal reasons which explain the
presence of so great a number of landlords. The election
of the ecclesiastics arose from similar causes, and also
from a different cause still worthier of consideration. This
cause was the almost general and very unexpected return
of a great part of the nation towards the concerns of
religion.

The Revolution of 1792, when striking the upper
classes, had cured them of their irreligiousness ; it had
taught them, if not the truth, at least the social usefulness
of belief. This lesson was lost upon the middle class,
which remained their political heir and their jealous
rival ; and the latter had even become more sceptical in
proportion as the former seemed to become more religious. The Revolution of 1848 had just done on a small
scale for our tradesmen what that of 1792 had done for
the nobility : the same reverses, the same terrors, the
same conversion ; it was the same picture, only painted
smaller and in less bright and, no doubt, less lasting
colours. The clergy had facilitated this conversion by
separating itself from all the old political parties, and
entering into the old, true spirit of the Catholic clergy,
which is that it should belong only to the Church. It
readily, therefore, professed republican opinions, while
at the same time it gave to long established interests the
guarantee of its traditions, its customs and its hierarchy.
It was accepted and made much of by all. The priests sent

to the Assembly were treated with very great consideration, and they deserved it, through their good sense, their
moderation and their modesty. Some of them endeavoured to speak from the tribune, but they were never
able to learn the language of politics. They had forgotten
it too long ago, and all their speeches turned imperceptibly into homilies.

For the rest, the universal franchise had shaken the
country from top to bottom without bringing to light a
single new man worthy of coming to the front. I have
always held that, whatever method be followed in a
general election, the great majority of the exceptional
men whom the nation possesses definitely succeed in
getting elected. The system of election adopted exercises
a great influence only upon the class of ordinary individuals in the Assembly, who form the ground-work of
every political body. These belong to very different
orders and are of very diverse natures, according to the
system upon which the election has been conducted.
Nothing confirmed me in this belief more than did the
sight of the Constituent Assembly. Almost all the men
who played the first part in it were already known to
me, but the bulk of the rest resembled nothing that I had
seen before. They were imbued with a new spirit, and
displayed a new character and new manners.

I will say that, in my opinion, and taken all round,
this Assembly compared favourably with those which I
had seen. One met in it more men who were sincere,
disinterested, honest and, above all, courageous than
in the Chambers of Deputies among which I had lived.

The Constituent Assembly had been elected to make a
stand against civil war. This was its principal merit ;
and, in fact, so long as it was necessary to fight, it was
great, and only became contemptible after the victory,
and when it felt that it was breaking up in consequence
of this very victory and under the weight of it.

I selected my seat on the left side of the House, on a bench from which it was easy for me to hear the speakers and to reach the tribune when I wished to speak myself. A large number of my old friends joined me there; Lanjuinais, Dufaure, Corcelles, Beaumont and several others sat near me.

Let me say a word concerning the House itself, although everybody knows it. This is necessary in order to understand the narrative; and, moreover, although this monument of wood and plaster is probably destined to last longer than the Republic of which it was the cradle, I do not think it will enjoy a very long existence; and when it is destroyed, many of the events that took place in it will be difficult to understand.

The house formed an oblong of great size. At one end, against the wall, was the President's platform and the tribune; nine rows of benches rose gradually along the three other walls. In the middle, facing the tribune, spread a huge, empty space, like the arena of an amphi-theatre, with this difference, that this arena was square, not round. The consequence was that most of the listeners only caught a side glimpse of the speaker, and the only ones who saw him full face were very far away: an arrangement curiously calculated to promote in-attention and disorder. For the first, who saw the speaker badly, and were continually looking at one another, were more engaged in threatening and apostrophizing each other; and the others did not listen any better, because, although able to see the occupant of the tribune, they heard him badly.

Large windows, placed high up in the walls, opened straight outside, and admitted air and light; the walls were decorated only with a few flags; time had, luckily, been wanting in which to add to them all those spiritless allegories on canvas or pasteboard with which the French love to adorn their monuments, in spite of their being insipid to those who can understand them and utterly incomprehensible to the mass of the people. The whole bore an aspect of immensity, together with an air that was cold, solemn, and almost melancholy. There were seats for nine hundred members, a larger number than that of any of the assemblies that had sat in France for sixty years.

I felt at once that the atmosphere of this assembly suited me. Notwithstanding the gravity of events, I experienced there a sense of well-being that was new to me. For the first time since I had entered public life, I felt myself caught in the current of a majority, and following in its company the only road which my tastes, my reason and my conscience pointed out to me : a new and very welcome sensation. I gathered that this majority would disown the Socialists and the Montagnards, but was sincere in its desire to maintain and organize the Republic. I was with it on these two leading points : I had no monarchic faith, no affection nor regrets for any prince ; I felt called upon to defend no cause save that of liberty and the dignity of mankind. To protect the ancient laws of Society against the innovators with the help of the new force which the republican principle might lend to the government ; to cause the evident will of the French people to triumph over the passions and desires of the Paris workmen ; to conquer demagogism by democracy—that was my only aim. I am not sure that the dangers to be passed through, before it could be attained, did not make it still more attractive to me ; for I have a natural inclination for adventure, and a spice of danger has always seemed to me the best seasoning that can be given to most of the actions of life.

CHAPTER VI

My Relations With Lamartine—His Subterfuges.

LAMARTINE was now at the climax of his fame : to all those whom the Revolution had injured or alarmed, that is to say, to the great majority of the nation, he appeared in the light of a saviour. He had been elected to the Assembly by the city of Paris and no fewer than eleven departments ; I do not believe that ever anybody inspired such keen enthusiasm as that to which he was then giving rise ; one must have seen love thus stimulated by fear to know with what excess of idolatry men are capable of loving. The transcendental favour which was shown him at this time was not to be compared with anything except, perhaps, the excessive injustice which he shortly afterwards received. All the deputies who came to Paris with the desire to put down the excesses of the Revolution and to combat the demagogic party regarded him beforehand as their only possible leader, and looked to him unhesitatingly to place himself at their head to attack and overthrow the Socialists and demagogues. They soon discovered that they were deceived and that Lamartine did not see the part he was called upon to play in so simple a light. It must be confessed that his was a very complex and difficult position. It was forgotten at the time, but he could not himself forget, that he had contributed more than any other to the success of the Revolution of February. Terror effaced this remembrance for the moment from the public mind ; but a general feeling of security could not fail soon to restore it. It was easy to foresee that, as soon as the current which had brought affairs to their present pitch was arrested, a contrary current would set in, which would impel the nation in the opposite direction, and drive it faster and further than Lamartine could or would go. The success of the Montagnards would involve his immediate ruin ; but their complete defeat would render him useless and must, sooner or later, remove the government from his hands. He saw, therefore, that for him there was almost as much danger and loss in triumph as in defeat.

As a matter of fact, I believe that if Lamartine had resolutely, from the first, placed himself at the head of the immense party which desired to moderate and regulate the course of the Revolution, and had succeeded in leading it to victory, he would before long have been buried beneath his own triumph ; he would not have been able to stop his army in time, and it would have left him behind and chosen other leaders.

I doubt whether, whatever line of conduct he had adopted, he could have retained his power for long. I believe his only remaining chance was to be gloriously defeated while saving his country. But Lamartine was the last man to sacrifice himself in this way. I do not know that I have ever, in this world of selfishness and ambition in which I lived, met a mind so void of any thought of the public welfare as his. I have seen a crowd of men disturbing the country in order to raise themselves : that is an everyday perversity ; but he is the only one who seemed to me always ready to turn the world upside down in order to divert himself. Neither have I ever known a mind less sincere, nor one that had a more thorough contempt for the truth. When I say he despised it, I am wrong : he did not honour it enough to heed it in any way whatever. When speaking or writing, he spoke the truth or lied, without caring which he did, occupied only with the effect he wished to produce at the moment.

I had not seen Lamartine since the 24th of February. I saw him the first time on the day before the opening of the Assembly in the new house, where I had gone to choose my seat, but I did not speak to him ; he was surrounded by some of his new friends. The instant he saw me, he pretended some business at the other end of the house, and hurried away as fast as he could. He sent me word afterwards by Champeaux (who belonged to him, half as a friend and half as a servant) that I must not take it ill of him that he avoided me ; that his position obliged him to act in this way towards the members of the late parliament ; that my place was, of course, marked out among the future leaders of the Republic ; but that we must wait till the first temporary difficulties were surmounted before coming to an agreement. Champeaux also declared that he was instructed to ask my opinion on the state of affairs ; I gave my views very readily, but to very little purpose. This established certain indirect relations between Lamartine and myself through the intermediary of Champeaux. The latter often came to see me, to inform me, on behalf of his patron, of the arrangements that were being prepared ; and I sometimes went to see him in a little room he had hired on the top floor of a house in the Rue Saint-Honoré, where he used to receive suspicious visitors, although he had a complete set of rooms at the Foreign Office.

I usually found him overwhelmed with place-hunters ; for in France political mendicancy exists under every form of government. It even increases through the very revolutions that are directed against it, because all revolutions ruin a certain number of men, and with us a ruined man always looks to the State to repair his fortunes. They were of all kinds, all attracted by the reflection of power which Lamartine's friendship very transiently cast over Champeaux. I remember among others a certain cook, not particularly distinguished in his calling, as far as I could see, who insisted upon entering the service of Lamartine, who had, he said, become President of the Republic.

" But he's not President yet ! " cried Champeaux.

" If he's not so yet, as you say", said the man, " he's going to be, and he must already be thinking of his kitchen."

In order to rid himself of this scullion's obstinate ambition, Champeaux promised to bring his name before Lamartine as soon as the latter should be President of the Republic. The poor man went away quite satisfied, dreaming no doubt of the very imaginary splendours of his approaching condition.

I frequented Champeaux pretty assiduously during that time, although he was exceedingly vain, loquacious, and tedious, because, in talking with him, I became better acquainted with Lamartine's thoughts and projects than if I had been talking to the great man himself. Lamartine's intelligence was seen through Champeaux' folly as you see the sun through a smoked glass, which shows you the luminary deprived of its heat-rays, but less dazzling to the eye. I easily gathered that in this world every one was feeding on pretty well the same chimeras as the cook of whom I have just spoken, and that Lamartine already tasted at the bottom of his heart the sweets of that sovereign power which was nevertheless at that very moment escaping from his hands. He was then following the tortuous road that was so soon to lead him to his ruin, struggling to dominate the Mountain without overthrowing it, and to slacken the revolutionary fire without extinguishing it, so as to give the country a feeling of security strong enough for it to bless him, not strong enough to cause it to forget him. What he dreaded above all was that the conduct of the Assembly should be allowed to fall into the hands of the former parliamentary leaders. This was, I believe, at the time his dominant passion. One could see this during the great discussion on the constitution of the Executive Power ; never did the different parties display more visibly the pedantic hypocrisy which induces them to conceal their interests beneath their ideas : an ordinary spectacle enough, but more striking at this time than usual, because the needs of the moment compelled each party to shelter itself behind theories which were foreign or even opposed to it. The old royalist party maintained that the Assembly itself should govern and choose its ministers : a theory that was almost demagogic ; and the demagogues declared that the Executive Power should be entrusted to a permanent commission, which should govern and select all the agents of the government : a system that approached the monarchic idea. All this verbiage only meant that one side wished to remove Ledru-Rollin from power, and the other to keep him there.

The nation saw in Ledru-Rollin the bloody image of the Terror ; it beheld in him the genius of evil as in Lamartine the genius of good, and it was mistaken in both cases. Ledru-Rollin was nothing more than a very sensual and sanguine heavy fellow, quite without principles and almost without brains, possessing no real courage of mind or heart, and even free from malice : for he naturally wished well to all the world, and was incapable of cutting the throat of any one of his adversaries, except, perhaps, for the sake of historical reminiscences, or to accommodate his friends.

The result of the debate remained long doubtful : Barrot turned it against us by making a very fine speech in our favour. I have witnessed many of these unforeseen incidents in parliamentary life, and have seen parties constantly deceived in the same way, because they always think only of the pleasure they themselves derive from their great orator's words, and never of the dangerous excitement he promotes in their opponents.

When Lamartine, who till then had kept silent and remained, I believe, in indecision, heard, for the first time since February, the voice of the ex-leader of the Left resounding with brilliancy and success, he suddenly made up his mind, and spoke. " You understand," said Champeaux to me the next day, " that before all it was necessary to prevent the Assembly from coming to a resolution upon Barrot's advice." So Lamartine spoke and, according to his custom, spoke in brilliant manner.

The majority, who had already adopted the course that Barrot had urged upon them, wheeled round as they listened to him (for this Assembly was more credulous and more submissive than any that I had ever seen to the wiles of eloquence : it was novice and innocent enough to seek for reasons for their decisions in the speeches of the orators). Thus Lamartine won his cause, but missed his fortune ; for he that day gave rise to the mistrust which soon arose and hurled him from his pinnacle of popularity more quickly than he had mounted it. Suspicion took a definite form the very next day, when he was seen to patronize Ledru-Rollin and force the hand of his own friends in order to induce them to appoint the latter as his colleague on the Executive Commission. At this sight there arose in the Assembly and in the nation inexpressible disappointment, terror and rage. For my part, I experienced these two last emotions in the highest degree ; I clearly perceived that Lamartine was turning out of the high-road that led us away from anarchy, and I could not guess into what abyss he might lead us if we followed the byways which he was treading. How was it possible, indeed, to foresee how far an always exuberant imagination might go, unrestrained by reason or virtue ? Lamartine's common-sense impressed me no more than did his disinterestedness ; and, in fact, I believed him capable of everything except cowardly behaviour or vulgar oratory.

I confess that the events of June to a certain extent modified the opinion I had formed of his manner of proceeding. They showed that our adversaries were more numerous, better organized and, above all, more determined than I had thought.

Lamartine, who had seen nothing but Paris during the last two months, and who had there, so to speak, lived in the very heart of the revolutionary party, exaggerated the power of the Capital and the inactivity of the rest of France. He over-estimated both. But I am not sure that I, on my side, did not strain a point on the other side. The road we ought to follow seemed to me so clearly and visibly traced that I would not admit the possibility of deviating from it by mistake ; it seemed obvious to me that we should hasten to profit by the moral force possessed by the Assembly in order to escape from the hands of the people, seize upon the government, and by a great effort establish it upon a solid basis. Every delay seemed to me calculated to diminish our power, and to strengthen the hand of our adversaries.

It was, in fact, during the six weeks that elapsed between the opening of the Assembly and the events of June that the Paris workmen grew bold, and took courage to resist, organized themselves, procured both arms and ammunition, and made their final preparations for the struggle. In any case, I am led to believe that it was Lamartine's tergiversations and his semi-connivance with the enemy that saved us, while it ruined him. Their effect was to amuse the leaders of the Mountain, and to divide them. The Montagnards of the old school, who were retained in the Government, separated themselves from the Socialists, who were excluded from it. Had all been united by a common interest, and impelled by common despair before our victory, as they became since, it is doubtful whether that victory would have been won. When I consider that we were almost effaced, although we were opposed only by the revolutionary party without its leaders, I ask myself what the results of the contest would have been if those leaders had come forward, and if the insurrection had been supported by a third of the National Assembly.

Lamartine saw these dangers more closely and clearly than I, and I believe to-day that the fear of arousing a mortal conflict influenced his conduct as much as did his ambition. I might have formed this opinion at the time had I listened to Madame de Lamartine, whose alarm for the safety of her husband, and even of the Assembly, amounted to extravagance. "Beware", she said to me, each time she met me, " beware of pushing things to extremes : you do not know the strength of the revolutionary party. If we enter into conflict with it, we shall perish." I have often reproached myself for not cultivating Madame de Lamartine's acquaintance, for I have always found her to possess real virtue, although she added to it almost all the faults which can cling to virtue, and which, without impairing it, render it less lovable : an imperious temper, great personal pride, an upright but unyielding, and sometimes bitter, spirit ; so much so that it was impossible not to respect her, and impossible to like her.

CHAPTER VII

The 15th of May, 1848.

THE revolutionary party had not dared to oppose the meeting of the Assembly, but it refused to be dominated by it. On the contrary, it well understood how to keep the Assembly in subjection, and to obtain from it by constraint what it refused to grant from sympathy. Already the clubs rang with threats and insults against the deputies. And as the French, in their political passions, are as argumentative as they are insensible to argument, these popular meeting-places were incessantly occupied in manufacturing theories that formed the ground-work of subsequent acts of violence. It was held that the people always remained superior to its representatives, and never completely surrendered its will into their hands : a true principle from which the false conclusion was drawn that the Paris workmen were the French people. Since our first sitting, a vague and widespread agitation had never ceased to reign in the town. Crowds met every day in the streets and squares ; they spread aimlessly, like the swell of the waves. The approaches to the Assembly were always filled with a gathering of these redoubtable idlers. A demagogic party has so many heads, chance always plays so great, and reason so small, a part in its actions that it is almost impossible to say, either before or after the event, what it wants or what it wanted. Nevertheless, my opinion then was, and has since remained, that the leading demagogues did not aim at destroying the Assembly, and that, as yet, they only sought to make use of it by mastering it. The attack directed against it on the 15th of May seemed intended rather to frighten than to overthrow it ; it was at least one of those equivocal enterprises which so frequently occur in times of popular excitement, in which the promoters themselves are careful not to trace or define precisely their plan or their aim, so as to remain free to limit themselves to a peaceful demonstration or force on a revolution, according to the incidents of the day.

Some attempt of this kind had been expected for eight days ; but the habit of living in a continual state of alarm ends in rendering both individuals and assemblies incapable of discerning, amid the signs announcing the approach of danger, that which immediately precedes it. We only knew that there was a question of a great popular demonstration in favour of Poland, and we were but vaguely disturbed at it. Doubtless the members of the Government were better informed and more alarmed than we, but they kept their own counsel, and I was not sufficiently in touch with them to penetrate into secret thoughts.

Thus it happened that, on the 15th of May, I reached the Assembly without foreseeing what was going to happen. The sitting began as any other sitting might have begun : and what was very strange, twenty thousand men already surrounded the chamber, without a single sound from the outside having announced their presence. Wolowski was in the tribune : he was mumbling between his teeth I know not what commonplaces about Poland, when the crowd at last betrayed its approach with a terrible shout, which penetrated from every side through the upper windows, left open because of the heat, and fell upon us as though from the sky. Never had I imagined that a number of human voices could together produce so immense a volume of sound, and the sight of the crowd itself, when it surged into the Assembly, did not seem to me so formidable as that first roar which it had uttered before showing itself. Many members, yielding to a first impulse of curiosity or fear, sprang to their feet ; others shouted violently, " Keep your seats ! " Everyone sat down again firmly on his bench, and kept silence. Wolowski resumed his speech, and continued it for some time. It must have been the first time in his life that he was listened to in silence ; and even now it was not he to whom we listened, but the crowd outside, whose murmurs grew momentarily louder and nearer.

Suddenly Degousée, one of our questors, solemnly mounted the steps of the tribune, silently pushed Wolowski aside, and said, " Contrary to the wishes of the questors, General Courtais has ordered the Gardes Mobiles guarding the doors of the Assembly to sheathe their bayonets ".

After uttering these few words he stopped. This Degousée, who was a very good man, had the most hang-dog look and the hollowest voice imaginable. The news, the man and the voice combined to create a curious impression. The Assembly was roused, but immediately grew calm again ; it was too late to do anything ; the chamber was forced.

Lamartine, who had gone out at the first noise, returned to the door with a disconcerted air ; he crossed the central gangway and regained his seat with great strides, as though pursued by some enemy invisible to us. Almost immediately, there appeared behind him a number of men of the people, who stopped still on the threshold, surprised at the sight of this immense seated assembly. At the same moment, as on the 24th of February, the galleries were noisily opened and invaded by a flood of people, who filled and more than filled them. Pressed forward by the crowd who followed and pushed them without seeing them, the first comers climbed over the balustrades of the galleries, trusting to find room in the Chamber itself, the floor of which was not more than ten feet beneath them, hung down along the walls, and dropped the distance of four or five feet into the Chamber. The fall of each of these bodies striking the floor in succession produced a dull concussion which at first, amid the tumult, I took for the distant sound of cannon. While one part of the people was thus falling into the house, the other, composed principally of the club-leaders, entered by every door. They carried various emblems of the Terror, and waved flags of which some were surmounted by a red cap.

In an instant the crowd had filled the large empty space in the centre of the Assembly ; and finding itself pressed for room, it climbed all the little gangways leading to our benches, and crowded more and more into these narrow spaces without ceasing its agitation. Amid this tumultuous and incessant commotion, the dust became very thick and the heat so oppressive that perhaps I would have gone out to breathe some fresh air, had it been merely a question of the public interest. But honour kept us glued to our seats.

Some of the intruders were openly armed, others showed glimpses of concealed weapons, but none seemed to entertain a fixed intention of striking us. Their expression was one of astonishment and ill-will rather than enmity ; with many of them a sort of vulgar curiosity in course of gratifying itself seemed to dominate every other sentiment ; for even in our most sanguinary insurrections there are always a number of people half scoundrels, half sightseers, who fancy themselves at the play. Moreover, there was no common leader whom they seemed to obey ; it was a mob of men, not a troop. I saw some drunken men among them, but the majority seemed to be the prey of a feverish excitement imparted to them by the enthusiasm and shouting without and the stifling heat, the close packing and general discomfort within. They dripped with sweat, although the nature and condition of their clothing was not calculated to make the heat very uncomfortable for them, for several were quite bare-breasted. There rose from this multitude a con-

fused noise from the midst of which one sometimes heard
very threatening observations. I caught sight of men who
shook their fists at us and called us their agents. This
expression was often repeated ; for several days the
ultra-democratic newspapers had done nothing but call
the representatives the agents of the people, and these
blackguards had taken kindly to the idea. A moment
after, I had an opportunity of observing with what
vivacity and clearness the popular mind receives and
reflects images. I heard a man in a blouse, standing next
to me, say to his fellow, " See that vulture down there ?
I should like to twist its neck ". I followed the movement
of his arm and his eyes and saw without difficulty that
he was speaking of Lacordaire, who was sitting in his
Dominican's frock on the top bench of the Left. The
sentiment struck me as very wicked, but the comparison
was admirable ; the priest's long, bony neck issuing from
its white cowl, his bald head surrounded only with a tuft
of black hair, his narrow face, his hooked nose and his
fixed, glittering eyes really gave him a striking resemblance to the bird of prey in question.

During all this disorder in its midst, the Assembly sat
passive and motionless on its benches, neither resisting
nor giving way, silent and firm. A few members of the
Mountain fraternized with the mob, but stealthily and in
whispers. Raspail had taken possession of the tribune
and was preparing to read the petition of the clubs ; a
young deputy, d'Adelsward, rose and exclaimed, " By
what right does Citizen Raspail claim to speak here ? "
A furious howling arose ; some of the people made a
rush at d'Adelsward, but were stopped and held back.
With great difficulty, Raspail obtained a moment's
silence from his friends, and read the petition, or rather
the orders, of the clubs which enjoined us to pronounce
forthwith in favour of Poland.

" No delay, we're waiting for the answer ! " was

shouted on every side. The Assembly continued to give no sign of life; the crowd, in its disorder and impatience, made a horrible noise, which by itself alone saved us from making a reply. Buchez, the President, whom some would make out to be a rascal and others a saint, but who undoubtedly, on that day, was a great blockhead, rang his bell with all his might to obtain silence, as though the silence of that multitude was not, under the present circumstances, more to be dreaded than its cries.

It was then that I saw appear, in his turn, in the tribune a man whom I have never seen since, but the recollection of whom has always filled me with horror and disgust. He had wan, emaciated cheeks, white lips, a sickly, wicked and repulsive expression, a dirty pallor, the appearance of a mouldy corpse; he wore no visible linen; an old black frock-coat tightly covered his lean, withered limbs; he seemed to have passed his life in a sewer and to have just left it. I was told it was Blanqui.

Blanqui said one word about Poland; then, turning sharply to domestic affairs, he asked for revenge for what he called the massacres of Rouen, recalled with threats the wretchedness in which the people had been left, and complained of the wrongs done to the latter by the Assembly. After thus exciting his hearers, he returned to Poland and, like Raspail, demanded an immediate vote.

The Assembly continued to sit motionless, the people to move about and utter a thousand contradictory exclamations, the President to ring his bell. Ledru-Rollin tried to persuade the masses to withdraw, but nobody was now able to exercise any influence over them. Ledru-Rollin, almost hooted, left the tribune.

The tumult was renewed, increased, multiplied itself as it were, for the crowd was no longer sufficiently master of itself to be able even to understand the necessity for a moment's self-restraint in order to attain the object of its passion. A long interval passed; at last Barbès darted up and climbed, or rather leapt into the tribune. He was one of those men in whom the demagogue, the madman and the knight-errant are so closely intermingled that it is not possible to say where one ends or the other commences, and who can only make their way in a society as sick and troubled as ours. I am inclined to believe that it was the madman that predominated in him, and his madness became raging when he heard the voice of the people. His soul boiled as naturally amid popular passion as water does on the fire. Since our invasion by this crowd, I had not taken my eyes from him ; I considered him by far the most formidable of our adversaries, because he was the most insane, the most disinterested, and the most resolute of them all. I had seen him mount the platform on which the President sat, and stand for a long time motionless, only turning his agitated gaze about the Assembly ; I had observed and pointed out to my neighbours the distortion of his features, his livid pallor, the convulsive excitement which caused him each moment to twist his moustache between his fingers ; he stood there as the image of irresolution, leaning already towards an extreme side. This time, Barbès had made up his mind ; he proposed in some way to sum up the passions of the people, and to make sure of victory by stating its object in terms of precision :

"I demand", said he, in panting, jerking tones, " that, immediately and before rising, the Assembly shall vote the departure of an army for Poland, a tax of a milliard upon the rich, the removal of the troops from Paris, and shall forbid the beating to arms ; if not, the representatives to be declared traitors to the country."

I believe we should have been lost if Barbès had succeeded in getting his motion put to the vote ; for if the Assembly had accepted it, it would have been dishonoured and powerless, whereas, if it had rejected it, which was probable, we should have run the risk of having our throats cut. But Barbès himself did not succeed in obtaining a brief space of silence so as to compel us to take a decision. The huge clamour that followed his last words was not to be appeased ; on the contrary, it continued in a thousand varied intonations. Barbès exhausted himself in his efforts to still it, but in vain, although he was powerfully aided by the President's bell, which, during all this time, never ceased to sound, like a knell.

This extraordinary sitting had lasted since two o'clock ; the Assembly held out, its ears pricked up to catch any sound from the outside, waiting for assistance to come. But Paris seemed a dead city. Listen as we might, we heard no rumour issue from it.

This passive resistance irritated and incensed the people ; it was like a cold, even surface upon which its fury glided without knowing what to catch hold of ; it struggled and writhed in vain, without finding any issue to its undertaking. A thousand diverse and contradictory clamours filled the air : " Let us go away," cried some. . . . " The organization of labour. . . . A ministry of labour. . . . A tax on the rich. . . . We want Louis Blanc ! " cried others ; they ended by fighting at the foot of the tribune to decide who should mount it ; five or six orators occupied it at once, and often all spoke together. As always happens in insurrections, the terrible was mingled with the ridiculous. The heat was so stifling that many of the first intruders left the Chamber ; they were forthwith replaced by others who had been waiting at the doors to come in. In this way I saw a fireman in uniform making his way down the gangway that passed along my bench. " We can't make them vote ! " they shouted to him. " Wait, wait," he replied, " I'll see to it, I'll give them a piece of my mind." Thereupon he pulled his helmet over his eyes with a determined air, fastened the strap, squeezed through the crowd, pushing aside all who stood in his way, and mounted the tribune. He imagined he would be as much at his ease there as upon a roof, but he could not find his words and stopped short. The people cried, " Speak up, fireman ! " but he did not speak a word, and they ended by turning him out of the tribune. Just then a number of men of the people caught Louis Blanc in their arms and carried him in triumph round the Chamber. They held him by his little legs above their heads ; I saw him make vain efforts to extricate himself : he twisted and turned on every side without succeeding in escaping from their hands, talking all the while in a choking, strident voice. He reminded me of a snake having its tail pinched. They put him down at last on a bench beneath mine. I heard him cry. " My friends, the right you have just won. . . ." but the remainder of his words were lost in the din. I was told that Sobrier was carried in the same way a little lower down.

A very tragic incident nearly put an end to these saturnalia : the benches at the bottom of the house suddenly cracked, gave way more than a foot, and threatened to hurl into the Chamber the crowd which overloaded it, and which fled off in terror. This alarming occurrence put a momentary stop to the commotion ; and I then first heard, in the distance, the sound of drums beating the call to arms in Paris. The crowd heard it too, and uttered a long yell of rage and terror. " Why are they beating to arms ? " exclaimed Barbès, beside himself, making his way to the tribune afresh. " Who is beating to arms ? Let those who have given the order be outlawed ! " Cries of " We are betrayed, to arms ! To the Hôtel de Ville ! " rose from the crowd.

The President was driven from his chair, whence if we are to believe the version he since gave, he caused himself to be driven voluntarily. A clubleader called Huber climbed to his seat and hoisted a flag surmounted by a red cap. The man had, it seemed, just recovered from a long epileptic swoon, caused doubtless by the excitement and the heat ; it was on recovering from this sort of troubled sleep that he came forward. His clothes were still in disorder, his look scared and haggard. He exclaimed twice over in a resounding voice, which, uttered from aloft, filled the house and dominated every other sound. " In the name of the people, betrayed by its representatives, I declare the National Assembly dissolved ! "

The Assembly, deprived of its President, broke up. Barbès and the bolder of the club politicians went out to go to the Hôtel de Ville. This conclusion to the affair was far from meeting the general wishes. I heard men of the people beside me say to each other, in an aggrieved tone, " No, no, that's not what we want". Many sincere Republicans were in despair. I was first accosted, amid this tumult, by Trétat, a revolutionary of the sentimental kind, a dreamer who had plotted in favour of the Republic during the whole existence of the Monarchy. Moreover, he was a physician of distinction, who was at that time at the head of one of the principal madhouses in Paris, although he was a little cracked himself. He took my hands effusively, and with tears in his eyes :

" Ah, monsieur", he said, " what a misfortune, and how strange it is to think that it is madmen, real madmen, who have brought this about ! I have treated or prescribed for each one of them. Blanqui is a madman, Barbès is a madman, Sobrier is a madman, Huber is the greatest madman of them all : they are all madmen, monsieur, who ought to be locked up at my Salpétrière instead of being here."

He would certainly have added his own name to the list, had he known himself as well as he knew his old friends. I have always thought that in revolutions, especially democratic revolutions, madmen, not those so called by courtesy, but genuine madmen, have played a very considerable political part. One thing at least is certain, and that is that a condition of semi-madness is not unbecoming at such times, and often even leads to success.

The Assembly had dispersed, but it will be readily believed that it did not consider itself dissolved.

Nor did it even regard itself as defeated The majority of the members who left the House did so with the firm intention of soon meeting again elsewhere ; they said so to one another, and I am convinced that they were, in fact, quite resolved upon it. As for myself, I decided to stay behind, kept back partly by the feeling of curiosity that irresistibly retains me in places where anything uncommon is proceeding, and partly by the opinion which I held then, as I did on the 24th of February, that the strength of an assembly in a measure resides in the hall it occupies. I therefore remained and witnessed the grotesque and disorderly, but meaningless and uninteresting, scenes that followed. The crowd set itself, amid a thousand disorders and a thousand cries, to form a Provisional Government. It was a parody of the 24th of February, just as the 24th of February was a parody of other revolutionary scenes. This had lasted some time, when I thought that among all the noise I heard an irregular sound coming from the outside of the Palace. I have a very quick ear, and I was not slow in distinguishing the sound of a drum approaching and beating the charge ; for in our days of civil disorder, everyone has learnt to know the language of these warlike instruments. I at once hurried to the door by which these new arrivals would enter.

It was, in fact, a drum preceding some forty Gardes Mobiles. These lads pierced through the crowd with a certain air of resolution, although one could not clearly say at first what they proposed to do. Soon they disappeared from sight and remained as though submerged; but a short distance behind them marched a compact column of National Guards, who rushed into the House with significant shouts of " Long live the National Assembly ! " I stuck my card of membership in my hat-band and entered with them. They first cleared the platform of five or six orators, who were at that moment speaking at once, and flung them, with none too great ceremony, down the steps of the little staircase that leads to it. At the sight of this, the insurgents at first made as though to resist ; but a panic seized them. Climbing over the empty benches, tumbling over one another in the gangways, they made for the outer lobbies and sprang into the court-yards from every window. In a few minutes there remained only the National Guards, whose cries of " Long live the National Assembly " shook the walls of the Chamber.

The Assembly itself was absent ; but little by little the members who had dispersed in the neighbourhood hastened up. They shook the hands of the National Guards, embraced each other, and regained their seats. The National Guards cried, " Long live the National Assembly ! " and the members, " Long live the National Guard ! and long live the Republic ! "

[In the first scramble which followed the entry of the National Guard, I had a little adventure which I should like to relate as a warning to judges against the errors to which their profession is liable. Coming to the Assembly that morning I had brought with me a sword-stick which I left standing inside the entrance door. A moment later I was swept by the crowd to the side of a young man who, brandishing a bare sword in one hand and my stick in the other, was shouting with all his might : " Long live the National Assembly."—" One moment," I said, " this stick is mine."—" No, it is mine," he answered.— " It is mine," I said, " so much that I know that it contains a sword."—" I know," he said, " I have had a sword put in two days ago. But who are you ? " he added. I told him my name. He at once took off his hat respectfully and offered me the stick by its knob : " Sir," he said, " this stick is mine, but I shall be glad to lend it to you for you may need it to-day more than I. I shall have the honour of coming to fetch it from you." Next day I found my stick in a corner of the Assembly. It was so exactly like that of my suspected thief that I could not tell the two apart. I never knew if it was my stick or his that I returned to him when he came to see me as he had announced.]

No sooner was the hall recaptured, than General Courtais, the original author of our danger, had the incomparable impudence to present himself ; the National Guards received him with yells of fury ; he was seized and dragged to the foot of the rostrum. I saw him pass before my eyes, pale as a dying man among the flashing swords : thinking they would cut his throat, I cried with all my might, " Tear off his epaulettes, but don't kill him ! " which was done.

Then Lamartine reappeared. I never learnt how he had employed his time during the three hours wherein we were invaded. I had caught sight of him during the first hour : he was seated at that moment on a bench below mine, and he was combing his hair, glued together with perspiration, with a little comb he drew from his pocket ; the crowd formed again and I saw him no more. Apparently he went to the inner rooms of the Palace, into which the crowd had also penetrated, with the intention of haranguing it, and was very badly received. I was given, on the next day, some curious details of this scene, which I would have related here if I had not resolved to set down only what I have myself observed. They say that, subsequently, he withdrew to the Palace then being built, close at hand, and destined for the Foreign Office. He would certainly have done better had he placed himself at the head of the National Guards and come to our release. I think he must have been seized with the faintness of heart that overcomes the bravest (and he was one of these) when possessed of a restless and lively imagination.

When he returned to the Chamber, he had recovered his energy and his eloquence. He told us that his place was not in the Assembly, but in the streets, and that he was going to march upon the Hôtel de Ville and crush the insurrection. This was the last time I heard him enthusiastically cheered. True, it was not he alone that they applauded, but the victory : those cheers and clappings were but an echo of the tumultuous passions that still agitated every breast. Lamartine went out. The drums, which had beat the charge half-an-hour before, now beat the march. The National Guards and the Gardes Mobiles, who were still with us in crowds, formed themselves into order and followed him. The Assembly, still very incomplete, resumed its sitting ; it was six o'clock.

I went home an instant to take some food ; I then returned to the Assembly, which had declared its sitting permanent. We soon learnt that the members of the new Provisional Government had been arrested. Barbès was impeached, as was that old fool of a Courtais, who deserved a sound thrashing and no more. Many wished to include Louis Blanc, who, however, had pluckily undertaken to defend himself ; he had just escaped with difficulty from the fury of the National Guards at the door, and still wore his torn clothes, covered with dust and all disordered. This time he did not send for the stool on which he used to climb in order to bring his head above the level of the rostrum balustrade (for he was almost a dwarf) ; he even forgot the effect he wished to produce, and thought only of what he had to say. In

spite of that, or rather because of that, he won his case
for the moment. I never considered him to possess talent
except on that one day ; for I do not call talent the art
of polishing brilliant and hollow phrases, which are like
finely chased dishes containing nothing.

For the rest, I was so tired by the excitement of the day
that I have retained but a dull indistinct remembrance
of the night sitting. I shall therefore say no more, for I
wish only to record my personal impressions : for facts
in detail it is the *Moniteur*, not I, that should be consulted.

CHAPTER VIII

The Feast of Concord and the Preparations for the Days of June.

THE revolutionaries of 1848, unwilling or unable to imitate the bloodthirsty follies of their predecessors, consoled themselves by imitating their ludicrous follies. They took it into their heads to give the people a series of grand allegorical festivals.

Despite the terrible condition of the finances, the Provisional Government had decided that a sum of one or two millions should be spent upon celebrating the Feast of Concord in the Champ-de-Mars.

According to the programme, which was published in advance and faithfully followed, the Champ-de-Mars was to be filled with figures representing all sorts of persons, virtues, political institutions, and even public services. France, Germany and Italy, hand in hand ; Equality, Liberty and Fraternity, also hand in hand ; Agriculture, Commerce, the Army, the Navy and, above all, the Republic ; the last of colossal dimensions. A car was to be drawn by sixteen plough-horses : " this car," said the programme aforesaid, " will be of a simple and rustic shape, and will carry three trees, an oak, a laurel, and an olive tree, symbolizing strength, honour, and plenty ; and, moreover, a plough in the midst of a group of flowers and ears of corn. Ploughmen and young girls dressed in white will surround the car, singing patriotic hymns." We were also promised oxen with gilded horns, but did not get them.

The National Assembly had not the smallest desire to see all these beautiful things ; it even feared lest the immense gathering of people which was sure to be occasioned should produce some dangerous disorder. Accordingly, it put the date as far back as possible ; but the preparations were made, there was no possibility of going back from it, and the date was fixed for the 21st of May.

On that day I went early to the Assembly, which was to proceed on foot, in a body, to the Champ-de-Mars. I had put my pistols in my pockets, and in talking to my colleagues I discovered that most of them were secretly armed, like myself : one had taken a sword-stick, another a dagger ; nearly all carried some weapon of defence. Edmond de la Fayette showed me a weapon of a peculiar kind. It was a ball of lead sewn into a short leathern thong which could easily be fastened to the arm: one might have called it a portable club. La Fayette declared that this little instrument was being widely carried by the National Assembly, especially since the 15th of May. It was thus that we proceeded to this Feast of Concord.

A sinister rumour ran that some great danger awaited the Assembly when it should cross through the crowd of the Champ-de-Mars and take up its place on the stage reserved for it outside the Military College. As a matter of fact, nothing could have been easier than to make it the object of an unexpected attack during this progress, which it made on foot and, so to speak, unguarded. Its real safeguard lay in the recollection of the 15th of May, and that sufficed. It very rarely happens, whatever opportunity may present itself, that a body is affronted the day after its triumph. Moreover, the French never do two things at a time. Their minds often change their object, but they are always devoted wholly to that occupying them at the moment, and I believe there is no precedent of their making an insurrection in the middle of a fête or even of a ceremony. On this day, therefore, the people seemed to enter willingly into the fictitious idea of its happiness, and for a moment to place on one side the recollection of its miseries and its hatreds. It was animated, without being turbulent. The programme had stated that a " fraternal confusion " was to prevail. There was, it is true, extreme confusion, but no disorder ; for we are strange people : we cannot do without the police when we are orderly, and so soon as we start a revolution, the police seem useless. The sight of this popular joyfulness enraptured the moderate and sincere Republicans, and made them almost maudlin.

Carnot observed to me, with that silliness which the honest democrat always mingles with his virtue :

" Believe me, my dear colleague, one should always trust the people."

I remember rather brusquely replying, " Ah ! why didn't you tell me that before the 15th of May ? "

The Executive Commission occupied one-half of the immense stage that had been erected along the Military College, and the National Assembly the other. There first defiled past us the different emblems of all nations, which took an enormous time, because of the fraternal confusion of which the programme spoke. Then came the car, and then the young girls dressed in white. There were at least three hundred of them, who wore their virginal costume in so virile a fashion that they might have been taken for boys dressed up as girls. Each had been given a big bouquet to carry, which they were so gallant as to throw to us as they passed. As these gossips were the owners of very nervous arms, and were more accustomed, I should think, to using the laundress's beetle than to strewing flowers, the bouquets fell down upon us in a very hard and uncomfortable hail-storm.

One tall girl left her companions and, stopping in front of Lamartine, recited an ode to his glory. Gradually she grew excited in talking, so much so that she pulled a terrible face and began to make the most alarming contortions. Never had enthusiasm seemed to me to come so near to epilepsy. When she had finished, the people in-

sisted at all costs that Lamartine should kiss her ; she
offered him two fat cheeks, streaming with perspiration,
which he touched with the tip of his lips and with indifferent bad grace.

The only serious portion of the fête was the review.
I have never seen so many armed men in one spot in my
life, and I believe that few have seen more. Apart from
the innumerable crowd of sight-seers in the Champ-de-
Mars, one saw an entire people under arms. The *Moniteur* estimated the number of National Guards and
soldiers of the line who were there at three hundred
thousand. This seemed to me to be exaggerated, but I do
not think that the number could be reduced to less than
two hundred thousand.

The spectacle of those two hundred thousand bayonets
will never leave my memory. As the men who carried
them were tightly pressed against one another, so as to
be able to keep within the slopes of the Champ-de-Mars,
and as we, from our but slightly raised position, could
only throw an almost horizontal glance upon them, they
formed, to our eyes, a flat and lightly undulating surface,
which flashed in the sun and made the Champ-de-Mars
resemble a great lake filled with liquid steel.

All these men marched past us in succession, and we
noticed that this army numbered many more muskets
than uniforms. Only the legions from the wealthier parts
of the town presented a large number of National Guards
clad in military uniform. They were the first to appear,
and shouted, " Long live the National Assembly ! "
with much enthusiasm. In the legions from the suburbs,
which formed in themselves veritable armies, one saw
little but jackets and blouses, though this did not prevent
them from marching with a very warlike aspect. Most of
them, as they passed us, were content to shout, " Long
live the Democratic Republic ! " or to sing the *Marseil-
laise* or the song of the *Girondins*. Next came the legions

of the outskirts, composed of peasants, badly equipped, badly armed, and dressed in blouses like the workmen of the suburbs, but filled with a very different spirit to that of the latter, as they showed by their cries and gestures. The battalions of the Garde Mobile uttered various exclamations, which left us full of doubt and anxiety as to the intention of these lads, or rather children, who at that time more than any other held our destinies in their hands.

The regiments of the line, who closed the review, marched past in silence.

I witnessed this long parade with a heart filled with sadness. Never at any time had so many arms been placed at once into the hands of the people. It will be easily believed that I shared neither the simple confidence nor the stupid happiness of my friend Carnot ; I foresaw, on the contrary, that all the bayonets I saw glittering in the sun would soon be raised against each other, and I felt that I was at a review of the two armies of the civil war that was just concluded. In the course of that day I still heard frequent shouts of " Long live Lamartine ! " although his great popularity was already waning. In fact, one might say it was over, were it not that in every crowd one meets with a large number of belated individuals who are stirred with the enthusiasm of yesterday, like the provincials who begin to adopt the Paris mode on the day when the Parisians abandon it.

Lamartine hastened to withdraw from this last ray of his sun : he retired long before the ceremony was finished. He looked weary and care-worn. Many members of the Assembly, also overcome with fatigue, followed his example, and the review ended in front of almost empty benches. It had begun early and ended at night-fall.

The whole time elapsing between the review of the 21st of May and the days of June was filled with the anxiety caused by the approach of these latter days. Every day fresh alarms came and called out the army and the National Guard ; the artisans and shopkeepers no longer lived at home, but in the public places and under arms. Each one fervently desired to avoid the necessity of a conflict and all vaguely felt that this necessity was becoming more inevitable from day to day. The National Assembly was so constantly possessed by this thought that one might have said that it read the words " Civil War " written on the four walls of the House.

On all sides great efforts of prudence and patience were being made to prevent, or at least delay, the crisis. Members who in their hearts were most hostile to the revolution were careful to restrain any expressions of sympathy or antipathy ; the old parliamentary orators were silent, lest the sound of their voices should give umbrage ; they left the rostrum to the new-comers, who themselves but rarely occupied it, for the great debates had ceased. As is common in all assemblies, that which most disturbed the members' minds was that of which they spoke least, though it was proved that each day they thought of it. All sorts of measures to help the misery of the people were proposed and discussed. We even entered readily into an examination of the different socialistic systems, and each strove in all good faith to discover in these something applicable to, or at least compatible with, the ancient laws of Society.

During this time, the national workshops continued to fill ; their population already exceeded one hundred thousand men. It was felt that we could not live if they were kept on and it was feared that we should perish if we tried to dismiss them. This burning question of the national workshops was treated daily, but superficially and timidly ; it was constantly touched upon, but never firmly taken in hand.

On the other hand, it was clear that, outside the

Assembly, the different parties, while dreading the contest, were actively preparing for it. The wealthy legions of the National Guard offered banquets to the army and to the Garde Mobile, in which they mutually urged each other to unite for the common defence.

The workmen of the suburbs, on their side, were secretly amassing that great number of cartridges which enabled them later to sustain so long a contest. As to the muskets, the Provisional Government had taken care that these should be supplied in profusion ; one could safely say that there was not a workman who did not possess at least one, and sometimes several.

The danger was perceived afar off as well as near at hand. The provinces grew indignant and irritated with Paris ; for the first time for sixty years they ventured to entertain the idea of resisting it ; the people armed themselves and encouraged each other to come to the assistance of the Assembly ; they sent it thousands of addresses congratulating it on its victory of the 15th of May. The ruin of commerce, universal war, the dread of Socialism made the Republic more and more hateful in the eyes of the provinces. This hatred manifested itself especially beneath the secrecy of the ballot. The electors were called upon to re-elect in twenty-one departments ; and in general they elected the men who in their eyes represented the Monarchy in some form or other. M. Molé was elected at Bordeaux, and M. Thiers at Rouen.

It was then that suddenly, for the first time, the name of Louis Napoleon came into notice. The Prince was elected at the same time in Paris and in several departments. Republicans, Legitimists and demagogues gave him their votes ; for the nation at that time was like a frightened flock of sheep, which runs in all directions without following any road. I little thought, when I heard that Louis Napoleon had been nominated, that exactly a year later I should be his minister. I confess that I observed the return of the old parliamentary leaders with considerable apprehension and regret ; not that I failed to do justice to their talent and discretion, but I feared lest their approach should drive back towards the Mountain the moderate Republicans who were coming towards us. Moreover, I knew them too well not to see that, as soon as they had returned to political life, they would wish to lead it, and that it would not suit them to save the country unless they could govern it. Now an enterprise of this sort seemed to me both premature and dangerous. Our duty and theirs was to assist the moderate Republicans to govern the Republic without seeking to govern it indirectly ourselves, and especially without appearing to have this in view.

For my part, I never doubted but that we were on the eve of a terrible struggle ; nevertheless, I did not fully understand our danger until after a conversation that I had about this time with the celebrated Madame Sand. I met her at an Englishman's of my acquaintance : Milnes,[1] a member of Parliament, who was then in Paris. Milnes was a clever fellow who did and, what is rarer, said many foolish things. What a number of those faces I have seen in my life of which one can say that the two profiles are not alike : men of sense on one side, fools on the other. I have always seen Milnes infatuated with something or somebody. This time he was smitten with Madame Sand, and notwithstanding the seriousness of events, had insisted on giving her a literary *déjeuner*. I was present at this *déjeuner*, and the image of the days of June, which followed so closely after, far from effacing the remembrance of it from my mind, recalls it.

The company was anything but homogeneous. Besides Madame Sand, I met a young English lady, very modest and very agreeable, who must have found the company invited to meet her somewhat singular ; some

[1] The Right Honble. Monckton Milnes—later Lord Houghton.

more or less obscure writers ; and Mérimée. [Some of the guests did not know each other and others knew each other too well. If I am not mistaken this was the case of Madame Sand and Mérimée. Shortly before this they had had a tender though rather ephemeral relationship. We were even assured that they had conducted their affair in accordance with Aristotle's rules as to unity of time and place. Our British host knew nothing of this and had clumsily brought them together without informing them in advance. Thus they met without warning for the first time since their adventure, and the embarrassment to both was at first great, especially as Madame Sand was rather angry with Mérimée for having triumphed so easily and availed himself so little of his triumph ; but they soon pulled themselves together, and nothing could be observed during the rest of the day.]

Milnes placed me next to Madame Sand. I had never spoken to her, and I doubt whether I had ever seen her (I had lived little in the world of literary adventurers which she frequented). One of my friends asked her one day what she thought of my book on America, and she answered, " Monsieur, I am only accustomed to read the books which are presented to me by their authors ". I was strongly prejudiced against Madame Sand, for I loathe women who write, especially those who systematically disguise the weaknesses of their sex, instead of interesting us by displaying them in their true character. Nevertheless, she pleased me. I thought her features rather massive, but her expression admirable : all her mind seemed to have taken refuge in her eyes, abandoning the rest of her face to matter ; and I was particularly struck at meeting in her with something of the naturalness of behaviour of great minds. She had a real simplicity of manner and language, which she mingled, perhaps, with some little affectation of simplicity in her dress. I confess that, more adorned, she would have appeared still more simple. We talked for a whole hour of public affairs ; it was impossible to talk of anything else in those days. Besides, Madame Sand at that time was a sort of politican, and what she said on the subject struck me greatly ; it was the first time that I had entered into direct and familiar communication with a person able and willing to tell me what was happening in the camp of our adversaries. Political parties never know each other : they approach, touch, seize, but never see one another. Madame Sand depicted to me, in great detail and with singular vivacity, the condition of the Paris workmen, their organization, their numbers, their arms, their preparations, their thoughts, their passions, their terrible resolves. I thought the picture overloaded, but it was not, as subsequent events clearly proved. She seemed to be alarmed for herself at the popular triumph, and to take the greatest pity upon the fate that awaited us.

" Try to persuade your friends, monsieur," she said, " not to force the people into the streets by alarming or irritating them. I also wish that I could instil patience into my own friends ; for if it comes to a fight, believe me, you will all perish."

With these consoling words we parted, and I have never seen her since.

CHAPTER IX

The Days of June.

I COME at last to the insurrection of June, the most extensive and the most singular that has occurred in our history, and perhaps in any other : the most extensive, because, during four days, more than a hundred thousand men were engaged in it ; the most singular, because the insurgents fought without a war-cry, without leaders, without flags, and yet with a marvellous harmony and an amount of military experience that astonished the oldest officers.

What distinguished it also, among all the events of this kind which have succeeded one another in France for sixty years, is that it did not aim at changing the form of government, but at altering the order of society. It was not, strictly speaking, a political struggle, in the sense which until then we had given to the word, but a struggle of class against class, a sort of Servile War. It represented the facts of the Revolution of February in the same manner as the theories of Socialism represented its ideas ; or rather it issued naturally from these ideas, as a son does from his mother. We beheld in it nothing more than a blind and rude, but powerful, effort on the part of the workmen to escape from the necessities of their condition, which had been depicted to them as one of unlawful oppression, and to open up by main force a road towards that imaginary comfort with which they had been deluded. It was this mixture of greed and false theory which first gave birth to the insurrection and then made it so formidable. These poor people had been told that the wealth of the rich was in some way the produce of a theft practised upon themselves. They had been assured that the inequality of fortunes was as opposed to morality and the welfare of society as it was to nature. Prompted by

150

their needs and their passions, many had believed this obscure and erroneous notion of right, which, mingled with brute force, imparted to the latter an energy, a tenacity and a power which it would never have possessed unaided.

It must also be observed that this formidable insurrection was not the enterprise of a certain number of conspirators, but the revolt of one whole section of the population against another. Women took part in it as well as men. While the latter fought the former prepared and carried ammunition ; and when at last the time had come to surrender, the women were the last to yield.

These women went to battle with, as it were, a housewifely ardour : they looked to victory for the comfort of their husbands and the education of their children. They took pleasure in this war as they might have taken pleasure in a lottery.

As to the strategic science displayed by this multitude, the warlike nature of the French, their long experience of insurrections, and particularly the military education which the majority of the men of the people in turn receive, suffice to explain it. Half of the Paris workmen have served in our armies, and they are always glad to take up arms again. Generally speaking, old soldiers abound in our insurrections. On the 24th of February, when Lamoricière was surrounded by his foes, he twice owed his life to insurgents who had fought under him in Africa, men in whom the recollection of their military life had been stronger than the fury of civil war.

As we know, it was the closing of the national workshops that occasioned the rising. Dreading to disband this formidable soldiery at one stroke, the Government had tried to disperse it by sending part of the workmen into the country. They refused to leave. On the 22nd of June, they marched through Paris in troops, singing in cadence, in a monotonous chant, " We won't be sent away, we won't be sent away. . . ." Their delegates waited upon the members of the Committee of the Executive Power with a series of arrogant demands, and on meeting with a refusal, withdrew with the announcement that next day they would have recourse to arms. Everything, indeed, tended to show that the long-expected crisis had come.

When this news reached the Assembly it caused the greatest alarm. Nevertheless, the Assembly did not interrupt its order of the day ; it continued the discussion of a commercial act, and even listened to it, despite its excited condition ; true, it was a very important question and a very eminent orator was speaking.

The Government had proposed to acquire all the railways by purchase. Montalembert opposed it ; his case was good, but his speech was excellent ; I do not think I ever heard him speak so well before or since. As a matter of fact, I thought as he did, this time ; but I believe that, even in the eyes of his adversaries, he surpassed himself. He made a vigorous attack without being as peevish and outrageous as usual. A certain fear tempered his natural insolence, and set a limit to his paradoxical and querulous humour ; for, like so many other men of words, he had more temerity of language than stoutness of heart.

The sitting concluded without any question as to what was occurring outside, and the Assembly adjourned.

On the 23rd, on going to the Assembly I saw a large number of omnibuses grouped round the Madeleine. This told me that they were beginning to erect barricades in the streets ; which was confirmed on my arrival at the Palace. Nevertheless, a doubt was expressed whether it was seriously contemplated to resort to arms. I resolved to go and assure myself of the real state of things, and, with Corcelles, went to the neighbourhood of the Hôtel de Ville. In all the little streets surrounding that building, I found the people engaged in making barricades ; they proceeded in their work with the cunning and regularity of an engineer, not unpaving more stones than were necessary to lay the foundations of a very thick, solid and even neatly-built wall, in which they generally left a small opening by the side of the houses to permit of ingress and egress. Eager for quicker information as to the state of the town, Corcelles and I agreed to separate. He went one way and I the other ; and his excursion very nearly turned out badly. He told me afterwards that after crossing several half-built barricades without impediment, he was stopped at the last one. The men who were building it, seeing a fine gentleman, in black clothes and very white linen, quietly trotting through the dirty streets round the Hôtel de Ville and stopping before them with a placid and inquisitive air, thought they would make use of this suspicious onlooker. They called upon him, in the name of the brotherhood, to assist them in their work. Corcelles was as brave as Caesar, but he rightly judged that, under these circumstances, there was nothing better to be done than to give way quietly. See him therefore lifting paving-stones and placing them as neatly as possible one atop the other. His natural awkwardness and his absentmindedness came to his aid ; and he was soon sent about his business as a useless workman.

To me no such adventure happened. I passed through the streets of the Saint-Martin and Saint-Denis quarters without coming across any barricades to speak of ; but the excitement was extraordinary. On my return I met, in the Rue des Jeuneurs, a National Guard covered with blood and fragments of brain. He was very pale and was going home. I asked him what was happening ; he told me that his battalion had just received the full force of a very murderous discharge of musketry at the Porte Saint-Denis. One of his comrades, whose name he mentioned to me, had been killed by his side, and he was

covered with the blood and brains of this unhappy
man.

I returned to the Assembly, astonished at not having
met a single soldier in the whole distance which I had
traversed. It was not till I came in front of the Palais-
Bourbon that I at last perceived great columns of infantry, marching, followed by cannon.

Lamoricière, in full uniform and on horseback, was at
their head. I have never seen a figure more resplendent
with aggressive passion and almost with joy ; and whatever may have been the natural impetuosity of his
humour, I doubt whether it was that alone which urged
him at that moment, and whether there was not mingled
with it an eagerness to avenge himself for the dangers and
outrages he had undergone.

" What are you doing ? " I asked him. " They have
already been fighting at the Porte Saint-Denis, and
barricades are being built all round the Hôtel de Ville."

" Patience," he replied, " we are going there. Do you
think we are such fools as to scatter our soldiers on such a
day as this over the small streets of the suburbs ? No, no !
we shall let the insurgents concentrate in the quarters
which we can't keep them out of, and then we will go
and destroy them. They sha'n't escape us this time."

As I reached the Assembly, a terrible storm broke
which flooded the town. I entertained a slight hope that
this bad weather would get us out of our difficulties for
the day, and it would, indeed, have been enough to put a
stop to an ordinary riot ; for the people of Paris need fine
weather to fight in, and are more afraid of rain than of
grape-shot.

But I soon lost this hope : each moment the news became more distressing. The Assembly found difficulty in
resuming its ordinary work. Agitated, though not overcome by the excitement outside, it suspended the order
of the day, returned to it, and finally suspended it for

good, giving itself over to the preoccupations of the civil war. Different members came and described from the rostrum what they had seen in Paris. Others suggested various courses of action. Falloux, in the name of the Committee of Public Assistance, proposed a decree dissolving the national workshops, and received applause. Time was wasted with empty conversations, empty speeches. Nothing was known for certain ; they kept on calling for the attendance of the Executive Commission, to inform them of the state of Paris, but the latter did not appear. There is nothing more pitiful than the spectacle of an assembly in a moment of crisis, when the Government itself fails it ; it resembles a man still full of will and passion, but impotent, and tossing childishly amid the helplessness of his limbs. At last appeared two members of the Executive Commission ; they announced that affairs were in a perilous condition, but that, nevertheless, it was hoped to crush the insurrection before night. The Assembly declared its sitting permanent, and adjourned till the evening.

When the sitting was resumed, we learnt that Lamartine had been received with shots at all the barricades he attempted to approach. Two of our colleagues, Bixio and Dornès, had been mortally wounded when trying to address the insurgents. Bedeau had been shot through the thigh at the entrance to the Faubourg Saint-Jacques, and many officers of distinction were already killed or dangerously wounded. One of our members, Victor Considérant, spoke of making concessions to the workmen. The Assembly, which was tumultuous and disturbed, but not weak, revolted at these words : " Order order ! " they cried on every side, with a sort of rage, " it will be time to talk of that after the victory ! " The rest of the evening and a portion of the night were spent in vaguely talking, listening, and waiting. About midnight, Cavaignac appeared. The Executive Commission had since that afternoon placed the whole military power in his hands. In a hoarse and jerky voice, and in simple and precise words, Cavaignac detailed the principal incidents of the day. He stated that he had given orders to all the regiments posted along the railways to converge upon Paris, and that all the National Guards of the outskirts had been called out ; he concluded by telling us that the insurgents had been beaten back to the barriers, and that he hoped soon to have mastered the city. The Assembly, exhausted with fatigue, left its officials sitting in permanence, and adjourned until eight o'clock the next morning.

When, on quitting this turbulent scene, I found myself at one in the morning on the Pont Royal, and from there saw Paris wrapped in darkness, and calm as a city asleep, it was with difficulty that I persuaded myself that all that I had seen and heard since the morning had existed in reality and was not a pure creation of my mind. The streets and squares which I crossed were absolutely deserted ; not a sound, not a cry ; one would have said that an industrious population, fatigued with its day's work, was resting before resuming the peaceful labours of the morrow. The security of the night ended by overmastering me ; I brought myself to believe that we had triumphed already, and on reaching home I went straight to sleep.

I woke very early in the morning. The sun had risen some time before, for we were in the midst of the longest days of the year. On opening my eyes, I heard a sharp, metallic sound, which shook the window-panes and immediately died out amid the silence of Paris.

" What is that ? " I asked.

My wife replied, " It is the cannon ; I have heard it for over an hour, but would not wake you, for I knew you would want your strength during the day."

I dressed hurriedly and went out. The drums were

beating to arms on every side; the day of the great battle had come at last. The National Guards left their homes under arms; all those I met seemed full of energy, for the sound of cannon, which brought the brave ones out, kept the others at home. But they were in bad humour: they thought themselves either badly commanded or betrayed by the Executive Power, against which they uttered terrible imprecations. This extreme distrust of its leaders on the part of the armed force seemed to me an alarming symptom. Continuing on my way, at the entrance to the Rue Saint-Honoré, I met a crowd of workmen anxiously listening to the cannon. These men were all in blouses, which, as we know, constitute their fighting as well as their working clothes; nevertheless, they had no arms, but one could see by their looks that they were quite ready to take them up. They remarked, with a hardly restrained joy, that the sound of the firing seemed to come nearer, which showed that the insurrection was gaining ground. I had augured before this that the whole of the working class was engaged, either in fact or in spirit, in the struggle; and this confirmed my suspicions. The spirit of insurrection circulated from one end to the other of this immense class, and in each of its parts, as the blood does in the body; it filled the quarters where there was no fighting, as well as those which served as the scene of battle; it had penetrated into our houses, around, above, below us. The very places in which we thought ourselves the masters swarmed with domestic enemies; one might say that an atmosphere of civil war enveloped the whole of Paris, amid which, to whatever part we withdrew, we had to live; and in this connection I shall violate the law I have imposed upon myself never to speak upon the word of another, and will relate a fact which I learnt a few days later from my colleague Blanqui.[1] Although

[1] Of the Institute, a brother of Blanqui of the 15th of May.

very trivial, I consider it very characteristic of the physiognomy of the time. Blanqui had brought up from the country and taken into his house, as a servant, the son of a poor man, whose wretchedness had touched him. On the evening of the day on which the insurrection began, he heard this lad say as he was clearing the table after dinner, " Next Sunday (it was Thursday then) *we* shall be eating the wings of the chicken " ; to which a little girl who worked in the house replied, " And *we* shall be wearing fine silk dresses". Could anything give a better idea of the general state of minds than this childish scene ? And to complete it, Blanqui was very careful not to seem to hear these little monkeys : they really frightened him. It was not until after the victory that he ventured to send back the ambitious pair to their hovels.

At last I reached the Assembly. The representatives were gathered in crowds, although the time appointed for the sitting had not yet come. The sound of cannon had attracted them. The Palace had the appearance of a fortified town : battalions were encamped around, and guns were levelled at all the approaches leading to it.

I found the Assembly very determined, but very ill at ease ; and it must be confessed there was enough to make it so. It was easy to perceive through the multitude of contradictory reports that we had to do with the most universal, the best armed, and the most furious insurrection ever known in Paris. The national workshops and various revolutionary bands that had just been disbanded supplied it with leaders. It was extending every moment, and it was difficult to believe that it would not end by being victorious, when one remembered that all the great insurrections of the last sixty years had triumphed. To all these enemies we were only able to oppose the battalions of the *bourgeoisie*, regiments which had been disarmed in February, and twenty thousand undisciplined lads of the Garde Mobile, who were all sons, brothers, or near relations of insurgents, and whose dispositions were doubtful.

But what alarmed us most was our leaders. The members of the Executive Commission filled us with profound distrust. On this subject I encountered, in the Assembly, the same feeling which I had observed among the National Guard. We doubted the good faith of some and the capacity of others. They were too numerous, besides, and too much divided to be able to act in complete harmony, and they were too much men of speech and the pen to be able to act to good purpose under such circumstances, even if they had agreed among themselves.

Nevertheless, we succeeded in triumphing over this so formidable insurrection; nay more, it was just that which rendered it so terrible which saved us. One might well apply in this case the famous phrase of the Prince de Condé, during the wars of religion : " We should have been destroyed, had we not been so near destruction". Had the revolt borne a less radical character and a less ferocious aspect, it is probable that the greater part of the *bourgeois* would have stayed at home ; France would not have come to our aid ; the National Assembly itself would perhaps have yielded, or at least a minority of its members would have advised it ; and the energy of the whole body would have been greatly unnerved. But the insurrection was of such a nature that any understanding with it became at once impossible, and from the first it left us no alternative but to defeat it or to be destroyed ourselves.

The same reason prevented any man of consideration from placing himself at its head. In general, insurrections—I mean even those which succeed—begin without a leader ; but they always end by securing one. This insurrection finished without having found one ; it embraced all popular classes, but never passed those limits. Even the Montagnards in the Assembly did not dare pronounce in its favour. Several pronounced against it. They did not even yet despair of attaining their ends by other means; they feared, moreover, that the triumph of the workmen would soon prove fatal to them. The greedy, blind and vulgar passions which induced the populace to take up arms alarmed them; for these passions are as dangerous to those who sympathize with them, without utterly abandoning themselves to them, as to those who reprove and combat them. The only men who could have placed themselves at the head of the insurgents had allowed themselves to be prematurely taken, like fools, on the 15th of May; and they only heard the sound of the conflict through the walls of the dungeon of Vincennes.

Preoccupied though I was with public affairs, I continued to be distressed with the uneasiness which my young nephews once more caused me. They had been sent back to the Little Seminary, and I feared that the insurrection must come pretty near, if it had not already reached, the place where they lived. As their parents were not in Paris, I decided to go and fetch them, and I accordingly again traversed the long distance separating the Palais-Bourbon from the Rue Notre-Dame-des-Champs. I came across a few barricades erected during the night by the forlorn hope of the insurrection; but these had been either abandoned or captured at daybreak.

All these quarters resounded with a devilish music, a mixture of drums and trumpets, whose rough, discordant, savage notes were new to me. In fact, I heard for the first time—and I have never heard it since—the rally, which it had been decided should never be beaten except in extreme cases and to call the whole population at once to arms. Everywhere National Guards were issuing from the houses; everywhere stood groups of workmen in blouses, listening with a sinister air to the rally and the cannon. The fighting had not yet reached so far as the Rue Notre-Dame-des-Champs, although it was very near it. I took my nephews with me, and returned to the Chamber.

As I approached, and when I was already in the midst of the troops which guarded it, an old woman, pushing a barrow full of vegetables, obstinately barred my progress. I ended by telling her pretty curtly to make way. Instead of doing so, she left her barrow and flew at me in such a frenzy that I had great difficulty in protecting myself. I was horrified at the hideous and frightful expression of her face, on which were depicted all the fury of demagogic passion and the rage of civil war. I mention this little fact because I saw in it, and with good cause, an important symptom. In violently critical times, even actions which have nothing to do with politics assume a singular character of anger and disorder, which does not escape the attentive eye, and which is an unfailing index of the general state of mind. These great public excitements form a sort of glowing atmosphere in which all private passions seethe and bubble.

I found the Assembly agitated by a thousand sinister reports. The insurrection was gaining ground in every direction. Its headquarters, or, so to speak, its trunk, was behind the Hôtel de Ville, whence it stretched its long arms further to right and left into the suburbs, and threatened soon to hug even us. The cannon was drawing appreciably nearer. And to this correct news were added a thousand lying rumours. Some said that our troops were running short of ammunition ; others, that a number of them had laid down their arms or gone over to the insurgents.

M. Thiers asked Barrot, Dufaure, Rémusat, Lanjuinais and myself to follow him to a private room. There he said :

"I know something of insurrections, and I tell you this is the worst I have ever seen. The insurgents may be here within an hour, and we shall be butchered one and all. Do you not think that it would be well for us to agree to propose to the Assembly, as soon as we think necessary and before it becomes too late, that it should call back the troops around it, in order that, placed in their midst, we may all leave Paris together and remove the seat of the Republic to a place where we could summon the army and all the National Guards in France to our assistance?"

He said this in very eager tones and with a greater display of excitement than is, perhaps, advisable in the presence of great danger. I saw that he was pursued by the ghost of February. Dufaure, who had a less vivid imagination, and who, moreover, never readily made up his mind to associate himself with people he did not care about, even to save himself, phlegmatically and somewhat sarcastically explained that the time had not yet come to discuss a plan of this kind ; that we could always talk of it later on ; that our chances did not seem to him so desperate as to oblige us to entertain so extreme a remedy ; that to entertain it was to weaken ourselves. He was undoubtedly right, and his words broke up the consultation. I at once wrote a few lines to my wife, telling her that the danger was hourly increasing, that Paris would perhaps end by falling entirely into the power of the revolt, and that, in that case, we should be obliged to leave it in order to carry on the civil war elsewhere. I charged her to go at once to Saint-Germain by the railroad, which was still free, and there to await my news ; told my nephews to take the letter ; and returned to the Assembly.

I found it discussing a decree to proclaim Paris in a state of siege, to abolish the powers of the Executive Commission, and to replace it by a military dictatorship under General Cavaignac.

162

The Assembly knew precisely that this was what it wanted. The thing was easily done : it was urgent, and yet it was not done. Each moment some little incident, some trivial motion interrupted and turned aside the current of the general wish ; for assemblies are very liable to that sort of nightmare in which an unknown and invisible force seems always at the last moment to interpose between the will and the deed and to prevent the one from influencing the other. Who would have thought that it was Bastide who should eventually induce the Assembly to make up its mind ? Yet he it was.

I had heard him say—and it was very true—speaking of himself, that he was never able to remember more than the first fifteen words of a speech. But I have sometimes observed that men who do not know how to speak produce a greater impression, under certain circumstances, than the finest orators. They bring forward but a single idea, that of the moment, clothed in a single phrase, and somehow they lay it down in the rostrum like an inscription written in big letters, which everybody perceives, and in which each instantly recognizes his own particular thought. Bastide, then, displayed his long, honest, melancholy face in the tribune, and said, with a mournful air :

"Citizens, in the name of the country I beseech you to vote as quickly as possible. We are told that perhaps within an hour the Hôtel de Ville will be taken."

These few words put an end to debate, and the decree was voted in the twinkling of an eye.

I protested against the clause proclaiming Paris in a state of siege ; I did so by instinct rather than reflection. I have such a contempt and so great a natural horror for military despotism that these feelings came rising tumultuously in my heart when I heard a state of siege suggested, and even dominated those prompted by our peril.

In this I made a mistake in which I fortunately found few to imitate me.

The friends of the Executive Commission have asserted in very bitter terms that their adversaries and the partisans of General Cavaignac spread ominous rumours on purpose to precipitate the vote. If the latter did really resort to this trick, I gladly pardon them, for the measures they caused to be taken were indispensable to the safety of the country.

Before adopting the decree of which I have spoken, the Assembly unanimously voted another, which declared that the families of those who should fall in the struggle should receive a pension from the Treasury and their children be adopted by the Republic.

It was decided that sixty members of the Chamber, appointed by the committees, should spread themselves over Paris, inform the National Guards of the different decrees issued by the Assembly, and re-establish their confidence, which was said to be uncertain and discouraged.

In the committee to which I belonged, instead of immediately appointing commissioners, they began an endless discussion on the uselessness and danger of the resolution adopted. [During this time I was wondering impatiently about our part in this affair, and thinking that it needed only a word to end this ridiculous chatter ; but according to our parliamentary usage, in order to say this word I had to ask to be appointed a commissioner, a task which was not to my liking. I thought it was a little hard to let myself be shot while making a speech, like Bixio and Dornès. I said to myself : let people like Cormenin and Crémieux, who are members of the Committee like myself, and who are responsible for all this, be the commissioners ; nothing could be better. But why should I, who was chased out from their midst only six months ago, be so foolish as to seek this office ? But it concerned not only them but all of us, and we were like honest travellers kidnapped by pirates, who must help to save the ship if they would not themselves be drowned. Reflecting on this I asked to speak] and stopped the discussion at once with this sentence : " Gentlemen," I said, " the Assembly may have been mistaken ; but permit me to observe that, having passed a two-fold resolution, it would be a disgrace for it to draw back, and a disgrace for us not to submit."

They voted on the spot ; and I was unanimously elected a commissioner, as I expected. My colleagues were Cormenin and Crémieux, to whom they added Goudchaux. The latter was then not so well known, although in his own way he was the most original of them all. He was at once a Radical and a banker, a rare combination ; and by dint of his business occupations, he had succeeded in covering with a few reasonable ideas the foundation of his mind, which was filled with mad theories that always ended by making their way to the top. [Although both his parents were Jews, he was quite unaware of looking Jewish, for he had round cheeks, thick and ruddy lips, and a short, plump body, which made him look like a cook from a good house.] It was impossible to be vainer, more irascible, more quarrelsome, petulant or excitable than he. He was unable to discuss the difficulties of the Budget without shedding tears ; and yet he was one of the most valiant little men it was possible to meet.

Thanks to the stormy discussion in our committee, the other deputations had already left, and with them the guides and the escort who were to have accompanied us. Nevertheless, we set out, after putting on our scarves, and turned our steps alone and a little at hazard towards the interior of Paris, along the right bank of the Seine. By that time the insurrection had made such progress that one could see the cannon drawn up in line and firing between the Pont des Arts and the Pont Neuf. The National Guards, who saw us from the top of the embankment, looked at us with anxiety ; they respectfully took off their hats, and said in an undertone, and with grief-stricken accents, " Long live the National Assembly ! " No noisy cheers uttered at the sight of a king ever came more visibly from the heart, or pointed to a more un-feigned sympathy. When we had passed through the gates and were on the Carrousel, I saw that Cormenin and Crémieux were imperceptibly making for the Tuileries, and I heard one of them, I forget which, say :

" Where can we go ? And what can we do of any use without guides ? Is it not best to content ourselves with going through the Tuileries gardens ? There are several battalions of the reserve stationed there ; we will inform them of the decrees of the Assembly."

" Certainly," replied the other ; " I even think we shall be executing the Assembly's instructions better than our colleagues ; for what can one say to people already engaged in action ? It is the reserves that we should prepare to fall into line in their turn."

I have always thought it rather interesting to follow the involuntary movements of fear in clever people. Fools coarsely display their cowardice in all its naked-ness ; but the others are able to cover it with a veil so delicate, so daintily woven with small, plausible lies, that there is some pleasure to be found in contemplating this ingenious work of our intelligence.

As may be supposed, I was in no humour for a stroll in the Tuileries gardens. I had set out in none too good a temper ; but it was no good crying over spilt milk. I therefore pointed out to Goudchaux the road our col-leagues had taken.

" I know," he said, angrily ; " I shall leave them and I will make public the decrees of the Assembly without them."

Together we made for the gate opposite. Cormenin and Crémieux soon rejoined us, a little ashamed of their attempt. Thus we reached the Rue Saint-Honoré, the appearance of which was perhaps what struck me most during the days of June. This noisy, populous street was at this moment more deserted than I had ever seen it at four o'clock on a winter morning. As far as the eye could reach, we perceived not a living soul ; the shops, doors and windows were hermetically closed. Nothing was visible, nothing stirred ; we heard no sound of a wheel, no clatter of a horse, no human footstep, but only the voice of the cannon, which seemed to resound through an abandoned city. Yet the houses were not empty ; for as we walked on, we could catch glimpses at the windows of women and children who, with their faces glued to the panes, watched us go by with a terrified air.

At last, near the Palais-Royal, we met some large bodies of National Guards, and our mission commenced. When Crémieux saw that it was only a question of talking, he became all ardour ; he told them of what had happened at the National Assembly, and held forth to them in a little *bravura* speech which was heartily applauded. We found an escort there, and passed on. We wandered a long time through the little streets of that district, until we came in front of the great barricade of the Rue Rambuteau, which was not yet taken and which stopped our further progress. From there we came back again through all those little streets, which were covered with blood from the recent combats : they were still fighting from time to time. For it was a war of ambuscades, whose scene was not fixed but every moment changed. When one least expected it, one was shot at through a garret window ; and on breaking into the house, one found the gun but not the marksman : the latter escaped by a back-door while the front-door was being battered in. For this reason the National

Guards had orders to have all the shutters opened, and to fire on all those who showed themselves at the windows ; and they obeyed these orders so literally that they narrowly escaped killing several merely inquisitive people whom the sight of our scarves tempted to put their noses outside.

During this walk of two or three hours, we had to make at least thirty speeches ; I refer to Crémieux and myself, for Goudchaux was only able to speak on finance, and as to Cormenin, he was always as dumb as a fish. To tell the truth, almost all the burden of the day fell upon Crémieux. He filled me, I will not say with admiration, but with surprise. Janvier has said of Crémieux that he was " an eloquent louse". If only he could have seen him that day, jaded, with uncovered breast, dripping with perspiration and dirty with dust, wrapped in a long scarf twisted several times in every direction round his little body, but constantly hitting upon new ideas, or rather new words and phrases, now expressing in gestures what he had just expressed in words, then in words what he had just expressed in gestures : always eloquent, always ardent ! I do not believe that anyone has ever seen, and I doubt whether anyone has ever imagined, a man who was uglier or more fluent.

I observed that when the National Guards were told that Paris was in a state of siege, they were pleased, and when one added that the Executive Commission was overthrown, they cheered. Never were people so delighted to be relieved of their liberty and their government. And yet this was what Lamartine's popularity had come to in less than two months.

When we had done speaking, the men surrounded us ; they asked us if we were quite sure that the Executive Commission had ceased to act ; we had to show them the decree to satisfy them.

Particularly remarkable was the firm attitude of these

men. We had come to encourage them, and it was rather they who encouraged us. " Hold on at the National Assembly," they cried, " and we'll hold on here. Courage ! no transactions with the insurgents ! We'll put an end to the revolt : all will end well." I had never seen the National Guard so resolute before, nor do I think that we could rely upon finding it so again ; for its courage was prompted by necessity and despair, and proceeded from circumstances which are not likely to recur.

Paris on that day reminded me of a city of antiquity whose citizens defended the walls like heroes, because they knew that if the city were taken they themselves would be dragged into slavery. As we turned our steps back towards the Assembly, Goudchaux left us. " Now that we have done our errand," said he, clenching his teeth, and in an accent half Gascon and half Alsatian, " I want to go and fight a bit." He said this with such a martial air, so little in harmony with his pacific appearance, that I could not help smiling.

He did, in fact, go and fight, as I heard the next day, and so well that he might have had his little paunch pierced in two or three places, had fate so willed it. I returned from my round convinced that we should come out victorious ; and what I saw on nearing the Assembly confirmed my opinion.

Thousands of men were hastening to our aid from every part of France, and entering the city by all the roads not commanded by the insurgents. Thanks to the railroads, some had already come from fifty leagues' distance, although the fighting had only begun the night before. On the next and the subsequent days, they came from distances of a hundred and two hundred leagues. These men belonged indiscriminately to every class of society ; among them were many peasants, many shop-keepers, many landlords and nobles, all mingled to-

gether in the same ranks. They were armed in an irregular and insufficient manner, but they rushed into
Paris with unequalled ardour : a spectacle as strange
and unprecedented in our revolutionary annals as that
offered by the insurrection itself. It was evident from
that moment that we should end by gaining the day,
for the insurgents received no reinforcements, whereas
we had all France for reserves.

On the Place Louis XV, I met, surrounded by the
armed inhabitants of his canton, my kinsman Lepel-
letier d'Aunay, who was Vice-President of the Chamber
of Deputies during the last days of the Monarchy. He
wore neither uniform nor musket, but only a little silver-
hilted sword which he had slung at his side over his coat
by a narrow white linen bandolier.

I was touched to tears on seeing this venerable white-
haired man thus accoutred.

" Won't you come and dine with us this evening ? "

" No, no," he replied ; " what would these good folk
who are with me, and who know that I have more to
lose than they by the victory of the insurrection—what
would they say if they saw me leaving them to take it
easy ? No, I will share their meal and sleep here at their
bivouac. The only thing I would beg you is, if possible,
to hurry the despatch of the provision of bread promised
us, for we have had no food since morning."

I returned to the Assembly, I believe at about three,
and did not go out again.

The remainder of the day was taken up by accounts
of the fighting : each moment produced its event and
its piece of news. The arrival of volunteers from one of
the departments was announced ; they were bringing
in prisoners ; flags captured on the barricades were
brought in. Deeds of bravery were described, heroic
words repeated ; each moment we learnt of some person of note being wounded or killed. As to the final issue

of the day, nothing had yet occurred to enable us to form an opinion.

The President only called the Assembly together at infrequent intervals and for short periods ; and he was right, for assemblies are like children, and idleness always makes them say or do a number of foolish things. Each time the sitting was resumed, he himself told us all that had been learnt for certain during the adjournment. This President, as we know, was Sénard, a well-known Rouen advocate and a man of courage ; but in his youth he had contracted so deep-seated a theatrical habit in the daily comedy played at the bar that he had lost the faculty of truthfully giving his true impressions of a thing, when by accident he happened to have any. It seemed always necessary that he should add some turgidity or other of his own to the feats of courage he described, and that he should express the emotion, which I believe he really felt, in hollow tones, a trembling voice, and a sort of tragic hiccough which reminded one of an actor on the stage. Never were the sublime and the ridiculous brought so close together : for the facts were sublime and the narrator ridiculous.

We did not adjourn till late at night to take a little rest. The fighting had stopped, to be resumed on the morrow. The insurrection, although everywhere held in check, had as yet been stifled nowhere.

CHAPTER X

The Days of June (continued).

THE porter of the house in which we lived in the Rue de la Madeleine was a man of very bad reputation in the neighbourhood, an old soldier, not quite in his right mind, a drunkard, and a great good-for-nothing, who spent at the wine-shop all the time which he did not employ in beating his wife. This man might be said to be a Socialist by birth, or rather by temperament.

The early successes of the insurrection had brought him to a state of exaltation and on the morning of the day of which I speak he visited all the wineshops around, and among other mischievous remarks of which he delivered himself, he said that he would kill me when I came home in the evening, if I came in at all. He even displayed a large knife which he intended to use for the purpose. A poor woman who heard him ran in great alarm to tell Madame de Tocqueville ; and she, before leaving Paris, sent me a note in which, after telling me of the facts, she begged me not to come in that night, but to go to my father's house, which was close by, he being away. This I determined to do ; but when I left the Assembly at midnight, I had not the energy to carry out my intention. I was worn out with fatigue, and I did not know whether I should find a bed prepared if I slept out. Besides, I had little faith in the performance of murders proclaimed beforehand ; and also I was under the influence of the sort of listlessness that follows upon any prolonged excitement. I accordingly went and knocked at my door, only taking the precaution to load the pistols which, in those unhappy days it was common to carry. My man opened the door, I entered, and, while he was carefully pushing the bolts behind me, I asked him if all the tenants had come home. He replied drily that they had all left Paris that morning, and that we two were alone in the house. I should have preferred another kind of *tête-à-tête*, but it was too late to go back ; I therefore looked him straight in the eyes and told him to walk in front and show a light.

He stopped at a gate that led to the court-yard, and told me that he heard a curious noise in the stables which alarmed him, begging me to go with him to see what it was. As he spoke, he turned towards the stables. All this began to seem very suspicious to me, but I thought that, as I had gone so far, it was better to go on. I accordingly followed him, carefully watching his movements, and making up my mind to kill him like a dog at the first sign of treachery. As a matter of fact, we did hear a very strange noise. It resembled the dull running of water or the distant rumble of a carriage, although it obviously came from somewhere quite near. I never learnt what it was ; though it was true I did not spend much time in trying to discover. I soon returned to the house and made my companion bring me to my threshold, keeping my eyes on him the whole time. I told him to open the door, and as soon as he had done so, I took the candle from his hand and went in. It was not until I was almost out of his sight that he brought himself to take off his hat and bow to me. Had the man really intended to kill me, and seeing me on my guard, with both hands in my pockets, did he reflect that I was better armed than he, and that he would be well advised to abandon his design? I thought at the time that the latter had never been very seriously intended, and I think so still. In times of revolution, people boast almost as much about the imaginary crimes they propose to commit as in ordinary times they do of the good intentions they pretend to entertain. I have always believed that this wretch would only have become dangerous if the fortunes of the fight had seemed to turn against us ; but they leant, on the contrary, to our side, although they were still undecided ; and this was sufficient to assure my safety.

At dawn I heard some one in my room, and woke with a start : it was my man-servant, who had let himself in with a private key of the apartment, which he carried. The brave lad had just left the bivouac (I had supplied him at his request with a National Guard's uniform and a good gun), and he came to know if I had come home and if his services were required. This one was certainly not a Socialist, either in theory or temperament. He was not even tainted in the slightest degree with the most general malady of the age, restlessness of mind, and even in other times than ours it would have been difficult to find a man more contented with his position and less sullen at his lot. Always very much satisfied with himself, and tolerably satisfied with others, he generally desired only that which was within his reach, and he generally attained, or thought he attained, all that he desired ; thus unwittingly following the precepts which philosophers teach and never observe, and enjoying by the gift of Nature that happy equilibrium between faculty and desire which alone gives the happiness which philosophy promises us.

" Well, Eugène," I said, when I saw him, " how are affairs going on ? "

" Very well, sir, perfectly well ! "

" What do you mean by very well ? I can still hear the sound of cannon ! "

" Yes, they are still fighting," he replied, " but every one says it will end all right."

With that he took off his uniform, cleaned my boots, brushed my clothes, and putting on his uniform again :

" If you don't require me any more, sir," said he, " and if you will permit me, I will go back to the fighting."

He pursued this two-fold calling during four days and

four nights, as simply as I am writing it down ; and I
experienced a sort of reposeful feeling, during these days
filled with turmoil and hate, when I looked at the young
man's peaceful and contented face.

Before going to the Assembly, where I did not think
there would be any important measures to take, I resolved to make my way to the places where the fighting
was still going on, and where I heard the sound of
cannon. It was not that I was longing " to go and fight a
bit", like Goudchaux, but I wanted to judge for myself
as to the state of things ; for, in my simple ignorance of
war, I could not understand what made the struggle last
so long. Besides, shall I confess it, a keen curiosity was
piercing through all the feelings that filled my mind, and
from time to time dominated them. I went along a great
portion of the boulevard without seeing any traces of the
battle, but there were plenty just beyond the Porte
Saint-Martin ; one stumbled over the *débris* left behind
by the retreating insurrection : broken windows, doors
smashed in, houses spotted by bullets or pierced by can-
non-balls, trees cut down, heaped-up paving-stones,
straw mixed with blood and mud. Such were these
melancholy vestiges.

I thus reached the Château-d'Eau, around which
were massed a number of troops of different sorts. At the
foot of the fountain was a piece of cannon which was
being discharged down the Rue Samson. I thought at
first that the insurgents were replying with cannon on
their side, but I ended by seeing that I was deceived by
an echo which repeated with a terrible crash the sound
of our own gun. I have never heard anything like it ;
one might have thought one's self in the midst of a great
battle. As a matter of fact, the insurgents were only
replying with an infrequent but deadly musketry fire.
It was a strange combat. The Rue Samson, as we knew
is not a very long one ; at the end runs the Canal Saint-

Martin, and behind the canal is a large house facing the street.

The street was absolutely deserted ; there was no barricade in sight, and the gun seemed to be firing at a target ; only from time to time a whiff of smoke issued from a few windows, and proclaimed the presence of an invisible enemy. Our sharp-shooters, posted along the walls, aimed at the windows from which they saw the shots fired. Lamoricière, mounted on a tall horse in full view of the enemy, gave his commands amid the whirl of bullets. I thought he was more excited and talkative than I had imagined a general ought to be in such a juncture ; he talked, shouted in a hoarse voice, gesticulated in a sort of rage. It was easy to see by the clearness of his thoughts and expressions that amid this apparent disorder he lost none of his presence of mind ; but his manner of commanding might have caused others to lose theirs, and I confess I should have admired his courage more if he had kept more quiet.

This conflict, in which one saw nobody before him, this firing, which seemed to be aimed only at the walls, surprised me strangely. I should never have pictured war to myself under this aspect. As the boulevard seemed clear beyond the Château-d'Eau, I was unable to understand why our columns did not pass further, nor why, if we wanted first to seize the large house facing the street, we did not capture it at a run, instead of remaining so long exposed to the deadly fire issuing from it. Yet nothing was more easily explained : the boulevard, which I thought clear from the Château-d'Eau onwards, was not so ; beyond the bend which it makes at this place, it was bristling with barricades, all the way to the Bastille. Before attacking the barricades, we wanted to become masters of the streets we left behind us, and especially to capture the house facing the street, which, commanding the boulevard as it did, would have impeded our communications. Finally, we did not take the house by assault, because we were separated from it by the canal, which I could not see from the boulevard. We confined ourselves, therefore, to efforts to destroy it by cannon-shots, or at least to render it untenable. This took a long time to accomplish, and after being astonished in the morning that the fighting had not finished. I now asked myself how at this rate it could ever finish. For what I was witnessing at the Château-d'Eau was at the same time being repeated in other forms in a hundred different parts of Paris.

As the insurgents had no artillery, the conflict did not possess the horrible aspect which it must have when the battle-field is ploughed by cannon balls. The men who were struck down before me seemed transfixed by an invisible shaft : they staggered and fell without one's seeing at first anything but a little hole made in their clothes. In the cases of this kind which I witnessed, I was struck less by the sight of physical pain than by the picture of moral anguish. It was indeed a strange and frightful thing to see the sudden change of features, the quick extinction of the light in the eyes in the terror of death.

After a certain period, I saw Lamoricière's horse sink to the ground, shot by a bullet ; it was the third horse the General had had killed under him since the day before yesterday. He sprang lightly to the ground, and continued bellowing his raging instructions.

I noticed that on our side the least eager were the soldiers of the Line. They were weakened and, as it were, dulled by the remembrance of February, and did not yet seem quite certain that they would not be told the next day that they had done wrong. The liveliest were undoubtedly the Gardes Mobiles of whom we had felt so uncertain ; and, in spite of the event, I maintain that we were right, at the time ; for it wanted but little for them to decide against us instead of taking our side. Until the end, they plainly showed that it was the fighting they loved rather than the cause for which they fought.

All these troops were raw and very subject to panic : I myself was a judge and almost a victim of this. At a street corner close to the Château-d'Eau was a large house in process of building. Some insurgents who doubtless entered from behind across the court-yards, had taken up their position there, unknown to us ; suddenly they appeared on the roof, and fired a great volley at the troops who filled the boulevard, and who did not expect to find the enemy posted so close at hand. The sound of their muskets reverberating with a great crash against the opposite houses gave reason to dread that a surprise of the same kind was taking place on that side. Immediately the most incredible confusion prevailed in our column : artillery, cavalry, and infantry were mingled in a moment, the soldiers fired in every direction, without knowing what they were doing, and tumultuously fell back sixty paces. This retreat was so disorderly and so impetuous that I was thrown against the wall of the houses facing the Rue du Faubourg-du-Temple, knocked down by the cavalry, and so hard pressed that I left my hat on the field, and very nearly left my body there. It was certainly the most serious danger I ran during the days of June. This made me think that it is not all heroism in the game of war. I have no doubt but that accidents of this kind often happen to the very best troops ; no one boasts about them, and they are not mentioned in the dispatches.

It was now that Lamoricière became sublime. He had till then kept his sword in the scabbard : he now drew it, and ran up to his soldiers, his features distorted with the most magnificent rage ; he stopped them with his voice, seized them with his hands, even struck them with the pummel of his sword, turned them, brought them back, and, placing himself at their head, forced them to pass at the trot through the fire in the Rue du Faubourg-du-Temple in order to take the house from which the firing had come. This was done in a moment and without striking a blow : the enemy had disappeared.

The combat resumed its dull aspect and lasted some time longer, until the enemy's fire was at length extinguished, and the street occupied. Before commencing the next operation, there was a moment's pause : Lamoricière went to his head-quarters, a wine-shop on the boulevard near the Porte Saint-Martin, and I was at last able to consult him on the state of affairs.

" How long do you think," I asked, " that all this will last ? "

" Why, how can I tell ? " he replied. " That depends on the enemy, not on us."

He then showed me on the map all the streets we had already captured and were occupying, and all those we had still to take, adding. " If the insurgents choose to defend themselves on the ground they still hold as they have done on that which we have won from them, we may still have a week's fighting before us, and our losses will be enormous, for we lose more than they do : the first side to lose its moral courage will be the first to be beaten."

I next reproached him with exposing himself so rashly, and, as I thought, so uselessly.

" What will you have me do ? " said he. " Tell Cavaignac to send generals able and willing to second me, and I will keep more in the background ; but you always have to expose yourself when you have only yourself to rely on."

M. Thiers then came up, threw himself on Lamoricière's neck, and told him he was a hero. I could not help smiling at this effusion, for there was no love lost between them : but a great danger is like wine, it makes men affectionate.

I left Lamoricière in M. Thiers' arms, and returned to the Assembly : it was growing late, and besides, I know no greater fool than the man who gets his head broken in battle out of curiosity.

The rest of the day was spent as the day before : the same anxiety in the Assembly, the same feverish inaction, the same firmness.

Volunteers continued to enter Paris ; every moment we were told of some tragic event or illustrious death. These pieces of news saddened, but animated and fortified, the Assembly. Any member who ventured to enter into negotiations with the insurgents was met with yells of rage.

In the evening I decided to go myself to the Hôtel de Ville, in order to obtain more certain news of the results of the day. The insurrection, after alarming me by its violence, now alarmed me by its long duration. For who could foresee the effect which the sight of so long and uncertain a conflict might produce in some parts of France, and especially in the great manufacturing towns, such as Lyons ? As I went along the Quai de la Ferraille, I met some National Guards from my neighbourhood, carrying on litters several of their comrades and two of their officers wounded. I observed, in talking with them, with what terrible rapidity, even in so civilized a century as our own, the most peaceful minds enter, as it were, into the spirit of civil war, and how quick they are, in these unhappy times, to acquire a taste for violence and a contempt for human life. The men with whom I was talking were peaceful, sober artisans, whose gentle and somewhat sluggish natures were still further removed from cruelty than from heroism. Yet they dreamt of nothing but massacre and destruction.

They complained that they were not allowed to use
bombs or to sap and mine the streets held by the insurgents, and they were determined to show no more quarter ; already that morning I had almost seen a poor
devil shot before my eyes on the boulevards, who had
been arrested without arms in his hands, but whose
mouth and hands were blackened by a substance which
they supposed to be, and which no doubt was, powder.
I did all I could to calm these rabid sheep. I promised
them that we should take terrible measures the next day.
Lamoricière, in fact, had told me that morning that he
had sent for shells to hurl behind the barricades ; and I
knew that a regiment of sappers was expected from
Douai, to pierce the walls and blow up the besieged
houses with petards. I added that they must not shoot
any of their prisoners, but that they should kill then and
there anyone who made as though to defend himself. I
left my men a little more contented, and, continuing
my road, I could not help examining myself and feeling
surprised at the nature of the arguments I had used, and
the promptness with which, in two days, I had become
familiarized with those ideas of inexorable destruction
which were naturally so foreign to my character.

As I passed in front of the little streets at the entrance
to which, two days before, I had seen such neat and
solid barricades being built, I noticed that the cannon
had considerably upset those fine works, although some
traces remained.

I was received by Marrast, the Mayor of Paris. He
told me that the Hôtel de Ville was clear for the present,
but that the insurgents might try in the night to recap-
ture the streets from which we had driven them. I found
him less tranquil than his bulletins. He took me to a
room in which they had laid Bedeau, who was dangerously wounded on the first day. This post at the Hôtel
de Ville was a very fatal one for the generals who com-

manded there. Bedeau almost lost his life. Duvivier and Négrier, who succeeded him, were killed. Bedeau believed he was but slightly hurt, and thought only of the situation of affairs : nevertheless, his activity of mind struck me as ill-omened, and alarmed me.

The night was well advanced when I left the Hôtel de Ville to go to the Assembly. I was offered an escort, which I refused, not thinking I should require it ; but I regretted it more than once on my way. In order to prevent the insurgent districts from receiving reinforcements, provisions, or communications from the other parts of the town, in which there were so many men prepared to embrace the same cause, it had very properly been resolved absolutely to prohibit circulation in any of the streets. Everyone was stopped who left his house without a pass or an escort. I was constantly stopped on my way and made to show my medal. I was aimed at more than ten times by those inexperienced sentries, who spoke every imaginable accent ; for Paris was filled with provincials, who had come from every part of the country, many of them for the first time.

When I arrived, the sitting was over, but the Palace was still in a great state of excitement. A rumour had got about that the workmen of the Gors-Caillou were about to take advantage of the darkness to seize upon the Palace itself. Thus the Assembly, which, after three days' fighting, had carried the conflict into the heart of the districts occupied by its enemies, was trembling for its own quarters. The rumour was void of foundation ; but nothing could better show the character of this war, in which the enemy might always be one's own neighbour, and in which one was never certain of not having his house sacked while gaining a victory at a distance. In order to secure the Palace against all surprise, barricades were hurriedly erected at the entrance to all the streets leading up to it. When I saw that it was only a question of a false rumour, I went home to bed.

I shall say no more of the June combats. The recollections of the last two days merge into and are lost in those of the first. As is known, the Faubourg Saint-Antoine, the last citadel of the civil war, did not lay down its arms until the Monday—that is to say, on the fourth day after the commencement of the conflict ; and it was not until the morning of that day that the volunteers from La Manche were able to reach Paris. They had hurried as fast as possible, but they had come more than eighty leagues across a country in which there were no railways. They were fifteen hundred in number. I was touched at recognizing among them many landlords, lawyers, doctors and farmers, who were my friends and neighbours. Almost all the old nobility of the country had taken up arms on this occasion and formed part of the column. It was the same over almost the whole of France. From the petty squire squatting in his den in the country to the useless, elegant sons of the great houses— all had at that moment remembered that they had once formed part of a warlike and governing class, and on every side they gave the example of vigour and resolution : so great is the vitality of those old bodies of aristocracy. They retain traces of themselves even when they appear to be reduced to dust, and spring up time after time from the shades of death before sinking back for ever.

It was in the midst of the days of June that the death occurred of a man who perhaps of all men in our day best preserved the spirit of the old races : M. de Chateaubriand, with whom I was connected by so many family ties and childish recollections. He had long since fallen into a sort of speechless stupor, which made one sometimes believe that his intelligence was extinguished. Nevertheless, while in this condition, he heard a rumour of the Revolution of February, and desired to be told what was happening. They informed him that Louis-Philippe's government had been overthrown. He said, " Well done ! " and nothing more. Four months later, the din of the days of June reached his ears, and again he asked what that noise was. They answered that people were fighting in Paris, and that it was the sound of cannon. Thereupon he made vain efforts to rise, saying, " I want to go to it", and was then silent, this time for ever ; for he died the next day.

Such were the days of June, necessary and disastrous days. They did not extinguish revolutionary ardour in France, but they put a stop, at least for a time, to what may be called the work appertaining to the Revolution of February. They delivered the nation from the tyranny of the Paris workmen and restored it to possession of itself.

Socialistic theories continued to penetrate into the minds of the people in the shape of envious and greedy desires, and to sow the seed of future revolutions ; but the socialist party itself was beaten and powerless. The Montagnards, who did not belong to it, felt that they were irrevocably affected by the blow that had struck it. The moderate Republicans themselves did not fail to be alarmed lest this victory had led them to a slope which might precipitate them from the Republic, and they made an immediate effort to stop their descent, but in vain. Personally I detested the Mountain, and was in-different to the Republic ; but I adored Liberty, and I conceived great apprehensions for it immediately after these days. I at once looked upon the June fighting as a necessary crisis, after which, however, the temper of the nation would undergo a certain change. The love of independence was to be followed by a dread of, and per-haps a distaste for, free institutions ; after such an abuse of liberty a return of this sort was inevitable. This retrograde movement began, in fact, on the 27th of June. At first very slow and invisible, as it were, to the naked eye, it grew swifter, impetuous, irresistible. Where will it stop? I do not know. I believe we shall have great difficulty in not rolling far beyond the point we had reached before February, and I foresee that all of us, Socialists, Montagnards and Liberal Republicans, will fall into common discredit until the particular recollections of the Revolution of 1848 are removed and effaced, and the general spirit of the times shall resume its empire.

CHAPTER XI[1]

The Committee for the Constitution.

(SORRENTO, *March* 1851).

I NOW change my subject, and am glad to leave the scenes of the civil war and to return to the recollections of my parliamentary life. I wish to speak of what happened in the Committee for the Constitution, of which I was a member. This will oblige us to retrace our steps a little, for the appointment and work of this committee date back to before the days of June ; but I did not mention it earlier, because I did not wish to interrupt the course of events which was leading us swiftly and directly to those days. The nomination of the Committee for the Constitution was commenced on the 17th of May ; it was a long performance, because it had been decided that the members of the committee should be chosen by the whole Assembly and by an absolute majority of votes. I was elected at the first voting[2] together with Cormenin, Marrast, Lamennais, Vivien and Dufaure. I do not remember how often the voting had to be repeated in order to complete the list, which was to consist of eighteen members.

Although the committee had been nominated before the victory of June, almost all its members belonged to the different moderate sections of the Assembly. The Mountain had only two representatives on it : Lamennais and Considérant ; and even these were little worse than chimerical visionaries, especially Considérant, who

---

[1] There is a great hiatus in this chapter, due to my not mentioning the discussions and resolutions relating to *general principles*. Many of the discussions were fairly thorough, and most of the resolutions were tolerably wise and even courageous. Most of the revolutionary and socialistic impulses of the time were combated in them. We were prepared and on our guard on these general questions.

[2] I received 496 votes.

would have deserved to be sent to a lunatic asylum had he been sincere—but I fear he deserved more than that.

Taking the Committee as a whole, it was easy to see that no very remarkable result was to be expected from it.

Some of its members had spent their lives in conducting or controlling the administration during the last government. They had never seen, studied, or understood anything except the Monarchy ; and even then they had, for the most part, applied rather than studied its principles. They had raised themselves but little above the practice of business. Now that they were called upon to realize the theories which they had always slighted or opposed, and which had defeated without convincing them, they found it difficult to apply any but monarchical ideas to their work ; or, if they adopted republican ideas, they did so now timidly, now rashly, always a little at haphazard, like novices.

As for the Republicans proper on the Committee, they had few ideas of any sort, except those which they had gathered in reading or writing for the newspapers ; for there were several journalists among them. Marrast had edited the *National* for ten years ; Dornès was at that time its editor-in-chief; Vaulabelle, a man of serious but coarse and even cynical cast of mind, habitually wrote for its columns. He was the man who, a month later, was himself vastly astonished at becoming Minister of Public Worship and Instruction.

All this bore very little resemblance to the men, so certain of their objects and so well acquainted with the measures necessary to attain them, who sixty years before, under Washington's presidency, so successfully drew up the American Constitution.

For that matter, even if the Committee had been capable of doing its work well, the want of time and the preoccupation of outside events would have prevented it.

There is no nation which attaches itself less to those who govern it than the French Nation, nor which is less able to dispense with government. As soon as it finds itself obliged to walk alone, it undergoes a sort of vertigo, which makes it dread an abyss at every step. At the time I speak of, it had a sort of frenzied desire for the work of framing the Constitution to be completed, and for the powers in command to be, if not solidly, at least permanently and regularly established. The Assembly shared this eagerness, and never ceased urging us on, although we required but little urging. The recollection of the 15th of May, the apprehensions entertained of the days of June and the sight of the divided, enervated and incapable government at the head of affairs were sufficient inducement to us to hasten our labours. But what especially deprived the Committee of its freedom of thought was, it must be confessed, the fear of outside matters and the excitement of the moment. It would be difficult to imagine the effect produced by this forcing of revolutionary ideas upon minds so little disposed to adopt them, and how the latter were being incessantly, and even almost unconsciously, impelled much further than they wished to go, when they were not pushed altogether out of the direction they desired to take. Certainly, if the Committee had met on the 27th of June instead of the 16th of May, its work would have been very different.

The discussion opened on the 22nd of May. The first question was to decide on which side we should tackle this immense work. Lamennais proposed to commence by regulating the state of the communes. He had proceeded in this way himself in a proposal for a Constitution which he had just published, so as to make certain of the first fruits of his discoveries. Then he passed from the question of sequence to that of the main point : he began to talk of administrative centralization, for his thoughts were incapable of sub-dividing themselves ; his mind was always wholly occupied by a single system, and all the ideas contained in it adhered so closely together that, as soon as one was uttered, the others seemed necessarily to follow. He therefore explained that a Republic whose citizens are not clever and experienced enough to govern themselves was a monster not fit to live.

Thereupon the Committee took fire : Barrot, who, amid the clouds of his mind, always pretty clearly perceived the necessity for local liberty, eagerly supported Lamennais. I did the same ; Marrast and Vivien opposed us. Vivien was quite consistent in defending centralization, for the movement of administrative affairs was his profession, and moreover he was quite naturally drawn towards it. He had all the qualities of a clever legist and an excellent commentator, and none of those necessary to a legislator or statesman. The danger in which he saw the institutions so dear to him inflamed him ; he grew so excited that he began to hold that the Republic, far from restraining centralization, ought even to increase it. One would have said that this was the side on which the Revolution of February pleased him.

Marrast belonged to the ordinary type of French revolutionaries, who have always understood the liberty of the people to mean despotism exercised in the name of the people. This sudden harmony between Vivien and Marrast did not, therefore, surprise me. I was used to the phenomenon, and I had long remarked that the only way to bring a Conservative and a Radical together was to attack the power of the central government, not in application, but in principle. One was then sure of throwing them into each other's arms.

When, therefore, people assert that nothing is safe from revolutions, I tell them they are wrong, and that centralization is one of those things. In France there is only one thing we can't set up : that is, a free government ; and only one institution we can't destroy : that is, centralization. How could it ever perish ? The enemies of government love it, and those who govern cherish it. The latter perceive, it is true, from time to time, that it exposes them to sudden and irremediable disasters ; but this does not disgust them with it. The pleasure it procures them of interfering with every one and holding everything in their hands atones to them for its dangers. They prefer this agreeable life to a more certain and longer existence, and say, " *Courte et bonne*", like the *roués* of the Regency : " A short life and a merry one."

The question could not be decided that day ; but it was settled in advance by the determination arrived at that we should not first occupy ourselves with the communal system.

Next day, Lamennais resigned. Under the circumstances, an occurrence of this sort was annoying. It was bound to increase and rooten the prejudices already existing against us. We took very pressing and even somewhat humble steps to induce Lamennais to reconsider his resolve. As I had shared his opinion, I was deputed to go and see him and press him to return. I did so, but in vain. He had only been beaten over a formal question, but he had concluded from this that he would not be the master. That was enough to decide him to be nothing at all. He was inflexible, in spite of all I could say in the interest of the very ideas which we held in common.

One should especially consider an unfrocked priest if one wishes to acquire a correct idea of the indestructible and, so to speak, infinite power which the clerical habit and method of thought wield over those who have once contracted them. It was useless for Lamennais to sport white stockings, a yellow waistcoat, a striped necktie, and a green coat : he remained a priest in character, and even in appearance. He walked with short, hurried and discreet steps, never turning his head or looking at anybody, and glided through the crowd with an awkward, modest air, as though he were leaving the sacristy. Add to this a pride great enough to walk over the heads of kings and bid defiance to God.

When it was found that Lamennais' obstinacy was not to be overcome, we proceeded with other business ; and so that no more time might be lost in premature discussions, a sub-committee was appointed to draw up rules for the regulation of our labours, and to propose them to the Committee. Unfortunately, this sub-committee was so constituted that Cormenin, our chairman, was its master and, in reality, substituted himself for it. The permanent power of initiative which he thus possessed, coupled with the conduct of the debates which belonged to him as chairman, had the most baneful influence upon our deliberations, and I am not sure if the faults in our work should not be mainly attributed to him.[1]

Like Lamennais, Cormenin had drawn up and published a Constitution after his own idea, and again, like the former, he expected us to adopt it. But he did not quite know how to put it to us. As a rule, extreme vanity makes the timidest very bold in speaking. Cormenin's did not permit him to open his mouth as soon as he had three listeners. He would have liked to do as one of my neighbours in Normandy did, a great lover of polemics, to whom Providence had refused the capacity of disputing *viva voce*. Whenever I opposed any of his opinions, he would hurry home and write to me all that he ought to have told me. Cormenin accordingly despaired of convincing us, but hoped to surprise us. He flattered himself that he would make us accept his system gradu-

[1] Cf. now Paul Bastid, *Un juriste pamphlétaire. Cormenin. Précurseur et Constituant de 1848*, Paris 1948. (M.)

ally, and, so to speak, unknown to ourselves, by presenting a morsel to us every day. He managed so cleverly that a general discussion could never be held upon the Constitution as a whole, and that even in each case it was almost impossible to trace back and find the primitive idea. He brought us every day five to six clauses ready drawn up, and patiently, little by little, drew back to this little plot of ground all those who wished to escape from it. We resisted sometimes ; but in the end, from sheer weariness, we yielded to this gentle, continuous restraint. The influence of the chairman upon the work of a committee is immense ; anyone who has closely observed these little assemblies will understand what I mean. Nevertheless, it must be admitted that if several of us had desired to withdraw ourselves from this tyranny, we should have ended by coming to an understanding and succeeding. But we had no time and no inclination for long discussions. The vastness and complexity of the subject alarmed and wearied the minds of the Committee beforehand : the majority had not even attempted to study it, or had only collected some very confused ideas ; and those who had formed clearer ones were ill at ease at having to expound them. They were afraid, besides, lest they should enter into violent, interminable disputes if they endeavoured to get to the bottom of things ; and they preferred to appear to be in harmony by keeping to the surface. In this way we ambled along to the end, adopting great principles explicitly for reasons of petty detail, and little by little building up the whole machinery of government without properly taking into account the relative strength of the various wheels and the manner in which they would work together.

In the moments of repose which interrupted this fine work, Marrast, who was a Republican of the Barras type, and who had always preferred the pleasures of luxury, the table and women to democracy in rags, told us little stories of gallantry, while Vaulabelle made broad jests. I hope, for the honour of the Committee, that no one will ever publish the minutes (very badly done, for that matter) which the secretary drew up of our sittings. The sterility of the discussions amid the exuberant fecundity of the subject-matter would assuredly provoke surprise. As for myself, I declare that I never witnessed a more wretched display in any committee on which I ever sat.

Nevertheless, there was one serious discussion. It referred to the system of a single Chamber. As a matter of fact, the two parties into which the Committee was silently divided only came to an issue on this one occasion. It was even less a question of the two Chambers than of the general character to be given to the new government : Were we to persevere in the learned and somewhat complicated system of counterpoises, and place powers held in check, and consequently prudent and moderate, at the head of the Republic ? Or were we to adopt the contrary course and accept the simpler theory, according to which affairs are placed in the hands of a single power, homogenous in all its parts, uncontrolled, and consequently impetuous in its measures, and irresistible ? This was the subject-matter of the debate. This general question might have cropped up as the result of a number of other clauses ; but it was better contained than elsewhere in the special question of the two Chambers.

The struggle was a long one and lasted for two sittings. The result was not for a moment in doubt ; for public opinion had pronounced strongly in favour of a single Chamber, not only in Paris, but in nearly every department. Barrot was the first to speak in favour of the two Chambers ; he took up my thesis and developed it with great talent, but intemperately ; for during the Revolution of February, his mind had lost its equilibrium and had never since been able to recover its self-possession. I supported Barrot and returned time after time to the charge. I was a little surprised to hear Dufaure pronouncing against us and doing so with a certain eagerness. Lawyers are rarely able to escape from one of two habits : they accustom themselves either to plead what they do not believe or to persuade themselves very easily of what they wish to plead. Dufaure came under the latter category. The drift of public opinion, of his own passions or interest, would never have led him to embrace a cause which he thought a bad one ; but it prompted him with a desire to think it a good one, and that was often sufficient. His naturally vacillating, ingenious and subtle mind turned gradually towards it ; and he sometimes ended by adopting it not only with conviction but with success. How often have I not been amazed to see him vehemently defending theories which I had seen him adopt with infinite hesitation !

His principal reason for voting this time in favour of a single Chamber in the Legislative Body (and it was the best, I think, that could be found) was that, with us, the Executive Power wielded by one man elected by the people would most certainly become preponderant if there were placed beside him only a legislative body weakened by being divided into two branches.

I remember that I replied that that might be the case, but that one thing was quite certain, and that was, that two great powers naturally jealous of one another, and placed in an eternal *tête-à-tête* (that was the expression I used), without ever having recourse to the arbitrament of a third power, would at once be on bad terms or at war with one another, and would constantly remain so until one had destroyed the other. I added that, if it was true that a President elected by the people, and possessing the immense prerogatives which in France belong to the chief of the public administration, was sometimes able to curb a divided legislative body, a President who should feel himself to possess this origin and these rights would always refuse to become a simple agent and to submit to the capricious and tyrannical will of a single assembly.

We were both in the right. The problem, thus propounded, was insoluble ; but the nation propounded it thus. To allow the President the same power that the King had enjoyed, and to have him elected by the people, would make the Republic impossible. As I said later, one must either infinitely narrow the sphere of his power, or else have him elected by the Assembly ; but the nation would hear of neither one nor the other.[1]

Dupin completed our defeat : he defended the single Chamber with surprising vigour. One would have thought that he had never held another opinion. I expected as much, I knew him to possess a heart that was habitually self-interested and cowardly, though subject at times to sudden leaps of courage and honesty. I had seen him for ten years prowling round every party without joining any, and attacking all the vanquished : half ape and half jackal, constantly biting, grimacing, gambolling, and always ready to fall upon the wretch who slipped. He showed himself in his true colours on the Committee of the Constitution, or rather he surpassed himself. I perceived in him none of those sudden leaps of which I have just spoken : he was uniformly commonplace from beginning to end. He usually remained silent while the majority were making up their minds ; but as soon as he saw them pronounce in favour of democratic opinions, he rushed to place himself at their head, and often went far beyond them. Once, he

[1] *See* also : *Œuvres Complètes*, vol. I, pp. 574 sqq : *Rapport fait a L'Assemblée Législative au nom de la Commission chargée d'examiner les propositions relatives à la Révision de la Constitution* (M.)

perceived, when he had gone half-way, that the majority were not going in the direction he had thought ; whereupon he immediately stopped short with a prompt and nimble effort of the intelligence, turned round, and hurried back at the same run towards the opinion from which he had been departing.

Almost all the old members of Parliament pronounced in this way against the dual Chamber. Most of them sought for more or less plausible pretexts for their votes. Some pretended that a Council of State would provide the counterpoise of which they acknowledged the necessity ; others purposed to subject the single assembly to forms whose slowness would safeguard it against its own impulses and against surprise ; but in the end the true reason was always given. On the committee was a minister of the Gospel, M. Coquerel, who, seeing that his colleagues of the Catholic clergy were entering the Assembly, wanted to appear there too, and he was wrong : from the much-admired preacher that he was, he suddenly transformed himself into a very ridiculous political orator. He could hardly open his mouth without uttering some pompous absurdity. On this occasion he was so naïve as to inform us that he continued to favour the dual Chamber, but that he would vote for the single Chamber because public opinion was pushing him on, and he did not wish, to use his own words, to fight against the current. This candour greatly annoyed those who were acting as he did, and mightily delighted Barrot and myself ; but this was the only satisfaction we received, for, when it came to voting, there were only three on our side.

This signal defeat disinclined me a little to continue the struggle, and threw Barrot quite out of humour. He no longer appeared except at rare intervals, and in order to utter signs of impatience or disdain rather than opinions.

We passed on to the Executive Power. In spite of all that I have said of the circumstances of the time and the disposition of the Committee, it will still be believed with difficulty that so vast, so perplexing, so novel a subject did not furnish the material for a single general debate, nor for any very profound discussion.

All were unanimous in the opinion that the Executive Power should be entrusted to one man alone. But what prerogatives and what agents should he be given, what responsibilities laid upon him? Clearly, none of these questions could be treated in an arbitrary fashion : each of them was necessarily in connection with all the others, and could, above all, be only decided by taking into special account the habits and customs of the country. These were old problems, no doubt ; but they were made young again by the novelty of the circumstances.

Cormenin, according to his custom, opened the discussion by proposing a little clause all ready drawn up, which provided that the head of the Executive Power, or the President, as he was thenceforward called, should be elected directly by the people by a relative majority, the minimum of votes necessary to carry his election being fixed at two millions. I believe Marrast was the only one to oppose it ; he proposed that the head of the Executive Power should be elected by the Assembly : he was at that time intoxicated with his own fortune, and flattered himself, strange though this may seem to-day, that the choice of the Assembly would fall upon himself. Nevertheless, the clause proposed by Cormenin was adopted without any difficulty, so far as I can remember ; and yet it must be confessed that the expediency of having the President elected by the people was not self-evident truth, and that the disposition to have him elected directly was as new as it was dangerous. In a country with no monarchical tradition, in which the Executive Power has always been feeble and continues to be very limited, nothing is wiser than to charge the nation with the choice of its representative. A President who had not the strength which he could draw from that origin would then become the plaything of the Assemblies ; but with us the conditions of the problem were very different. We were emerging from the Monarchy, and the habits of the Republicans themselves were still monarchical. Moreover, our system of centralization made our position an unique one : according to its principles, the whole administration of the country, in matters of the greatest and of the smallest moment, belonged to the President ; the thousands of officials who held the whole country in their hands were dependent upon him alone ; this was so according to the laws, and even the ideas, which the 24th of February had allowed to continue in force ; for we had retained the spirit of the Monarchy, while losing the taste for it. Under these conditions, what could a President elected by the people be other than a pretender to the Crown ? The office could only suit those who hoped to make use of it in order to assist in transforming the Presidential into Royal powers ; it seemed clear to me then, and it seems evident to me now, that if it was desired that the President should be elected by the people without danger to the Republic, it was necessary to limit prodigiously the circle of his prerogatives ; and even then, I am not sure that this would have sufficed, for his sphere, although thus confined in point of law, would, in habit and remembrance, have preserved its former extent. If, on the other hand, the President was allowed to retain his power, he should not be elected by the people. These truths were not put forward ; I doubt whether they were even perceived in the heart of the Committee. However, Cormenin's clause, although adopted at first, was later made the object of a very lively attack ; but it was attacked for reasons different to those I have just given. It was on the day after the 4th of June. Prince Louis Napoleon, of whom no one had thought a few days before, had just been elected to the Assembly by Paris and three departments. They began to fear that he would be placed at the head of the Republic if the choice were left to the people. The various pretenders and their friends grew excited, the question was raised afresh in the Committee, and the majority persisted in its original vote.

I remember that, during all the time that the Committee was occupied in this way, my mind was labouring to divine to which side the balance of power would most generally lean in a Republic of the kind which I saw they were going to make. Sometimes I thought that it would be on the side of the Assembly, and then again on that of the elected President; and this uncertainty made me very uneasy. The fact is, that it was impossible to tell beforehand. The victory of one or other of these two great rivals must necessarily depend upon circumstances and dispositions of the moment. There were only two things certain : the war which they would wage together, and the eventual ruin of the Republic.

Of all the ideas which I have expounded, not one was sifted by the Committee ; I might even say that not one was discussed. Barrot one day touched upon them in passing, but did not linger over them. His mind (which was sleepy rather than feeble, and which was even able to see far ahead when it took the trouble to look) caught a glimpse of them, as it were, between sleeping and waking, and thought no more of them.

I myself only pointed them out with a certain hesitation and reserve. My rebuff in the matter of the dual Chamber left me little heart for the fight. Moreover, I confess, I was more anxious to reach a quick decision, and place a powerful leader at the head of the Republic, than to organize a perfect republican Constitution. We were then under the divided and uncertain government of the Executive Committee; Socialism was at our gates, and we were approaching the days of June, as we must not forget. Later, after these days, I vigorously supported in the Assembly the system of electing the President by the people, and in a certain measure contributed to its acceptance. The principal reason which I gave was that, after announcing to the nation that we would grant it that right, which it had always ardently desired, it was no longer possible to withhold it. This was true. Nevertheless, I regret having spoken on this occasion.

To return to the Committee : unable and even unwilling to oppose the adoption of the principle, I endeavoured at least to make its application less dangerous. I first proposed to limit in various directions the sphere of the Executive Power ; but I soon saw that it was useless to attempt anything serious on that side. I then fell back upon the method of election itself, and raised a discussion on that portion of Cormenin's clause which treated of it. The clause, as I said above, laid down that the President should be elected directly, by a relative majority, the minimum of this majority being fixed at two million votes. This method had several very serious drawbacks.

Since the President was to be elected directly by the citizens, the enthusiasm and infatuation of the people was very much to be feared ; and moreover, the prestige and moral power which the newly elected would possess would be much greater. Since a relative majority was to be sufficient to make the election valid, it might be possible that the President should only represent the wishes of a minority of the nation. I asked that the President might not be elected directly by the citizens, but that this should be entrusted to delegates whom the people would elect.

In the second place, I proposed to substitute an actual for a relative majority ; if an absolute majority was not obtained at the first vote, it would fall to the Assembly to make a choice. These ideas, were I think sound, but they were not new ; I had borrowed them from the American Constitution. I doubt whether anyone would have suspected this, had I not said so ; so little was the Committee prepared to play its great part.

The first part of my amendment was rejected. I expected this : our great men were of opinion that this system was not sufficiently simple, and they considered it tainted with a touch of aristocracy. The second was accepted, and is part of the actual Constitution.

Beaumont proposed that the President should not be re-eligible ; I supported him vigorously, and the proposal was carried. On this occasion we both fell into a great mistake which will, I fear, lead to very sad results. We had always been greatly struck with the dangers threatening liberty and public morality at the hands of a re-eligible president, who in order to secure his re-election would infallibly employ beforehand the immense resources of constraint and corruption which our laws and customs allow to the head of the Executive Power. Our minds were not supple or prompt enough to turn in time or to see that, as soon as it was decided that the citizens themselves should directly choose the President, the evil was irreparable, and that it would be only increasing it rashly to undertake to hinder the people in their choice. This vote, and the great influence I brought to bear upon it, is my most unpleasant memory of that period.

Each moment we came up against centralization, and instead of removing the obstacle, we stumbled over it. It was of the essence of the Republic that the head of the Executive Power should be responsible ; but responsible for what, and to what extent ? Could he be made responsible for the thousand details of administration with which our administrative legislation is overcharged, and over which it would be impossible, and moreover dangerous, for him to watch in person ? That would have been unjust and ridiculous ; and if he was not to be responsible for the administration proper, who would be? It was decided that the responsibility of the President should be shared by the ministers, and that their counter-signature should be necessary, as in the days of the Monarchy. Thus the President was responsible, and yet he was not entirely free in his own actions, and he was not able to protect his agents.

We passed to the constitution of the Council of State. Cormenin and Vivien took charge of this ; it may be said that they set to work like people who are building up a house for themselves. They did their utmost to make the Council of State a third power, but without success. It became something more than an administrative council, but infinitely less than a legislative assembly.

The only part of our work which was at all well thought out, and arranged, as I think, with wisdom, was that which related to justice. Here the committee felt at home, most of its members being, or having been, lawyers. Thanks to these, we were able to save the principle of the irremovability of the judges ; as in 1830, it held good against the current which swept away all the rest. Those who had been Republicans from the commencement attacked it nevertheless, and very stupidly, in my opinion ; for this principle is much more in favour of the independence of one's fellow-citizens than of the power of those who govern. The Court of Appeal and especially, the tribunal charged with judging political crimes, were constituted at once just as they are to-day (1851). Beaumont drew up most of the articles which refer to these two great courts. What we did in these matters is far in advance of all that had been attempted in the same direction during sixty years. It is probably the only part of the Constitution of 1848 which will survive.[1]

It was decided at the instance of Vivien that the Constitution could only be revised by a Constituent Assembly which was right ; but they added that this revision could only take place if the National Assembly demanded it by an express vote, given three times consecutively by a majority of four-fifths, which rendered any regular revision almost impossible. I took no part in this vote. I had long been of opinion that, instead of aiming to make our governments eternal, we should tend to make it possible to change them in an easy and regular manner. Taken all round, I thought this less dangerous than the opposite course ; and I thought it best to treat the French people like those madmen whom one should be careful not to bind lest they become infuriated by the restraint.

I noticed casually a number of curious opinions that were emitted. Martin (of Strasburg), who, not content with being a Republican of yesterday, one day declared so absurdly in the tribune that he was a Republican by birth, nevertheless proposed to give the President the right to dissolve the Assembly, and failed to see that a right of this kind would easily make him master of the Republic ; Marrast wanted a section to be added to the Council of State charged to elaborate " new ideas", to be called a section of progress ; Barrot proposed to leave to a jury the decision of all civil suits, as though a judiciary revolution of this sort could possibly be improvised. And Dufaure proposed to prohibit substitution in the conscription, and to compel everyone personally to perform his military service, a measure which would have destroyed all liberal education unless the time of service had been greatly reduced, or have disorganized the army if this reduction had been effected.

[1] Cf. *Les Constitutions et les principales Lois politiques de la France depuis* 1789 par Duguit et Monnier, Paris 1932. (M.)

In this way, pressed by time and ill prepared to treat such important subjects, we approached the time appointed for the end of our labours. What was said was : Let us adopt, in the meantime, the articles proposed to us ; we can afterwards retrace our steps ; we can judge from this sketch how to fix the definitive features and to adjust the portions among themselves. But we did not retrace our steps, and the sketch remained the picture.

We appointed Marrast our secretary. The way in which he acquitted himself of this important office soon exposed the mixture of idleness, giddiness and impudence which formed the basis of his character. He was first several days without doing anything, though the Assembly was constantly asking to know the result of our deliberations, and all France was anxiously awaiting to learn it. Then he hurriedly wrote his report in one night immediately preceding the day on which he was to communicate it to the Assembly. In the morning, he spoke of it to one or two of his colleagues whom he met by chance, and then boldly appeared in the tribune and read, in the name of the Committee, a report of which hardly one of its members had heard a single word. This reading took place on the 19th of June. The draft of the Constitution contained one hundred and thirty-nine articles ; it had been drawn up in less than a month. We could not have been quicker, but we might have done better. We had adopted many of the little articles which Cormenin had brought us in turns ; but we had rejected a yet greater number, which caused their author an irritation, which was so much the greater in that he had never had an opportunity of giving vent to it. He turned to the public for consolation. He published, or caused to be published, I forget which it was, in all the newspapers an article in which he related what had passed in the Committee, attributing all the good it had done to M. de Cormenin, and all the harm to his adversaries. A publication of this sort displeased us greatly, as may be imagined ; and it was decided to acquaint Cormenin with the feeling inspired by his procedure. But no one cared to be the spokesman of the company.

We had among us a workman (for in those days they put workmen into everything) called Corbon, a tolerably right-minded man of firm character. He readily undertook the task. On the next morning, therefore, as soon as the sitting of the Committee had opened, Corbon stood up and, with cruel simplicity and conciseness, gave Cormenin to understand what we thought. Cormenin grew confused, and cast his eyes round the table to see if anybody would come to his aid. Nobody moved. He then said, in a hesitating voice, " Am I to conclude from what has just happened that the Committee wishes me to leave it ? " We made no reply. He took his hat and went, without anyone interfering. Never was so great an outrage swallowed with less effort or grimace. I believe that, although enormously vain, he was not very sensitive to insults in secret ; and as long as his self-love was well tickled in public, he would not have made many bones about receiving a few cuffs in private.

Many have believed that Cormenin, who from a viscount had suddenly become a Radical, while remaining a devout Catholic, never ceased to play a part and to betray his opinions. I would not venture to say that this was the case, although I have often observed strange inconsistencies between the things he said when talking and those he wrote ; and, to tell the truth, he always seemed to me to be more sincere in the dread he entertained of revolutions than in the opinions he had borrowed from them. What always especially struck me in him was the shortcomings of his mind. No writer ever to a greater extent preserved in public business the habits and peculiarities of that calling. When he had established a certain agreement between the different clauses of a law and drawn it up in a certain ingenious and striking manner, he thought he had done all that was necessary : he was absorbed in questions of form, of symmetry, and cohesion.

But what he especially sought for was novelty. Institutions which had already been tried elsewhere or elsewhen seemed to him as hateful as commonplaces, and the first merit of a law in his eyes was to resemble in no way that which had preceded it. It is known that the law laying down the Constitution was his work. At the time of the General Election I met him and he said, with a certain complacency, "Has anything in the world ever been seen like what is seen to-day ? Where is the country that has gone so far to give votes to servants, paupers and soldiers ? Confess that no one has ever thought of it before." And, rubbing his hands, he added, "It will be very curious to see the result". He spoke of it as though it were an experiment in chemistry.

PART THREE

MY TERM OF OFFICE

This part was commenced at Versailles on the 16th of September, 1851, during the prorogation of the National Assembly.

To come at once to this part of my recollections, I pass over the previous period, which extends from the end of the days of June 1848 to the 3rd of June 1849. I will return to it later if I have time. I have thought it more important, while my recollections are still fresh in my mind, to recall the five months during which I was a Member of the Government.

CHAPTER I

My Return to France—Formation of the Cabinet.

WHILE I was thus occupied in witnessing upon the private stage of Germany one act of the great drama of the European Revolution, my attention was suddenly drawn towards France and fixed upon our affairs by unexpected and alarming news.[1] I heard of the almost incredible check received by our army beneath the walls of Rome, the violent debates which followed in the Constituent Assembly, the excitement produced throughout the country by these two causes, and lastly, the General Election, whose result deceived the expectations of both parties and brought over one hundred and fifty Montagnards into the new Assembly. However, the demagogic wind which had suddenly blown over a part of France had not prevailed in the Department of La Manche. All the former members for the department who had separated from the Conservative Party in the Assembly had gone under in the *scrutin*. Of thirteen representatives only four had survived ; as for me, I had received more votes than all the others, although I was absent and silent, and although I had openly voted for Cavaignac in the previous month of December. Nevertheless, I was almost unanimously elected, less because of my opinions than of the great personal consideration which I enjoyed outside politics, an honourable position no doubt, but difficult to retain in the midst of parties, and destined to become very precarious on the day when the latter should themselves become exclusive as they became violent.

I set out as soon as I received this news. At Bonn a

[1] Concerning Tocqueville's relation to Germany and German problems *see* Werner Ohaus : *Volk und Voelker im Urteil von Alexis de Tocqueville,* Berlin 1938, pp. 60 sqq. (M.)

sudden indisposition obliged Madame de Tocqueville to stop. She herself urged me to leave her and to continue my journey, and I did so, although with regret ; for I was leaving her alone in a country still agitated by civil war ; and moreover, it is in moments of difficulty that her courage and her great sense are so helpful to me.

I arrived in Paris, if I am not mistaken, on the 25th of May, 1849, four days before the meeting of the Legislative and during the last convulsions of the Constituent Assembly. A few weeks had sufficed to make the aspect of the political world entirely unrecognizable, owing less to the changes which had taken place in outside facts, than to the prodigious revolution which had in a few days taken place in men's minds.

The party which was in power at my departure was so still, and the material result of the elections should, I thought, have strengthened its hands. This party, composed of so many different parties, and wishing either to stop or drive back the Revolution, had obtained an enormous majority in the electoral colleges, and would command more than two-thirds of the new Assembly. Nevertheless, I found it seized with so profound a terror that I can only compare it with that which followed February : so true is it that in politics one must argue as in war, and never forget that the effect of events should be measured less by what they are in themselves than by the impressions they give.

The Conservatives, who for six months had seen all the by-elections invariably turning to their advantage, who filled and dominated almost all the local councils, had placed an almost unlimited confidence in the system of universal suffrage, after professing unbounded distrust of it. In the General Election which was just decided, they had expected, not only to conquer but to annihilate, so to speak, their adversaries, and they were as much cast down at not attaining the absolute triumph which they had dreamt of as though they had really been beaten. On the other hand, the Montagnards, who had thought themselves lost, were as intoxicated with joy and mad audacity as though the elections had assured them a majority in the new Assembly. Why had the event thus at the same time deceived the hopes and fears of both parties? It is difficult to say for certain, for great masses of men move by virtue of causes almost as unknown to humanity itself as those which rule the movements of the sea. In both cases the reasons of the phenomenon are concealed and, in a sense, lost in the midst of its immensity.

We are, at any rate, entitled to believe that the Conservatives owed their rebuff mainly to the faults which they themselves committed. The intolerance, when they thought their triumph assured, of those who, without sharing their ideas, had assisted them in fighting the Montagnards; the violent administration of the new Minister of the Interior, M. Faucher; and more than all, the poor success of the Roman expedition prejudiced against them a portion of the people who were naturally disposed to follow them, and threw these into the arms of the agitators.

One hundred and fifty Montagnards, as I said, had been elected. A part of the peasantry and the majority of the army had voted for them: it was the two anchors of mercy which had snapped in the midst of the tempest. Terror was universal: it taught anew to the various monarchical parties the tolerance and modesty which they had practised immediately after February, but which they had to a great extent forgotten during the past six months. It was recognized on every hand that there could no longer be any question, for the present, of emerging from the Republic, and that all that remained to be done was to oppose the moderate Republicans to the Montagnards.

The same ministers whom they had created and instigated they now accused, and a modification of the Cabinet was loudly demanded. The Cabinet itself saw that it was insufficient, and implored to be replaced. At the time of my departure I had seen the committee of the Rue de Poitiers refuse to admit the name of M. Dufaure to its lists ; I now saw every glance directed towards M. Dufaure and his friends, who were called upon in the most pathetic manner to take office and save society.

On the very night of my arrival, I heard that some of my friends were dining together at a little restaurant in the Champs-Elysées. I hastened to join them, and found Dufaure, Lanjuinais, Beaumont, Corcelles, Vivien, Lamoricière, Bedeau, and one or two more whose names are not so well known. I was informed in a few words of the position of affairs. Barrot, who had been invited by the President to form a cabinet, had for some days been exhausting himself in vain efforts to do so. M. Thiers, M. Molé and the more important of their friends had refused to undertake the government. They had made up their minds, nevertheless, as will be seen, to remain its masters, but without becoming ministers. The uncertainty of the future, the general instability, the difficulties and perhaps the dangers of the moment kept them aloof. They were eager enough for power, but not for responsibility. Barrot, repulsed on that side, had come to us. He asked us, or rather he besought us, to become his colleagues. But which among us to choose ? What ministries to allot to us ? What colleagues to give us ? What general policy to adopt ? From all these questions had arisen difficulties in execution which, till then, seemed insurmountable. Already, more than once, Barrot had returned towards the natural chiefs of the majority ; and repelled by them, had fallen back upon us.

Time passed amid these sterile labours ; the dangers and difficulties increased ; the news became each day more alarming, and the Ministry were liable at any moment to be impeached by the dying but furious Assembly.

I returned home greatly preoccupied, as will be believed, by what I had heard. I was convinced that it only depended upon the wishes of myself and my friends to become ministers. We were the necessary and obvious men. I knew the leaders of the majority well enough to be sure that they would never commit themselves to taking charge of affairs under a government which seemed to them so ephemeral, and that, even if they had the disinterestedness, they would not have the courage to do so. Their pride and their timidity assured me of their abstention. It was enough for us, therefore, to stand firm on our ground to compel them to come and fetch us. But ought we to wish to become ministers ? I asked myself this very seriously. I think I may do myself the justice to say that I did not indulge in the smallest illusion respecting the true difficulties of the enterprise, and that I looked upon the future with a clearness of view which we rarely possess except when we consider the past.

Everybody expected to see fighting in the streets. I myself regarded it as imminent ; the furious audacity which the result of the elections had imparted to the Mountain and the opportunity afforded to it by the Rome affair seemed to make an event of this kind inevitable. I was not, however, very anxious about the issue. I was convinced that, although the majority of the soldiers had voted for the Mountain, the army would fight against it without hesitation. The soldier who individually votes for a candidate at an election and the soldier acting under pressure of *esprit de corps* and military discipline are two different men. The thoughts of the one do not regulate the actions of the other. The

Paris garrison was very numerous, well commanded, experienced in street warfare, and still filled with the memory of the passions and examples which had been left to it by the days of June. I therefore felt certain of victory. But I was very anxious as to the eventual results of this victory : what seemed to others the end of the difficulties I regarded as their commencement. I considered them insurmountable, as I believe they really were.

In whichever direction I looked, I saw no solid or lasting standpoint for us.

Public opinion looked to us, but it would have been unsafe to rely upon it for support ; fear drove the country in our direction, but its memories, its secret instincts, its passions could scarcely fail soon to withdraw it from us, as soon as the fear should have vanished. Our object was, if possible, to found the Republic, or at least to maintain it for some time, by governing it in a regular, moderate, conservative and absolutely constitutional way ; and this could not allow us to remain popular for long, since everybody wanted to evade the Constitution. The Mountain wanted more, the Monarchists much less.

In the Assembly it was much worse still. The same general causes were aggravated by a thousand accidents arising from the interests and vanities of the party leaders. The latter were quite content to allow us to assume the government, but we must not expect them to allow us to govern. As soon as the crisis was passed, we might expect every sort of ambush on their part.

As to the President, I did not know him yet, but it was evident that we could not rely upon him to support us in his Council, except where the jealousy and hatred were concerned with which our common adversaries inspired him. His sympathies must always lie in an opposite direction ; for our views were not only different, but naturally opposed to one another. We wanted to make the Republic live : he longed for its inheritance. We only supplied him with ministers where he wanted accomplices.

To these difficulties, which were in a sense inherent to the situation and consequently permanent, were added passing ones which it was not at all easy to surmount : the revolutionary agitation revived in part of the country ; the spirit and habits of exclusion spread and already rooted in the public administration ; the Roman expedition, so badly conceived and so badly conducted that it was now as difficult to bring it to an end as to get out of it ; in fact, the whole legacy of mistakes committed by our predecessors.

There were reasons enough for hesitation ; and yet I did not hesitate.

The idea of taking a post from which fear kept so many people off, and of relieving society from the bad pass in which it had been involved, flattered at the same time my sense of honour and my pride. I was quite aware that I should only be passing through power, and that I should not stay there ; but I hoped to stay long enough to be able to render some signal service to my country and to raise myself. This was enough to attract me.

I at once took three resolutions :

First, not to refuse office if an opportunity offered ;

Second, only to enter the Government together with my principal friends, directing the principal offices, so that we might always remain the masters of the Cabinet ;

Third and last, to behave every day when in office as though I was to be out of it the next day—that is to say, without ever subordinating to the necessity of maintaining my position that of remaining true to myself.

The next five or six days were wholly taken up in fruitless endeavours to form a ministry. The attempts made were so numerous, so overlapping, so full of small

incidents—great events of one day forgotten the next—
that I find it difficult to retrace them in my memory, in
spite of the prominent part which I myself played in
some of them. The problem was undoubtedly a difficult
one to solve under its given conditions. The President
was willing enough to change the appearance of his
ministry, but he was determined to retain in it the men
whom he considered his principal friends. The leaders
of the Monarchical parties refused themselves to take the
responsibility of government ; but they were not willing
either that it should be entrusted entirely to men over
whom they had no hold. If they consented to admit us,
it was only in a very small number and in second-rate
offices. We were looked upon as a necessary but disagreeable remedy, which it was preferable only to ad-
minister in very small doses.

Dufaure was first asked to join alone, and to be satisfied with the Public Works. He refused, demanded the
Interior, and two other offices for his friends. After much
difficulty they agreed to give him the Interior, but they
refused the rest. I have reason to believe that he was at one
time on the point of accepting this proposal and of again
leaving me in the lurch, as he had done six months ago.
Not that he was treacherous or indifferent in his friendships ; but the sight of this important office almost
within reach, which he could honestly accept, possessed
a strange attraction for him. It did not precisely cause
him to abandon his friends, but it distracted his thoughts
from them, and made him ready to forget them. He was
firm, however, this time ; and not being able to get him
by himself, they offered to take me with him. I was most
in view at that time, because the new Legislative Assembly had just elected me one of its vice-presidents.[1] But
what office to give me ? I only thought myself fit to fill
the Ministry of Public Instruction. Unfortunately that

[1] 1 June, 1849, by 336 votes to 261.

was in the hands of M. de Falloux, an indispensable man, whom it was equally important to the Legitimists to retain, of whom he was one of the leaders ; to the religious party, who saw in him a protector ; and finally to the President, of whom he had become the friend; I was offered Agriculture, and refused it. At last, in despair, Barrot came and asked me to accept the Foreign Office. I myself had made great efforts to persuade M. de Rémusat to accept this office, and what happened on this occasion between him and me is so characteristic that it is worthy of being retold. I was very anxious that M. de Rémusat should join the ministry with us. He was at once a friend of M. Thiers and a man of honour, a rather unusual combination; he alone was able to assure us, if not of the support, at least of the neutrality of that statesman, without infesting us with his spirit. Overcome by the insistency of Barrot and the rest of us, Rémusat one evening yielded. He had pledged us his word, but the next morning he came to withdraw it. I knew for certain that he had seen M. Thiers in the interval, and he confessed to me himself that M. Thiers, who was then loudly proclaiming the necessity of our accepting office, had dissuaded him from joining us. " I fully saw," he said, " that to become your colleague would not be to give you his assistance, but only to expose myself to be quarrelling with him before long." Those were the sort of men we had to deal with.

I had never thought of the Foreign Office, and my first impulse was to refuse it. I thought myself unsuited to fill an office for which nothing had prepared me. Among my papers I have found a trace of these hesitations, in the notes of a conversation which took place at a dinner which some of my friends and I had at that time. . . .

I decided at last, however, to accept the Foreign Office, but I made it a condition that Lanjuinais should enter the Council at the same time as myself. I had many very strong reasons for acting as I did. In the first place, I thought that three ministers were indispensable to us in order to acquire the preponderance in the Cabinet which we needed in order to do any good. I thought, moreover, that Lanjuinais would be very useful to keep Dufaure himself within the lines I wished to follow. I did not consider myself to have enough hold over him. Above all, I wanted to have near me a friend with whom I could talk openly of all things : a great advantage at any time, but especially in such times of suspicion and variableness as ours, and for a work as hazardous as that which I was undertaking.

From all these different points of view Lanjuinais suited me admirably, although we were of very dissimilar natures. His temper was as calm and placid as mine was restless and anxious. He was methodical, slow, indolent, prudent, and even over-scrupulous, and he was very backward to enter upon any undertaking ; but having once entered upon it he never drew back, and showed himself until the end as resolved and stubborn as a Breton of the true stamp. He was very slow in giving his opinion, and very explicit, and even candid to the verge of rudeness, when he did give it. One could not expect from his friendship either enthusiasm, ardour, or *abandon* ; on the other hand, one need not dread either faintheartedness, treachery, or after-thoughts. In short, he was a very safe associate, and taken all round, the most honourable man I ever met in public life. Of all of us, it was he who seemed to me least to mix his private or interested views with his love of the public good.

No one objected to the name of Lanjuinais ; but the difficulty was to find him a portfolio. I asked for him that of Commerce and Agriculture, which had been held since the 20th of December by Buffel, a friend of Falloux. The latter refused to let his colleague go ; I insisted ;

and the new Cabinet, which was almost complete, remained for twenty-four hours as though dissolved. To conquer my resolution, Falloux attempted a direct measure : he came to my house, where I lay confined to my bed, urged me, begged me to give up Lanjuinais and to leave his friend Buffet at the Ministry of Agriculture. I had made up my mind, and I closed my ears. Falloux was vexed, but retained his self-control and rose to go. I thought everything had gone wrong : on the contrary, everything had gone right.

" You are determined," he said, with that aristocratic good grace with which he was able to cover all feelings, even the bitterest ; " you are determined, and so I must yield. It shall not be said that a private consideration has, at so difficult and critical a period, made me break off so necessary a combination. I shall remain alone in the midst of you. But I hope you will not forget that I shall be not only your colleague, but your prisoner ! "

One hour later the Cabinet was formed,[1] and Dufaure, who told me of it, invited me to take immediate possession of the Foreign Office.

Thus was born this Ministry which was so painfully and slowly formed and which was destined to have so short an existence. During the long childbirth that preceded it, the man who was at the greatest trouble in France was certainly Barrot : his sincere love for the public weal inclined him to desire a change of cabinet, and his ambition, which was more intimately and norrowly bound up with his honesty than might have been believed, made him long with unequalled ardour to remain at the head of the new Cabinet. He therefore went incessantly to and fro from one to the other, addressing very pathetic and sometimes very eloquent objurgations to everyone, now turning to the leaders of the majority, now to us, now again to the new Republicans,

[1] The Presidential decree is dated 2 June, 1849.

whom he regarded as more moderate than the others. And, for that matter, he was equally inclined to carry either one or other with him ; for in politics he was incapable of either hatred or friendship. His heart is an evaporating vase, in which nothing remains. [He reminded me of an excited hen running after its lost chicks, but just as liable to bring back a brood of ducklings.]

CHAPTER II

Aspect of the Cabinet—Its First Acts until after the Insurrectionary Attempts of the 13th of June.

THE ministry was composed as follows :

Minister of Justice and President of the Council	.	Barrot.
Finance . . .	.	Passy.
War	.	Rulhière.
Navy	.	Tracy.
Public Works . .	.	Lacrosse.
Public Instruction . .	.	Falloux.
Interior . . .	.	Dufaure.
Agriculture . .	.	Lanjuinais.
Foreign Affairs . .	.	Tocqueville.

Dufaure, Lanjuinais and I were the only new ministers ; all the others had belonged to the previous Cabinet.

Passy was a man of real merit, but not of a very attractive merit. His mind was narrow, maladroit, provoking, disparaging and ingenious rather than just. Nevertheless, he was more inclined to be just when it was really necessary to act than when it was only a question of talking ; for he was more fond of paradox than liable to put it into practice. I never knew a greater talker, nor one who so easily consoled himself for trouble-some events by explaining the causes which had pro-duced them and the consequences likely to ensue. When he had finished drawing the most sombre picture of the state of affairs, he concluded with a smiling and placid air, saying : " So that there is practically no means of saving ourselves, and we have only to look forward to the total overthrow of Society." In other respects he was a cultured and experienced minister ; his courage and honesty were proof against everything ; and he was as incapable of vacillation as of treachery. His ideas, his feelings, his former intimacy with Dufaure and, above all, his eager animosity against Thiers made us certain of him.

Rulhière would have belonged to the monarchic and ultra-conservative party if he had belonged to any, and especially if Changarnier had not been in the world ; but he was a soldier who only thought of remaining Minister for War. We perceived at the first glance his extreme jealousy of the Commander-in-Chief of the Army in Paris ; and the intimacy between the latter and the leaders of the majority, and his influence over the President, obliged Rulhière to throw himself into our arms, and forcibly drove him to depend upon us.

Tracy had by nature a weak character which was, as it were, enclosed and confined in the very precise and systematic theories which he owed to the ideological education he had received from his father. But in the end, contact with every-day events and the shock of revolutions had worn out this rigid envelope, and all that remained was a wavering intelligence and a sluggish, but always honest and kindly heart.

Lacrosse was a poor devil whose private affairs were more or less involved. The chances of the Revolution had driven him into office from an obscure corner of the Opposition, and he never grew weary of the delight of being a minister. He gladly leant upon us, but he endeavoured at the same time to make sure of the goodwill of the President of the Republic by rendering him all sorts of little services and small compliments. To tell the truth, it would have been difficult for him to recommend himself in any other way, for he was a rare nonentity, and understood nothing about anything. We were reproached for taking office in company with such incapable ministers as Tracy and Lacrosse, and not without justice, for it was a great cause of ruin : not only because they did their work badly, but because their notorious insufficiency kept their succession always open, so to speak, and created a sort of permanent ministerial crisis.

As to Barrot, he adhered naturally to us from feeling and ideas. His old liberal associations, his republican tastes, his Opposition memories attached him to us. Had he been differently connected, he might have become, however regretfully, our adversary ; but, having him once among us, we were sure of him.

Of all the Ministry, therefore, only Falloux was a stranger to us by his starting-point, his engagements, and his inclinations. He alone represented the leaders of the majority on the Council, or rather he seemed to represent them, for in reality, as I will explain later, he represented, besides himself, nothing but the Church. This isolated position, together with the secret aims of his policy, drove him to seek support beyond us ; he strove to establish it in the Assembly and with the President, but discreetly and cleverly, as he did everything.

Thus constituted, the Cabinet had one great weakness : it was about to govern with the aid of a composite majority, without itself being a coalition ministry. But, on the other hand, it possessed the very great strength which ministers derive from uniform origin, identical instincts, old bonds of friendship, mutual confidence, and common ends.

I shall doubtless be asked what these ends were, where we were going, what we wanted. We live in times so uncertain and so obscure that I should hesitate to reply to that question in the name of my colleagues ; but I will readily reply for myself. I did not believe then, any more than I do now, that the republican form of government is the best suited to the needs of France. What I mean when I say the republican form of government, is the

Executive Power. With a people among whom habit, tradition, custom have assured so great a place to the Executive Power, its instability will always be, in periods of excitement, a cause of revolution, and, in peaceful times, a cause of great uneasiness. Moreover, I have always considered the Republic an ill-balanced form of government, which always promised more, but gave less, liberty than the Constitutional Monarchy. And yet I sincerely wished to maintain the Republic ; and although there were, so to speak, no Republicans in France, I did not look upon the maintenance of it as absolutely impossible.

I wished to maintain it because I saw nothing ready or fit to set in its place. The old Dynasty was profoundly antipathetic to the majority of the country. Amid this flagging of all political passion, which was the result of the fatigue of the revolutions and their vain promises, one genuine passion remained alive in France : hatred of the Ancien Régime and mistrust of the old privileged classes who represented it in the eyes of the people. This sentiment passes through revolutions without dissolving in them, like the water of those marvellous fountains which, according to the ancients, passed across the waves of the sea, without mixing with or disappearing in them. As to the Orleans Dynasty, the experience the people had had of it did not particularly incline them to return to it so soon. It was bound once more to throw into Opposition all the upper classes and the clergy, and to separate itself from the people, as it had done before, leaving the cares and profits of government to those same middle classes whom I had already seen during eighteen years so inadequate for the good government of France. Moreover, nothing was ready for its triumph.

Louis Napoleon alone was ready to take the place of the Republic, because he already held the power in his hands. But what could come of his success, except a bastard Monarchy, despised by the enlightened classes, hostile to liberty, governed by intriguers, adventurers and valets ? [Not one of these results would justify a new revolution.]

The Republic was doubtless difficult to maintain ; for those who favoured it were, for the most part, incapable or unworthy of governing it, while those who were fit to conduct it detested it. But it was also rather difficult to pull down. The hatred borne for it was an easy-going hatred, as were all the passions which the country then entertained. Besides, the Government was found fault with, but no other was moved in its place. Three parties, mutually irreconcilable, more hostile to one another than either of them was to the Republic, contended with each other for the future. As to a majority, there was no such thing.

I thought, therefore, that the Government of the Republic, having existence in its favour, and having no adversaries except minorities difficult to coalesce, would be able to maintain its position amid the inertia of the masses, if it was conducted with moderation and wisdom. For this reason, I was resolved not to lend myself to any steps that might be taken against it, but rather to defend it. Almost all the members of the Council thought as I did. Dufaure believed more than I did in the soundness of republican institutions and in their future. Barrot was less inclined than I to keep them always respected ; but we all wished at the present time firmly to maintain them. This common resolution was our political bond and standard.

As soon as the Ministry was formed, it went to the President of the Republic to hold a Council. It was the first time I had come into contact with him. I had only seen him at a distance at the time of the Constituent Assembly. He received us with politeness. It was all we could expect from him, for Dufaure had acted vigorously against him, and had spoken almost outrageously of his candidature no longer than six months ago, while both Lanjuinais and myself had openly voted for his opponent.

Louis Napoleon plays so great a part in the rest of my narrative that he seems to me to deserve a special portrait amid the host of contemporaries of whom I have been content to sketch the features. Of all his ministers, and perhaps of all the men who refused to take part in his conspiracy against the Republic, I was the one who was most advanced in his good graces, who saw him closest, and who was best able to judge him.

He was vastly superior to what his preceding career and his mad enterprises might very properly have led one to believe of him. This was my first impression on conversing with him. In this respect he deceived his adversaries, and perhaps still more his friends, if this term can be applied to the politicians who patronized his candidature. The greater part of these, in fact, elected him, not because of his merits, but because of his presumed mediocrity. They expected to find him an instrument which they could handle as they pleased, and which it would always be lawful for them to break when they wished to. In this they were greatly deceived.

As a private individual, Louis Napoleon possessed certain attractive qualities : an easy and kindly humour, a mind which was gentle, and even tender, without being delicate, great confidence in his intercourse, perfect simplicity, a certain personal modesty amidst the immense pride derived from his origin. He was capable of showing affection, and able to inspire it in those who approached him. His conversation was brief and unsuggestive. He had not the art of drawing others out or of establishing intimate relations with them ; nor any facility in expressing his views. He had the writer's habit, and a certain amount of the author's self-love. His dissimulation, which was the deep dissimulation of a man who has spent his life in plots, was assisted in a remarkable way by the immobility of his features and his want of expression : for his eyes were dull and opaque, like the thick glass used to light the cabins of ships, which admits the light but cannot be seen through. Careless of danger, he possessed a fine, cool courage in days of crisis ; and at the same time—a common thing enough—he was very vacillating in his plans. He was often seen to change his direction, to advance, hesitate, draw back, to his great detriment : for the nation had chosen him in order to dare all things, and what it expected from him was audacity and not prudence. It was said that he had always been greatly addicted to pleasures, and not very delicate in his choice of them. This passion for vulgar enjoyment and this taste for luxury had increased still more with the facilities offered by his position. Each day he wore out his energy in indulgence, and deadened and degraded even his ambition. His intelligence was incoherent, confused, filled with great but ill-assorted thoughts, which he borrowed now from the examples of Napoleon, now from socialistic theories, sometimes from recollections of England, where he had lived : very different, and often very contrary, sources. These he had laboriously collected in his solitary meditations, far removed from the contact of men and facts, for he was naturally a dreamer and a visionary. But when he was forced to emerge from these vague, vast regions in order to confine his mind to the limits of a piece of business, it showed itself to be capable of justice, sometimes of subtlety and compass, and even of a certain depth, but never sure, and always prepared to place a grotesque idea by the side of a correct one.

Generally, it was difficult to come into long and very close contact with him without discovering a little vein of madness running through his better sense, the sight of which always recalled the escapades of his youth, and served to explain them.

It may be admitted, for that matter, that it was his madness rather than his reason which, thanks to circumstances, caused his success and his force : for the world is a strange theatre. There are moments in it when the worst plays are those which succeed best. If Louis Napoleon had been a wise man, or a man of genius, he would never have become President of the Republic.

He trusted in his star ; he firmly believed himself to be the instrument of destiny and the necessary man. I have always believed that he was really convinced of his right, and I doubt whether Charles X was ever more infatuated with his legitimism than he with his. Moreover, he was quite as incapable of alleging a reason for his faith ; for, although he had a sort of abstract adoration for the people, he had very little taste for liberty. The characteristic and fundamental feature of his mind in political matters was his hatred of and contempt for assemblies. The rule of the Constitutional Monarchy seemed to him even more insupportable than that of the Republic. His unlimited pride in the name he bore, which willingly bowed before the nations, revolted at the idea of yielding to the influence of a parliament.

Before attaining power he had had time to strengthen his natural taste for the footman class, which is always displayed by mediocre princes, by the habits of twenty years of conspiracy spent amid low-class adventurers, men of ruined fortunes or blemished reputations, and young debauchees, the only persons who, during all this time, could have consented to serve him as go-betweens or accomplices. He himself, in spite of his good manners, allowed a glimpse to pierce through of the adventurer and the prince of fortune. He continued to take pleasure in this inferior company after he was no longer obliged to live in it. I believe that his difficulty in expressing his thoughts otherwise than in writing attached him to people who had long been familiar with his current of thought and with his dreamings, and that his inferiority in conversation rendered him generally averse to contact with clever men. Moreover, he desired above all things to meet with devotion to his person and his cause, as though his person and his cause were such as to be able to arouse devotion : merit annoyed him when it displayed ever so little independence. He wanted believers in his star, and vulgar worshippers of his fortune. [One could not approach him except through a group of special, intimate friends and servants, of whom General Changarnier told me that all could be described by these two words which go together : cheats and scoundrels. Nothing was more base than these intimates, except perhaps his family, which consisted, for the most part, of rogues and *femmes galantes*.]

This was the man whom the need of a chief and the power of a memory had placed at the head of France, and with whom we would have to govern.

It would be difficult to imagine a more critical moment in which to assume the direction of affairs. The Constituent Assembly, before ending its turbulent existence, had passed a resolution, on the 7th of May 1849, prohibiting the Government from attacking Rome. The first thing I learnt on entering the Cabinet was that the order to attack Rome had been sent to the army three days before. This flagrant disobedience of the injunctions of a sovereign Assembly, this war undertaken against a people in revolution, because of its revolution, and in defiance of the terms of the Constitution which commanded us to respect all foreign nationalities, made inevitable and brought nearer the conflict which we dreaded. What would be the issue of this new struggle ? All the letters from prefects of departments that were laid before us, all the police reports that reached us were calculated to throw us into great alarm. I had seen, at the end of the Cavaignac Administration, how a government can be supported in its visionary hopes by the self-interested complaisance of its agents. This time I saw, and much more closely, how these same agents can work to increase the terror of those who employ them: contrary effects produced by the same cause. Each one of them, judging that we were uneasy, wished to signalize himself by the discovery of new plots, and in his turn to supply us with some fresh indication of the conspiracy which threatened us. The more they believed in our success, the more readily they talked to us of our danger. For it is one of the dangerous characteristics of this sort of information, that it becomes rarer and less explicit in the measure that the peril increases and the need for information becomes greater. The agents in that case, doubting the duration of the government which employs them, and already fearing its successor, either scarcely speak at all or keep absolute silence. But now they made a great noise. To listen to them, it was impossible not to think that we were on the edge of an abyss, and yet I did not believe a word of it. I was quite convinced then, as I have been ever since, that official correspondence and police reports, which may be useful for purposes of consultation when there is question of discovering a particular plot, only serve to give exaggerated and incomplete and invariably false notions when one wishes to judge or foresee great movements of parties. In a matter of this kind, it is the aspect of the whole country, the knowledge of its needs, its passions and its ideas, that can instruct us, general *data* which one can procure for one's self, and which are never supplied by even the best placed and best accredited agents.

The sight of these general facts had led me to believe that at this moment no armed revolution was to be feared : but a combat was ; and the expectation of civil war is always cruel, especially when it comes in time to join its fury to that of pestilence. Paris was at that time ravaged by cholera. Death struck at all ranks. Already a large number of members of the Constituent Assembly had succumbed ; and Bugeaud, whom Africa had spared, was dying.

Had I entertained a moment's doubt as to the imminence of the crisis, the aspect alone of the new Assembly would have clearly announced it to me. It is not too much to say that one breathed the atmosphere of civil war in its midst. The speeches were short, the gestures violent, the words extravagant, the insults outrageous and direct. We met for the present in the old Chamber of Deputies. This room, built for 460 members, had difficulty in containing 750. The members, therefore, sat touching, while detesting, each other ; they pressed one against each other in spite of the hatred which divided them ; the discomfort increased their anger. It was a duel in a barrel. How would the Montagnards be able to restrain themselves ? They saw that they were sufficiently numerous to entitle them to believe themselves very strong in the country and in the army. Yet they remained too weak in Parliament to hope to prevail or even to count there. They were offered a fine occasion of resorting to force. All Europe, which was still in commotion, might with one great blow, struck in Paris, be thrown into revolution anew. This was more than was necessary for men of such savage temper.

It was easy to foresee that the movement would burst forth at the moment when it should become known that the order had been given to attack Rome and that the attack had taken place. And this was what in fact occurred.

The order given had remained secret. But on the 10th of June, the report of the first combat became current. On the 11th, the Mountain burst into furious speech.

Ledru-Rollin made an appeal from the tribune for civil war, saying that the Constitution had been violated and that he and his friends were ready to defend it by every method, including that of arms. The indictment was demanded of the President of Republic and of the preceding Cabinet.

On the 12th, the Committee of the Assembly, instructed to examine the question raised the day before, rejected the impeachment and called upon the Assembly to pronounce, where it sat, upon the fate of the President and Ministers. The Mountain opposed this immediate discussion and demanded that documents should be laid before it. What was its object in thus postponing the debate ? It was difficult to say. Did it hope that this delay would complete the general irritation, or did it in its heart of hearts wish to give it time to calm down ? One thing is certain, that its principal leaders, those who were more accustomed to speaking than to fighting, and who were passionate rather than resolute, displayed that day, amid all the intemperance of their language, a sort of hesitation of which they had given no sign the day before. After half drawing the sword from the scabbard, they appeared to wish to replace it ; but it was too late, the signal had been observed by their friends outside, and thence-forward they no longer led, but were led in their turn.

During these two days, my position was most cruel. As I have already stated, I disapproved entirely of the manner in which the Roman expedition had been undertaken and conducted. Before joining the Cabinet, I had solemnly declared to Barrot that I declined to take any responsibility except for the future, and that he must himself be prepared to defend what had up to that time been done in Italy. I had only accepted office on this condition. I therefore kept silent during the discussion on the 11th, and allowed Barrot to bear the brunt of the battle alone. But when, on the 12th, I saw my colleagues threatened with an impeachment, I considered that I could no longer abstain. The demand for fresh documents gave me an opportunity to intervene, without having to express an opinion upon the original question. I did so vigorously, although in very few words.

On reading over this speech in the *Moniteur*, I cannot but think it very insignificant and badly turned. Nevertheless, I was applauded by the majority, because in moments of crisis, when one is in danger of civil war, it is the movement of thought and the accent of one's words which make an impression, rather than their value. I directly attacked Ledru-Rollin. I accused him with violence of only wanting troubles and of spreading lies in order to create them. The feeling which impelled me to speak was an energetic one, the tone was determined and aggressive, and although I spoke very badly, being as yet unaccustomed to my new part, I met with much favour.

Ledru replied to me, and told the majority that they were on the side of the Cossacks. They answered that he was on the side of the plunderers and the incendiaries. Thiers, commenting on this thought, said that there was an intimate relation between the man they had just listened to and the insurgents of June. The Assembly rejected the demand for an impeachment by a large majority, and broke up.

Although the leaders of the Mountain continued to be outrageous, they had not shown any great firmness, so that we were able to flatter ourselves that the decisive moment for the struggle had not yet arrived. But this was a mistake. The reports which we received during the night told us that the people were preparing to take up arms.

On the next day, in fact, the language of the demagogic papers proclaimed that the editors no longer relied upon justice, but upon a revolution, to acquit them. All of them called either directly or indirectly for civil war. The National Guard, the schools, the entire population was summoned by them, unarmed, to a certain locality, in order to go and present themselves in mass before the doors of the Assembly. It was a 23rd of June which they wished to commence with a 15th of May ; and, in fact, seven or eight thousand people did meet at about eleven o'clock at the Château-d'Eau. We on our side held a Council under the President of the Republic. The latter was already in uniform, and prepared to go out on horseback as soon as he should be told that the fighting had commenced. For the rest, he had changed nothing except his clothes. He was exactly the same man as on the day before : the same rather dejected air, his speech no less slow and no less embarrassed, his eye no less dull. He showed none of that sort of warlike excitement and of rather feverish gaiety which the approach of danger so often gives : an attitude which is perhaps, after all, no more than the sign of a mind disturbed. [For myself, I would have liked him better if he had assumed a more heroic attitude. On this day all his faults appeared to me to his advantage.]

We sent for Changarnier, who explained his preparations to us, and guaranteed a victory. Dufaure communicated to us the reports he had received, all of which told of a formidable insurrection. He then left for the Ministry of the Interior, which was the centre of action, and at about midday I went to the Assembly.

The House took some time before it met, because the President, without consulting us, had declared, when arranging the Order of the Day on the evening before, that there would be no public sitting on the next day, a strange blunder which would have looked like treachery in anyone else. While messengers were being dispatched to inform the members at their own houses, I went to see the President of the Assembly in his private room :

most of the leaders of the majority were there before me,
Every face bore traces of excitement and anxiety ; the
contest was both feared and demanded. They began by
vehemently accusing the Ministry of slackness. Thiers,
lying back in a big arm-chair, with his legs crossed one
over the other, sat rubbing his stomach (for he felt certain symptoms of the prevailing epidemic), loudly and
angrily exclaiming, in his shrillest *falsetto*, that it was very
strange that no one seemed to think of declaring Paris
in a state of siege. I replied gently that we had thought
of it, but that the moment had not yet come to do so,
since the Assembly had not yet met.

The members arrived from every side, attracted less
by the messages dispatched to them, which most of
them had not even received, than by the rumours prevalent in the town. The sitting was opened at two
o'clock. The benches of the majority were well filled,
but the top of the Mountain was deserted. The gloomy
silence which reigned in this part of the House was more
alarming than the shouts which came from that quarter
as a rule. It was a proof that discussion had ceased, and
that the civil war was about to commence.

At three o'clock, Dufaure came and asked that the
stage of siege should be proclaimed in Paris. Cavaignac
seconded him in one of those short addresses which he
sometimes delivered, and in which his mind, which was
naturally mediocre and confused, reached the level of his
soul and approached the sublime. Under these circumstances he became, for a moment, the man of the most
genuine eloquence that I have ever heard speak in our
Assemblies : he left all the mere orators far behind him.

"You have just said," he exclaimed, addressing the
Montagnard[1] who was leaving the tribune, "that I have
fallen from power. That is not true : I retired volun-

[1] Pierre Leroux.

tarily. The national will does not overthrow ; it commands, and we obey. I add—and I want the republican party always to be able to say so with justice : I retired voluntarily, and, in so doing, my conduct did honour to my republican convictions. You said that we lived in terror : history is observing us, and will pronounce when the time comes. But what I say to you myself is this, that although you have not succeeded in inspiring me with a feeling of terror, you have inspired me with a feeling of profound sorrow. Shall I tell you one thing more ? You are Republicans of long standing ; whereas I have not worked for the Republic before its foundation, I have not suffered for it, and I regret that this is so ; but I have served it faithfully, and I have done more : I have governed it, I shall serve nothing else, understand me well ! Write it down, take it down in shorthand, so that it may remain engraved upon the annals of our deliberations : *I shall serve nothing else* ! Between you and me, I take it, it is a question as to which of us will serve the Republic best. Well then, my regret is, that you have served it very badly. I hope, for the sake of my country, that it is not destined to fall ; but if we should be condemned to undergo so great a blow, remember—remember distinctly—that we shall accuse your exaggerations and your fury as being the cause of it."

Shortly after the state of siege had been proclaimed, we learnt that the insurrection had been extinguished. Changarnier and the President, charging at the head of the cavalry, had cut in two and dispersed the column which was making its way towards the Assembly. A few newly-erected barricades had been destroyed, without striking a blow. The Montagnards, surrounded in the Conservatoire of Arts and Crafts, which they had turned into their head-quarters, had either been arrested or taken to flight. We were the masters of Paris.

The same movement took place in several of the large towns, with more vigour but no less success. At Lyons, the fighting lasted stubbornly for five hours, and the victory was for a moment in doubt. But for that matter, when we were once victorious in Paris, we distressed ourselves very little about the provinces ; for we knew that in France, in matters both of order and of disorder, Paris lays down the law.

Thus ended the second Insurrection of June, very different to the first by the extent of its violence and its duration, but similar in the causes which led to its failure. At the time of the first, the people, carried away less by their own opinions than by their appetites, had fought alone, without being able to attract their representatives to their head. This time the representatives had been unable to induce the people to follow them into battle. In June 1848, the army had no leaders ; in June 1849, the leaders had no army.

They were singular personages, those Montagnards : their quarrelsome nature and their self-conceit were displayed even in measures which least allowed of it. Among those who, in their newspapers and in their own persons, had spoken most violently in favour of civil war, and who had done the most to cover us with insults, was Considérant, the pupil and successor of Fourier, and the author of so many socialistic dreams which would only have been ridiculous at any other time, but which were dangerous in ours. Considérant succeeded in escaping with Ledru-Rollin from the Conservatoire, and in reaching the Belgian frontier. I had formerly had social relations with him, and when he arrived in Brussels, he wrote to me :

" MY DEAR TOCQUEVILLE,
(Here followed a request for a service which he asked me to do for him, and then went on) :

" Rely upon me at all times for any personal service. You are good for two or three months perhaps, and the pure Whites who will follow you are good for six months at the longest. You will both of you, it is true, have well deserved what is infallibly bound to happen to you a little sooner or a little later. But let us talk no more politics and respect the very legal, and very loyal, and very Odilon Barrotesque state of siege."

To this I replied :

" MY DEAR CONSIDÉRANT,

" I have done what you ask. I do not wish to take advantage of so small a service, but I am very pleased to ascertain, by the way, that those odious oppressors of liberty, the Ministers, inspire their adversaries with so much confidence that the latter, after outlawing them, do not hesitate to apply to them to obtain what is just. This proves that there is some good left in us, whatever may be said of us. Are you quite sure that if the position had been inverted, I should have been able to act in the same way, I will not say towards yourself, but towards such and such of your political friends whom I might mention ? I think the contrary, and I solemnly declare to you that if ever they become the masters, I shall consider myself quite satisfied if they only leave my head upon my shoulders, and ready to declare that their virtue has surpassed my greatest expectations."

CHAPTER III

*Our Domestic Policy—Internal Quarrels in the Cabinet
—Its Difficulties in its Relations with the Majority and
the President.*

WE were victorious, but our real difficulties were only
about to commence, and I expected them. I have always
held as a maxim, moreover, that it is after a great success
that one generally comes across the most dangerous
chances of ruin : so long as the peril lasts one has only
his adversaries to deal with and one triumphs ; but after
the victory, one begins to have to reckon with oneself,
one's slackness, one's pride, the imprudent security
inspired by victory, and one succumbs.

I was exposed to this last danger, for I never imagined
that we had surmounted our principal obstacles. I knew
that these lay with the very men with whom we would
have to govern the country, and that the rapid and signal
defeat of the Montagnards, instead of guaranteeing us
against the ill-will of the former, would expose us to it
without delay. We should have been much stronger if
we had less succeeded.

The majority consisted in the main, at that time, of
three parties (the President's party in Parliament was
as yet too few in number and of too evil repute to
count). Sixty to eighty members at the utmost were
sincerely with us in our endeavours to found a moderate
Republic, and these formed the only body we could rely
upon in that huge Assembly. The remainder of the
majority consisted of Legitimists, to the number of some
one hundred and sixty, and of old friends or supporters
of the Monarchy of July, for the most part representing
those middle classes who had governed, and above all
exploited, France during eighteen years. I felt at once
that of these two parties, that of which we could most

easily make use in our plans was the Legitimist party. The Legitimists had been excluded from power under the last government ; they therefore had no places and no salaries to regret. Moreover, being for the most part considerable land-owners, they had not the same need of public functions as the middle class : or, at least, custom had not taught them the sweetness of place. Although in principles more irreconcilable to the Republic than the others, they were better able than most to accept its duration, for it had destroyed their destroyer, and had opened up to them a prospect of power ; it had served at once their ambition and their desire for revenge ; and it only aroused against itself their fear, which was, in truth, very great. The old Conservatives, who formed the bulk of the majority, were much more eager to do away with the Republic ; but as the furious hatred which they bore it was strongly held in check by the fear of the risk they would run in endeavouring prematurely to abolish it, and as, moreover, they had long been accustomed to follow in the wake of power, it would have been easy for us to lead them, had we been able to obtain the support, or even the mere neutrality of their leaders, of whom the principal were then, as is known, M. Thiers and M. Molé.

Appreciating this position of affairs, I understood that it was necessary to subordinate all secondary objects to the principal end in view, which was to prevent the overthrow of the Republic and especially to hinder the establishment of the bastard monarchy of Louis Napoleon. This was at the time the nearest threatening danger.

I thought first of guaranteeing myself against the mistakes of my friends, for I have always considered as profoundly sensible the old Norman proverb which says, " Lord, preserve me from my friends : I will preserve myself from mine enemies".

At the head of our adherents in the National Assembly

was General Lamoricière, and I greatly dreaded his petulancy, his imprudent observations, and especially his idleness. I endeavoured to appoint him to an important and distant embassy. Russia had spontaneously recognized the new Republic ; it was proper that we should resume the diplomatic relations with her which had been almost interrupted under the last Government. I cast my eyes upon Lamoricière in order to entrust him with this extraordinary and distant mission. He was, besides, a man cut out for a post of this kind, in which few but generals, and celebrated generals, succeed. I had some difficulty in persuading him, but the most difficult thing was to persuade the President of the Republic. He at first resisted, and told me on that occasion, with a sort of simplicity which pointed less to candour than to his difficulty in finding words in which to express himself (these very rarely gave utterance to his thoughts, but sometimes permitted them to glimmer through), that he wished to be represented at the principal Courts by ambassadors devoted to himself. This was not my view of the matter ; for I, who was called upon to instruct the ambassadors, was quite determined to devote myself only to France. I therefore insisted, but I should have failed if I had not summoned M. de Falloux to my aid. Falloux was the only man in the Ministry in whom the President at that time had confidence. He persuaded him with arguments, of which I do not know the purport, and Lamoricière left for Russia. I shall say later what he did.

His departure reassured me as to the conduct of our friends, and I thought of winning or retaining the necessary allies. Here the task was more difficult on all points ; for, outside my own department, I was unable to do anything without the consent of the Cabinet, which contained a number of the most honest minds that one could meet, but so inflexible and narrow in matters of politics, that I have sometimes gone so far as to regret not having rather had to do with intelligent rascals.

As to the Legitimists, my opinion was that they should be allowed to retain great influence in the direction of Public Instruction. This proposal had its drawbacks, but it was the only one which could satisfy them, and which could ensure us their support in return, when it should become a question of restraining the President and preventing him from upsetting the Constitution. This plan was followed. Falloux was given a free hand in his own department, and the Council allowed him to bring before the Assembly the plan of Public Instruction, which since became law on the 15th of March, 1850. I also advised my colleagues to all the extent of my power to keep up good relations individually with the principal members of the Legitimist party, and I followed this line of conduct myself. I soon became and remained, of all the members of the Cabinet, the one who lived in the best understanding with them. I even ended by becoming the sole intermediary between them and ourselves.

It is true that my birth and the society in which I had been brought up gave me great facilities for this which the others did not possess ; for, although the French nobility have ceased to be a class, they have yet remained a sort of freemasonry, of which all the members continue to recognize one another through certain invisible signs, whatever may be the opinions which makes them strangers to one another, or even adversaries. [This bond which still exists between all its members is so close that I have found myself a hundred times more at ease in dealing with aristocrats who differed from me entirely in their interests and opinions than with bourgeois whose ideas and instincts were analogous to mine. With the former I was in disagreement but I knew what language I had to speak, and I felt instinctively what I had to say and when to keep silent.]

It so happened, therefore, that after annoying Falloux more than anyone else had done before entering the Cabinet, I had no sooner joined it than I easily became his friend. For that matter, he was a man worth taking the trouble of gaining. I do not think that during my whole political career I ever met anyone of a rarer nature. He possessed the two essentials necessary for good leadership : an ardent conviction, which constantly drove him towards his aim without allowing itself to be turned aside by mortifications or dangers, and a mind which was both firm and supple, and which applied a great multiplicity and prodigious variety of means to the execution of a single plan. He was sincere in this sense, that he only considered, as he declared, his cause and not his private interest ; but otherwise very sly, with a very uncommon and very effective slyness, for he succeeded, for the time being, in mingling truth and falsehood in his own belief, before serving up the mixture to the minds of others. This is the great secret which gives falsehood all the advantages of sincerity, and which permits its exponent to persuade to the error which he considers beneficial those whom he works upon or directs.

In spite of all my efforts, I was never able to bring about, I will not say a good understanding, but even a polite understanding between Falloux and Dufaure. It must be admitted that these two men had precisely the opposite qualities and defects. Dufaure, who in the bottom of his heart had remained a good west-country bourgeois, hostile to the nobles and the priests, was unable to put up with either Falloux's principles or his charming, refined manners, however agreeable they might seem to me. I succeeded, however, with great difficulty, in persuading him that he must not interfere with him in his own department : but as to allowing him to exercise the smallest influence upon what went on at the Ministry of the Interior (even within the limits where this was permissible and necessary), he would never hear speak of it. Falloux had in Anjou, where he came from, a prefect with whom he had reason to find fault. He did not ask that he should be dismissed, or even refused promotion ; all he wanted was that he should be transferred, as he thought his own position compromised so long as no change took place, a change which was, moreover, demanded by the majority of the deputies for Maine-et-Loire. Unfortunately, this prefect was a declared friend to the Republic ; and this was enough to fill Dufaure with distrust, and to persuade him that Falloux's only object was to compromise him by making use of him to strike at those of the Republicans whom he had not been able to reach till then. He refused, therefore ; the other insisted ; Dufaure grew still more obstinate. It was very amusing to watch Falloux spinning round Dufaure, pirouetting cleverly and gracefully, without finding a single opening by which to penetrate into his mind.

Dufaure let him have his say, and then confined himself to laconically replying, without looking at him or only turning a dull, wry glance in his direction :

" I should like to know why you did not take advantage of your friend M. Faucher's period at the Home Office to rid yourself of your prefect."

Falloux contained himself, although he was naturally, I believe, of a very hasty temper ; he came and told me his troubles, and I saw the most bitter rancour trickling through the honey of his speech. I thereupon intervened, and tried to make Dufaure understand that this was one of those demands which one cannot refuse a colleague unless one wishes to quarrel with him. I spent a month in this way, acting as a daily intermediary between the two, and expending more effort and diplomacy than I had employed, during the same period, in treating the

great affairs of Europe. The Cabinet was more than once
on the verge of breaking up over this puny incident.
Dufaure gave way at last, but with such bad grace that
it was impossible to thank him for it ; so that he gave up
his prefect without getting Falloux in exchange.

But the most difficult portion of our rôle was the conduct we had to display towards the old Conservatives
who formed the bulk of the majority, as I have already
said.

These had at one and the same time general opinions
which they wished to force through and a number of
private passions which they desired to satisfy. They
wanted us to re-establish order energetically : in this we
were their men ; we wanted it as much as they did, and
we did it as well as they could wish, and better than they
could have done. We had proclaimed the state of siege in
Lyons and several of the neighbouring departments, and
by virtue of the state of siege we had suspended six Paris
revolutionary papers, cashiered the three regiments of
the Paris National Guard which had displayed indecision on the 13th of June, arrested seven representatives
on the spot, and applied for warrants against thirty
others. Analogous measures were taken all over France.
Circulars addressed to all the agents showed them that
they had to do with a Government which knew how to
make itself obeyed, and which was determined that
everything should give way before the law.

Whenever Dufaure was attacked on account of these
different acts by the Montagnards remaining in the
Assembly, he replied with that masculine, nervous, and
sharp-edged eloquence of which he was so great a
master, and in the tone of a man who fights after burning
his boats.

The Conservatives not only wanted us to govern
with vigour ; they wished us to take advantage of our
victory to pass preventive and repressive laws. We our-

selves felt the necessity of moving in this direction, although we were not willing to go as far as they.

For my part, I was convinced that it was both wise and necessary to make great concessions in this respect to the fears and the legitimate resentment of the nation, and that the only means which remained, after so violent a revolution, of saving liberty was to restrict it. My colleagues were of the same opinion : we therefore brought in successively a law to suspend the clubs ; another to suppress, with even more energy than had been done under the Monarchy, the vagaries of the press ; and a third to regulate the state of siege.

"You are establishing a military dictatorship," they cried.

"Yes", replied Dufaure, "it is a dictatorship, but a parliamentary dictatorship. There are no individual rights which can prevail against the inalienable right of Society to protect itself. There are imperious necessities which are the same for all governments whether monarchies or republics ; and who has given rise to these necessities ? To whom do we owe the cruel experience which has given us eighteen months of violent agitations, incessant conspiracies, formidable insurrections ? Yes, no doubt you are quite right when you say that, after so many revolutions undertaken in the name of liberty, it is deplorable that we should be once again compelled to veil her statue and to place terrible weapons in the hands of the public powers. But whose fault is it, if not yours, and who is it that serves the Republic best, those who favour insurrections, or those who, like ourselves, apply themselves to suppressing them ?"

These measures, these laws and this language pleased the Conservatives without satisfying them ; and to tell the truth, nothing would have contented them short of the destruction of the Republic. Their instinct constantly impelled them in that direction, although their prudence and their reason restrained them on the road.

But what they desired above all things was to oust their enemies from place and to install in their stead their partisans or their private friends. We were again brought face to face with all the passions which had brought about the fall of the Monarchy of July. The Revolution had not destroyed them, but only made them the more greedy ; this was our great and permanent danger. Here again, I considered that we ought to make concessions. There were still in the public offices a very large number of those Republicans of indifferent capacity or bad character whom the chances of the Revolution had driven into power. My advice was to get rid of these at once, without waiting to be asked for their dismissal, in such a way as to inspire confidence in our intentions and to acquire the right to defend all the honest and capable Republicans ; but I could never induce Dufaure to consent to this. He had already held the Ministry of the Interior under Cavaignac. Many of the public servants whom it would be necessary to dismiss had been either appointed or supported by him. His vanity was involved in the question of maintaining them in their positions, and his mistrust of their detractors would in any event have sufficed to persuade him to oppose their representations. He accordingly resisted. It was, therefore, not long before he himself became the object of all their attacks. No one dared tackle him in the tribune, for he was too sturdy a swordsman there ; but he was constantly struck at from a distance and in the shade of the lobbies, and I soon saw a great storm gathering against him.

" What is it we have undertaken to do ? " I often asked him. " To save the Republic with the assistance of the Republicans ? No, for the majority of those who bear that name would assuredly kill us together with it ; and those who deserve to bear the name do not number one hundred in the Assembly. We have undertaken to save the Republic with the assistance of parties which do not love it. We can only, therefore, govern with the aid of concessions ; only, we must never yield anything substantial. In this matter, everything depends upon the degree. The best, and perhaps the only guarantee which the Republic at this moment possesses lies in our continuance in power. Every honourable means should therefore be taken to keep us there."

To this he replied that fighting, as he did every day, with the greatest energy, against socialism and anarchy, he must satisfy the majority ; as though one could ever satisfy men by thinking only of their general welfare, without taking into account their vanity and their private interests. If even, while refusing, he had been able to do so gracefully : but the form of his refusal was still more disobliging than the matter of it. I could never conceive how a man who was so much the master of his words in the tribune, so clever in the art of selecting his arguments and the words best calculated to please, so certain of always keeping to the expressions which would compel most agreement with his thought, could be so embarrassed, so sullen, and so awkward in conversation. This came, I believe, from his original education. He was a man of much intelligence, or rather talent—for of intelligence properly so-called he had hardly any—but of no knowledge of the world. In his youth he had led a laborious, concentrated, and almost savage life. His entrance into political life had not to any extent changed his habits. He had held aloof not only from intrigues, but from the contact of parties, assiduously occupying himself with affairs, but avoiding men, detesting the movement of assemblies, and dreading the tribune, which was his only strength. Nevertheless, he was ambitious after his fashion, but with a measured and somewhat inferior ambition, which aimed at the management rather than at the domination of affairs. His manner, as a minister, of treating people was sometimes very strange. One day, General Castellane, who was then in great credit, asked for an audience. He was received, and explained at length his pretensions and what he called his rights. Dufaure listened to him long and attentively ; and then rose, led the general with many bows to the door, and left him standing aghast, without having answered a single word. When I reproached him with this conduct: " I should only have had to say disagreeable things to him ", he replied ; " it was more reasonable to say nothing at all ! "

It is easy to believe that one rarely left a man of this kind except in a very bad temper.

Unfortunately, he had as a sort of double a permanent secretary who was as uncouth as himself, and very stupid besides ; so that when the solicitants passed from the Minister's office into the secretary's, in the hope of meeting with a little comfort, they found the same unpleasantness, minus the intelligence. It was like falling from a quickset hedge on to a bundle of thorns. In spite of these disadvantages, Dufaure obtained the support of the Conservatives ; but he was never able to win over their leaders.

The latter, as I had indeed foreseen, would neither undertake the government themselves nor allow anyone else to govern with a free hand. They were unable to see without jealousy ministers at the head of affairs who were not their creatures, and who refused to be their instruments. I do not believe that, between the 13th of June and the last debates on the Roman question, in other words, during almost the whole life of the Cabinet, a single day passed without some ambush being laid for us. They did not fight us in the tribune, I admit ; but they incessantly excited the majority secretly against us,

blamed our decisions, criticized our measures, put un-
favourable interpretations upon our speeches ; unable
to make up their minds to overthrow us, they arranged
in such a way that, finding us wholly unsupported, they
were always in a position, with the smallest effort, to hurl
us from power. After all, Dufaure's mistrust was not
always without grounds. The leaders of the majority
wanted to make use of us in order to take rigorous
measures, and to obtain repressive laws which would
make the task of government easy to our successors, and
our Republican opinions made us fitter for this, at that
moment, than the Conservatives. They did not fail to
count on soon bowing us out, and on bringing their sub-
stitutes upon the scene. Not only did they wish us not to
impress our influence upon the Assembly, but they
laboured unceasingly to prevent us from establishing it
in the mind of the President. They persisted in the delu-
sion that Louis Napoleon was still happy in their
leading-strings. They continued to beset him, therefore.
We were informed by our agents that most of them, but
especially M. Thiers and M. Molé, were constantly
seeing him in private, and urging him with all their
might to overthrow, in concert with them, and at their
common expense and to their common profit, the Republic. They formed, as it were, a secret ministry at the
side of the responsible Cabinet. Commencing with the
13th of June, I lived in a state of continuous alarm, fearing every day that they would take advantage of our
victory to drive Louis Napoleon to commit some violent
usurpation, and that one fine morning, as I said to
Barrot, the Empire should slip in between his legs. I have
since learnt that my fears were even better founded than
I at that time believed. Since leaving the ministry, I have
learnt from an undoubted source that a plot was formed
towards the month of July 1849 to alter the Constitution
by force by the combined enterprise of the President and

the Assembly. The leaders of the majority and Louis Napoleon had come to an agreement, and the blow only failed because Berryer, who no doubt feared lest he should be making a fool's bargain, refused his support and that of his party. Nevertheless, the idea was not renounced, but only adjourned ; and when I think that at the time when I am writing these lines, that is to say, two years only after the period of which I speak, the majority of these same men are growing indignant at seeing the people violate the Constitution by doing for Louis Napoleon precisely what they themselves at that time proposed to him to do, I find it difficult to imagine a more noteworthy example of the versatility of men and of the vanity of the great words " Patriotism " and " Right " beneath which petty passions are apt to cloak themselves.

We were no more certain, as has been seen, of the President than of the majority. In fact, Louis Napoleon was, for ourselves as well as for the Republic, the greatest and the most permanent danger.

I was convinced of this ; and yet, when I had very attentively studied him, I did not despair of the possibility of establishing ourselves in his mind, for a time at least, in a fairly solid fashion. I soon discovered that although he never refused to admit the majority leaders to his presence and to receive their advice, which he sometimes followed, and although he plotted with them when it suited his purpose, he nevertheless endured their yoke with great impatience ; that he felt humiliated at seeming to walk in their leading-strings ; and that he secretly burned to be free of them. This gave us a point of contact with him and a hold upon his mind ; for we ourselves were quite resolved to remain independent of these great wire-pullers, and to uphold the Executive Power against their attacks.

It did not seem impossible to me, moreover, for us to enter partly into Louis Napoleon's designs without emerging from our own. What had always struck me, when I reflected upon the situation of that extraordinary man (extraordinary, not through his genius, but through the circumstances which had combined to raise his mediocrity to so high a level), was the need which existed to feed his mind with hope of some kind if we wished to keep him quiet. That a man of this stamp could, after governing France for four years, be dismissed into private life, seemed very doubtful to me ; that he would consent to withdraw into private life, seemed very chimerical ; that he could even be prevented, during the length of his term of office, from plunging into some dangerous enterprise seemed very difficult, unless, indeed, one were able to place before his ambition some point of view which might, if not charm, at least restrain him. This is to what I, for my part, applied myself from the beginning.

" I will never serve you," I said to him, " in overthrowing the Republic ; but I will gladly strive to assure you a great position in it, and I believe that all my friends will end by entering into my plan. The Constitution can be revised ; Article 45, which prohibits reelection, can be changed. This is an object which we will gladly help you to attain."

And as the chances of revision were doubtful, I went further, and I hinted to him as to the future that, if he governed France peacefully, wisely, modestly, not aiming at more than being the first magistrate of the nation, and not its corrupter or its master, he might possibly be re-elected at the end of his term of office, in spite of Article 45, by an almost unanimous vote, since the Monarchical parties did not see the ruin of their hopes in the limited prolongation of his power, and the Republican party itself looked upon a government such as his as the best means of accustoming the country to the Republic and giving it a taste for it.

I told him all this in a tone of sincerity, because I was sincere in saying it. What I advised him seemed to me, in fact, and still seems to me, the best thing to be done in the interest of the country, and perhaps in his own. He readily listened to me, without giving a glimpse of the impression my language made upon him : this was his habit. The words one addressed to him were like stones thrown down a well; their sound was heard, but one never knew what became of them. I believe, however, that they were not entirely lost ; for there were two distinct men in him, as I was not long in discovering. The first was the ex-conspirator, the fatalistic dreamer, who thought himself called to govern France, and through it to dominate Europe. The other was the epicurean, who luxuriously made the most of his new state of well-being and of the facile pleasures which his present position gave him, and who did not dream of risking it in order to ascend still higher. In any case, he seemed to like me better and better. I admit that, in all that was compatible with the good of the public service, I made great efforts to please him. Whenever, by chance, he recommended for a diplomatic appointment a cap-able and honest man, I showed great alacrity in placing him. Even when his *protégé* was not very capable, if the post was an unimportant one, I generally arranged to give it to him; but most often the President honoured with his recommendations a set of gaol-birds, who had formerly thrown themselves in desperation into his party, not knowing where else to betake themselves, and to whom he thought himself to be under obligations ; or else he attempted to place at the principal embassies those whom he called "his own men", which most frequently meant intriguers and rascals. In that case I went and saw him, I explained to him the regulations, which were opposed to his wish, and the political reasons which prevented me from complying with it. I sometimes even went so far as to let him see that I would rather resign than retain office by doing as he wished. As he was not able to see any particular reasons for my refusal, nor any systematic desire to oppose him, he either yielded without complaining or postponed the business.

I did not get off as cheaply with his friends. These were unspeakably eager in their rush for the spoil. They incessantly assailed me with their demands, with so much importunity, and often impertinence, that I frequently felt inclined to have them thrown out of the window. I strove, nevertheless, to restrain myself. On one occasion, however, when one of them, a real gallows-bird, haughtily insisted, and said that it was very strange that the Prince should not have the power of rewarding those who had suffered for his cause, I replied :

" Sir, the best thing for the President to do is to forget that he was ever a pretender, and to remember that he is here to attend to the affairs of France and not to yours."

The Roman affair, in which, as I shall explain later, I firmly supported his policy, until the moment when it became extravagant and unreasonable, ended by putting me entirely into his good graces : of this he one day gave me a great proof. Beaumont, during his short embassy in England at the end of 1848, had spoken very strongly about Louis Napoleon, who was at that time a candidate for the Presidency. These remarks, when repeated to the latter, had caused him extreme irritation. I had several times endeavoured, since I had become a minister, to re-establish Beaumont in the President's mind; but I should never have ventured to propose to employ him, capable as he was, and anxious though I was to do so. The Vienna embassy was to be vacated in September 1849. It was at that time one of the most important posts in our diplomatic service, because of the affairs of Italy and Hungary. The President said to me of his own accord ;

" I suggest that you should give the Vienna embassy

to M. de Beaumont. True, I have had great reason to complain of him ; but I know that he is your best friend, and that is enough to decide me."

I was delighted. No one was better suited than Beaumont for the place which had to be filled, and nothing could be more agreeable to me than to offer it to him.

All my colleagues did not imitate me in the care which I took to gain the President's good-will without doing violence to my opinions and my wishes.

Dufaure however, against every expectation, was always just what he should be in his relations towards him. I believe the President's simplicity of manners had half won him over. But Passy seemed to take pleasure in being disagreeable to him. I believe that he considered that he had degraded himself by becoming the minister of a man whom he looked upon as an adventurer, and that he endeavoured to regain his level by impertinence. He annoyed him every day unnecessarily, rejecting all his candidates, ill-treating his friends, and contradicting his opinions with ill-concealed disdain. No wonder that the President cordially detested him.

Of all the ministers, the one who was most in his confidence was Falloux. I have always believed that the latter had gained him by means of something more substantial than that which any of us were able or willing to offer him. Falloux, who was a Legitimist by birth, by training, by society, and by taste, if you like, belonged at bottom to none but the Church. He did not believe in the triumph of the Legitimism which he served, and he only sought, amid all our revolutions, to find a road by which he could bring back the Catholic religion to power. He had only remained in office so that he might watch over its interests, and, as he said to me on the first day with well-calculated frankness, by the advice of his confessor. I am convinced that from the beginning Falloux had suspected the advantages to be gained from

Louis Napoleon towards the accomplishment of this design, and that, familiarizing himself at an early date with the idea of seeing the President become the heir of the Republic and the master of France, he had only thought of utilizing this inevitable event in the interest of the clergy. He had offered the support of his party without, however, compromising himself.

From the time of our entrance into affairs until the prorogation of the Assembly, which took place on the 13th of August, we did not cease to gain ground with the majority, in spite of their leaders. They saw us every day struggling with their enemies before their eyes ; and the furious attacks which the latter at every moment directed against us advanced us gradually in their good graces. But, on the other hand, during all that time we made no progress in the mind of the President, who used to suffer our presence in his counsels rather than to admit us to them.

Six weeks later it was just the opposite. The representatives had returned from the provinces incensed by the clamour of their friends, to whom we had refused to hand over the control of local affairs ; and on the other hand, the President of the Republic had drawn closer to us ; I shall show later why. One would have said that we had advanced on that side in the exact proportion to that in which we had gone back on the other.

Thus placed between two props badly joined together and always tottering, the Cabinet leant now upon one, now upon the other, and was always liable to tumble between the two. It was the Roman affair which brought about the fall.

Such was the state of things when the parliamentary session was resumed on the 1st of October 1849, and when the Roman affair was handled for the second and last time.[1]

[1] For a suggestive account of the Roman affair cf. *Louis Napoleon and the Recovery of France*, 1848—1856 by F. A. Simpson, London 1923, pp. 44 sqq. Cf. also *The Cambridge Modern History*, Vol. IX, pp. 121 sqq. (M.)

CHAPTER IV

Foreign Affairs.

I DID not wish to interrupt the story of our home misfortunes to speak of the difficulties which we encountered abroad, and of which I had to bear the brunt more than any other. I shall now retrace my steps and return to that part of my subject.

When I found myself installed at the Foreign Office, and when the state of affairs had been placed before my eyes, I was alarmed at the number and extent of the difficulties which I perceived. But what caused me more anxiety than anything else was myself.

I possess a great natural distrust of myself. The nine years which I had spent rather wretchedly in the last Assemblies of the Monarchy had tendered greatly to increase this natural infirmity, and although the manner in which I had just undergone the trial of the Revolution of February had helped to raise me a little in my own opinion, I nevertheless accepted this great task, at a time like the present, only after much hesitation, and I did not enter into it without great fear.

Before long, I was able to make a certain number of observations which tranquillized if they did not entirely reassure me. I began by perceiving that affairs did not always increase in difficulty as they increased in size, as would naturally appear at a cursory glance : the contrary is rather the truth. Their complications do not grow with their importance ; it even often happens that they assume a simpler aspect in the measure that their consequences become wider and more serious. Besides, a man whose will influences the destiny of a whole people always finds ready to hand more men willing to enlighten him, to assist him, to relieve him of details, more prepared to encourage, to defend him, than would be met with in second-rate affairs or inferior positions. And lastly, the size itself of the object pursued stimulates all the mental forces to such an extent, that though the task may be a little harder, the workman becomes much more expert.

I should have felt perplexed, full of care, discouragement and disordered excitement, in presence of petty responsibilities. I felt a peace of mind and a singular feeling of calm when brought face to face with larger ones. The sentiment of importance attached to the things I then did at once raised me to their level and kept me there. The idea of a rebuff had until then seemed insupportable to me ; the prospect of a dazzling fall upon one of the greatest stages in the world, on which I was mounted, did not disconcert me ; which showed that my weakness was not timidity but pride. I also was not long before perceiving that in politics, as in so many other matters—perhaps in all—the vivacity of impressions received was not in a ratio with the importance of the fact which produced it, but with the more or less frequent repetition of the latter. One who grows troubled and excited about the handling of a trifling piece of business, the only one which he happens to have taken in hand, ends by recovering his self-possession among greater ones, if they are repeated every day. Their frequency renders their effect, as it were, insensible. I have related how many enemies I used formerly to make by holding aloof from people who did not attract my attention by any merit ; and as people had often taken for haughtiness the boredom they caused me, I strongly dreaded this reef in the great journey I was about to undertake. But I soon observed that, although insolence increases with certain persons in the exact proportion of the progress of their fortunes, it was different with me, and that it was much easier for me to display affability and even cordiality when I felt myself above, than when

I was one of the common herd. This comes from the fact that, being a minister, I no longer had the trouble of running after people, nor to fear lest I should be coldly received by them, men making it a necessity themselves to approach those who occupy posts of that sort, and being simple enough to attach great importance to their most trivial words. It comes also from this that, as a minister, I no longer had to do only with the ideas of fools, but also with their interests, which always supply a ready-made and easy subject of conversation.

I saw, therefore, that I was not so ill fitted as I had feared for the part I had undertaken to play. This discovery encouraged me, not only for the present, but for the rest of my life ; and should I be asked what I gained in this Ministry, so troubled, so thwarted, and so short that I was only able to commence affairs in it and to finish none, I would answer that I gained one great advantage, perhaps the greatest advantage in the world— confidence in myself.

At home and abroad, our greatest obstacles came less from the difficulty of business than from those who had to conduct it with us. I saw this from the first. Most of our agents were creatures of the Monarchy, who, at the bottom of their hearts, furiously detested the Government they served ; and in the name of democratic and republican France, they extolled the restoration of the old aristocracies and secretly worked for the re-establishment of all the absolute monarchies of Europe. Others, on the contrary, whom the Revolution of February had dragged from an obscurity in which they should have always remained, clandestinely supported the demagogic parties which the French Government was combating. But the chief fault of most of them was timidity. The greater number of our ambassadors were afraid to attach themselves to any particular policy in the countries in which they represented us, and even feared to display to their own Government opinions which might sooner or later have been counted as a crime against them. They therefore took care to keep themselves covertly concealed beneath a heap of little facts with which they crammed their correspondence (for in diplomacy you must always write, even when you know nothing and wish to say nothing), and they were very careful not to show what they thought of the events they chronicled, and still less to give any indication as to what we were to conclude from them.

This condition of nullity to which our agents voluntarily reduced themselves, and which, to tell the truth, was in the case of most of them no more than an artificial perfection of nature, induced me, as soon as I had realized it, to employ new men at the great Courts.

I should have liked in the same way to be able to get rid of the leaders of the majority ; but not being able to do this, I endeavoured to live on good terms with them, and I did not even despair of pleasing them, while at the same time remaining independent of their influence : a difficult undertaking in which I nevertheless succeeded ; for, of all the Cabinet, I was the minister who most strongly opposed their policy and yet the only one who retained their good graces. My secret, if I must confess it, lay in flattering their self-conceit while neglecting their advice.

I had made an observation in small affairs which I deemed very applicable to greater ones : I had found that the most advantageous negotiations are those conducted with human vanity ; for one often obtains very substantial things from it, while giving very little substance in return. One never does so well when treating with ambition or cupidity. At the same time, it is a fact that in order to deal advantageously with the vanity of others, one must put his own entirely on one side and think of nothing but the success of his plans, an essential which will always prove a difficulty in the way of this sort of commerce. I practised it very happily at this time and to my great advantage. Three men thought themselves specially entitled to direct our foreign policy, owing to the position they had formerly occupied : these were M. de Broglie, M. Molé and M. Thiers. I overwhelmed all three of them with deference ; I often sent for them to see me, and sometimes called upon them to consult them and to ask them, with a sort of modesty, for advice which I hardly ever followed. But this did not prevent these great men from displaying every satisfaction. I pleased them more by asking their opinion without following it than if I had followed it without asking it. Especially in the case of M. Thiers, this manoeuvre of mine succeeded admirably. Rémusat, who, although without any personal pretentions, sincerely wished the Cabinet to last, and who had become familiarized through an intercourse extending over twenty-five years with all M. Thiers' weaknesses, said to me one day :

" The world does not know M. Thiers well ; he has much more vanity than ambition ; and he prefers consideration to obedience, and the appearance of power to power itself. Consult him constantly, and then do just as you please. He will take more notice of your deference to him than of your actions."

This is what I did, and with great success. In the two principal affairs that I had to conduct during my time of office, those of Piedmont and Turkey, I did precisely the opposite to what M. Thiers wished, and, nevertheless, we remained excellent friends till the end.

As to the President, it was especially in the conduct of foreign affairs that he showed how badly prepared he still was for the great part to which blind fortune had called him. I was not slow in perceiving that this man, whose pride aimed at leading everything, had not yet taken the smallest steps to inform himself of anything. I proposed to have an analysis drawn up every day of all the dispatches and to submit it to his inspection. Before this, he knew what happened in the world only by hear-say, and only knew what the Minister for Foreign Affairs had thought fit to tell him. The solid basis of facts was always lacking to the operations of his mind, and this was easily seen in all the dreams with which the latter was filled.

I was sometimes frightened at perceiving how much there was in his plans that was vast, chimerical, un-scrupulous, and confused ; although it is true that, when explaining the real state of things to him, I easily made him recognize the difficulties which they presented, for discussion was not his strong point. He was silent, but never yielded.

One of his myths was an alliance with one of the two great powers of Germany, of which he proposed to make use to alter the map of Europe and erase the limits which the treaties of 1815 had traced for France. As he saw that I did not believe it possible to find either of these powers inclined for an alliance of this sort, and with such an object, he undertook himself to sound their ambassadors in Paris. One of them came to me one day in a state of great excitement to tell me that the President of the Republic had asked him if, in consideration of an equivalent, his Court would not consent to allow France to seize Savoy. On another occasion, he conceived the idea of sending a private agent, one of his own men, as he called them, to come to a direct understanding with the German Princes. He chose Persigny, and asked me to give him his credentials ; and I consented, knowing well that nothing could come of a negotiation of this sort. I believe that Persigny had a two-fold mission : it was a question of facilitating the usurpation at home and an extension of territory abroad. He went first to Berlin and then to Vienna ; as I expected, he was very well received, handsomely entertained, and politely bowed out.

But I have spoken enough of individuals ; let us come to politics.

At the time when I took up office, Europe was, as it were, on fire, although the conflagration was already extinguished in certain countries.

Sicily was conquered and subdued ; the Neapolitans had returned to their obedience and even to their servitude ; the battle of Novara had been fought and lost ; the victorious Austrians were negotiating with the son of Charles Albert, who had become King of Piedmont by his father's abdication ; their armies, issuing from the confines of Lombardy, occupied Parma, a portion of the Papal States, Placentia, and Tuscany, which they had entered unasked, and in spite of the fact that the Grand Duke had been restored by his subjects, who have been but ill rewarded since for their zeal and fidelity. But Venice still resisted, and Rome, after repelling our first attack, was calling all the demagogues of Italy to its assistance and exciting all Europe with its clamour. Never, perhaps, since February, had Germany seemed more divided or disturbed. Although the dream of German unity had been dispelled, the reality of the old Teutonic organization had not yet resumed its place. Reduced to a small number of members, the National Assembly, which had till then endeavoured to promote this unity, fled from Frankfort and hawked round the spectacle of its impotence and its ridiculous fury. But its fall did not restore order ; on the contrary, it left a freer field for anarchy.

The moderate, one may say the innocent, revolutionaries, who had cherished the belief that they would be able, peacefully, and by means of arguments and decrees, to persuade the peoples and princes of Germany to submit to a single government, made way for the violent revolutionaries, who had always maintained that Germany could only be brought to a state of unity by the complete ruin of its old systems of government, and the entire abolition of the existing social order. Riots therefore followed in every land upon parliamentary discussion. Political rivalries turned into a war of classes ; the natural hatred and jealousy entertained by the poor for the rich developed into socialistic theories in many quarters, but especially in the small states of Central Germany and in the great Rhine Valley. Wurtemberg was in a state of agitation ; Saxony had just experienced a terrible insurrection, which had only been crushed with the assistance of Prussia ; insurrections had also occurred in Westphalia ; the Palatinate was in open revolt ; and Baden had expelled its Grand Duke, and appointed a Provisional Government. And yet the final victory of the Princes, which I had foreseen when travelling through Germany, a month before, was no longer in doubt ; the very violence of the insurrections hastened it. The larger monarchies had recaptured their capitals and their armies. Their heads had still difficulties to conquer, but no more dangers ; and themselves masters, or on the point of becoming so, at home, they could not fail soon to triumph in the second-rate States. By thus violently disturbing public order, the insurgents gave them the wish, the opportunity and the right to intervene.

Prussia had already commenced to do so. The Prussians had just suppressed the Saxon insurrection by force of arms ; they now entered the Rhine Palatinate, offered their intervention to Wurtemberg, and prepared to invade the Grand-Duchy of Baden, thus occupying almost the whole of Germany with their soldiers or their influence.

Austria had emerged from the terrible crisis which had

threatened its existence, but it was still in great travail. Its armies, after conquering in Italy, were being defeated in Hungary.

Despairing of mastering its subjects unaided, it had called Russia to its assistance and the Tsar, in a manifesto dated 13 May, had announced to Europe that he was marching against the Hungarians. The Emperor Nicholas had till then remained at rest amid his uncontested might. He had viewed the agitation of the nations from afar in safety, but not with indifference. Henceforward, he alone among the great powers of Europe represented the old state of society and the old traditional principle of authority. He was not only its representative: he considered himself its champion. His political theories, his religious belief, his ambition and his conscience, all urged him to adopt this part. He had, therefore, made for himself out of the cause of authority throughout the world a second empire yet vaster than the first. He encouraged with his letters and rewarded with his honours all those who, in whatever corner of Europe, gained victories over anarchy and even over liberty, as though they were his subjects and had contributed to strengthening his own power. He had thus sent, to the extreme South of Europe, one of his orders to Filangieri, the conqueror of the Sicilians, and had written that general an autograph letter to show to him that he was satisfied with his conduct. From the lofty position which he occupied, and whence he peacefully watched the various incidents of the struggle which shook Europe, the Emperor judged freely, and followed with a certain tranquil disdain, not only the follies of the revolutionaries whom he pursued, but also the vices and the faults of the parties and princes whom he assisted. He expressed himself on this subject simply and as the occasion required, without showing any eagerness to disclose his thoughts or taking any pains to conceal them.

Lamoricière wrote to me on the 11th of August, 1894, in a secret dispatch :

" The Tsar said to me this morning: ' You believe, general, that your dynastic parties would be capable of uniting with the Radicals to overthrow a dynasty which they disliked, in the hope of setting their own in its place ; I am certain of it. Your Legitimist Party especially would not hesitate to do so. I have long since thought that it is the Legitimists who make the Elder Branch of the Bourbons impossible. This is one of the reasons why I recognized the Republic ; and also because I perceive in your nation a certain common sense which is wanting in the Germans.'

" Later, the Emperor also said: ' The King of Prussia, my brother-in-law, with whom I was on very close terms of friendship, has not taken the slightest heed of my advice. The result is that our political relations have become remarkably cool, to such an extent that they have affected even our family relations. Look at the things he has done : did he not put himself at the head of those fools who dream of an United Germany, and now that he has broken with the Frankfort Parliament, has he not brought himself to the necessity of fighting the troops of the Schleswig-Holstein Duchies, which were levied under his patronage ! Is it possible to imagine anything more disgraceful ? And now, who knows how far he will go with his constitutional proposals ? ' He added: ' Do not think that, because I intervene in Hungary, I wish to justify the conduct of Austria in this affair. She heaped up, one on the other, the most serious faults and the greatest follies ; but when all is said and done, it had allowed the country to be invaded by subversive doctrines, and the government had fallen into the hands of disorderly persons. This was not to be endured.'

" Speaking of the affairs of Italy, ' We others ', he said,

' see nothing in those temporal functions fulfilled in Rome by ecclesiastics ; but it matters little to us how those priests arrange things among themselves, provided that something is set up which will last and that you constitute the power in such a way that it can stand.' "

Hereupon Lamoricière, wounded by this supercilious tone, which smelt somewhat of the autocrat and betrayed a sort of rivalry as between pope and pope, began to defend Catholic institutions.

" ' Very well, very well,' said the Emperor, ending the conversation, ' let France be as Catholic as she pleases, only let her protect herself against the insane theories and passions of innovators.' "

Though hard and austere in the exercise of his power, the Tsar was simple and almost *bourgeois* in his habits, keeping only the substance of sovereign power and rejecting its pomp and worries. On the 17th of July, the French Ambassador at St. Petersburg wrote to me :

" The Emperor is here ; he arrived from Warsaw without suite of any kind, in an ordinary post-cart—his carriage had broken down sixty leagues from here—so as to be in time for the Empress's saint's-day, which has just taken place. He did the journey with extraordinary rapidity, in two days and a half, and he leaves again tomorrow. Every one here is touched with this contrast of power and simplicity, with the sight of this Sovereign who, after hurling one hundred and twenty thousand men on to the battle-field, races along the roads like a *feld-jaeger*, so as not to miss his wife's saint's-day. Nothing is more in keeping with the spirit of the Slavs, among whom one might say that the principal element of civilization is the spirit of family."

267

It would, in fact, be a great mistake to think that the Tsar's immense power was only based upon force. It was founded, above all, on the wishes and the ardent sympathies of the Russians. For the principle of the sovereignty of the people lies at the root of all government whatever may be said to the contrary, and is hidden beneath the least independent institutions. The Russian nobles had adopted the principles and still more the vices of Europe ; but the people were not in touch with our West and with the new spirit which animated it. They saw in the Emperor not only their lawful Prince, but the envoy of God, and almost God Himself.

In the midst of this Europe which I have depicted, the position of France was one of weakness and embarrassment. Nowhere had the Revolution succeeded in establishing a regular and stable system of liberty. On every side, the old powers were rising up again from amid the ruins which it had made—not, it is true, the same as when they fell, but very similar. We could not assist the latter in establishing themselves nor ensure their victory, for the system which they were setting up was antipathetic, I will say not only to the institutions created by the Revolution of February, but, at the root of our ideas, to all that was most permanent and unconquerable in our new habits. They, on their side, distrusted us, and rightly. The great part of restorers of the general order in Europe was therefore forbidden us. This part, moreover, was already played by another : it belonged by right to Russia, and only the second remained for us. As to placing France at the head of the innovators, this was to be still less thought of, for two reasons : first, that it would have been absolutely impossible to advise these latter or to hope to lead them, because of their extravagance and their detestable incapacity ; secondly, that it was not possible to support them abroad without falling beneath their blows at home. The contact of their passions and doctrines would have put all France in flame, revolutionary doctrines at that time dominating all others. Thus we were neither able to unite with the nations, who accused us of urging them on and then betraying them, nor with the princes, who reproached us with shaking thrones. We were reduced to accepting the sterile good-will of the English : it was the same isolation as before February, with the Continent more hostile to us and England more lukewarm. It was therefore necessary, as it had been then, to reduce ourselves to leading a small life, from day to day ; but this was difficult. The French Nation, which had made and, in a certain way, still made so great a figure in the world, kicked against this necessity of the time: it had remained haughty while it ceased to be preponderant ; it feared to act and tried to talk loudly ; and it also expected its Government to be proud, without, however, permitting it to run the risks which such conduct entailed. [A sorry condition for a Ministry of Foreign Affairs in such a country and at such a time !

Having thought out deeply what I am about to say, I adopted two maxims which were to be of great use to me during my short term of office. I believed that they should be followed by any man charged with the direction of French Foreign Affairs in times like ours.

The first was to break without reservations with the revolutionary party abroad ; for we were not living in a time like that of Richelieu, who could bring low the Protestants in France while helping them to rise in Germany. At the same time I promised myself never to disown our principles of liberty and toleration ; and to favour the restoration of order without surrendering ourselves to the passions of the prince, whom it was, in any case, impossible to win over. Thus France, while at war with the revolution, did not lose her liberal attitude by which she was known among the peoples. It is true that this attitude was not of a kind to bring her immediate good fortune, for she had rather discredited the cause of liberty ; but it helped nevertheless and the hope of fair dealings in the future increased her prestige.

A second maxim was never to touch things which were clearly beyond our strength ; never to promise anything which we could not give, nor to encourage anyone whom we could not beat. In short, not to aspire to a rank which we had occupied in the past, but which the present state of affairs no longer permitted us to hold ; but to hold with pride the high place which was still left to us, and to maintain it against all risks in case of dispute. Should the President or the Assembly restrain me, I would have to resign at once. "Gentlemen", I said to our ambassadors the first time they came to see me, " I am not a diplomat, and what I tell you now is my last word ; it will not be changed now or later. I know that France is not in a position to dominate Europe, or to make her will prevail in distant affairs. Consequently let us not interest ourselves in them. Be assured that we leave you absolutely free in those affairs which do not concern us, and I shall not even encourage you to give us any concern in them or to create the impression that we might interfere. But in all countries which are close to us and in all questions which are directly related to us France has a right to exert not only a great, but a predominating influence. We shall not interfere in events which happen at the other end of Europe, in the Principalities, in Poland or in Hungary. But in Switzerland, in Belgium or in the Piedmont I warn you to do nothing without consulting us and without our agreement. In these foreign territories we shall exert our right, not only by negotiation but, if necessary, also by force ; we shall risk everything to maintain our influence. I do not wish to hide from you that a war would be difficult for us and very dangerous. The social order might collapse and bury ourselves and our fortunes under its ruins. Yet you may be certain that in such circumstances we would resort to war. Be assured at any rate that I would resign my office if the President and the Assembly did not support me". I gave similar instructions to our ambassadors at all courts.]

Never had France been looked upon with more anxiety than at the moment when the Cabinet had just been formed. The easy and complete victory which we had won in Paris on the 13th of June had extraordinary rebounds throughout Europe. A new insurrection in France was generally expected. The revolutionaries, half destroyed, relied only upon this occurrence to recover themselves and they redoubled their efforts in order to be able to take advantage of it. The governments, half victorious, fearing to be surprised by this crisis, stopped before striking their final blow. The day of the 13th of June gave rise to cries of pain and joy from one end of the Continent to the other. It decided fortune suddenly, and precipitated it towards the Rhine.

The Prussian army, already master of the Palatinate, at once burst into the Grand-Duchy of Baden, dispersed the insurgents, and occupied the whole country, with the exception of Rastadt, which held out for a few weeks.[1]

[1] Nothing was ever more despicable than the conduct of those revolutionaries. The soldiers who, at the commencement of the insurrection, had put to flight or killed their officers, turned tail before the Prussians. The ringleaders did nothing but dispute among themselves and defame one another instead of defending themselves, and took refuge in Switzerland after pillaging the public treasury and levying contributions upon their own country.

While the struggle lasted, we took strong measures to prevent the insurgents from receiving any assistance from France. Those among them who crossed the Rhine, in great numbers, received asylum from us, but were disarmed and placed in confinement. The victors, as it was easy to foresee, at once abused their victory. Many prisoners were put to death, all liberty was indefinitely suspended, and even

The Baden revolutionaries took refuge in Switzerland. Refugees were then arriving in that country from Italy, France, and to tell the truth, from every corner of Europe, for all Europe, with the exception of Russia, had undergone or was undergoing a revolution. Their number soon amounted to ten or twelve thousand. It

the government which had been restored was kept in very close tutelage. I soon perceived that the French representative in the Grand-Duchy of Baden not only did not strive to moderate these violences, but thoroughly approved of them. I at once wrote to him as follows :

" SIR,

" I am informed that a number of military executions have taken place, and that many more are announced. I do not understand why these facts have not been reported by you, nor why you have not sought to prevent them, without even waiting for instructions. We have assisted as much as we could, without taking up arms, in suppressing the rebellion ; all the more reason for desiring that the victory to which we have given our aid should not be sullied by acts of violence of which France disapproves, and which we regard as both odious and impolitic. There is another point which causes us much anxiety, and which does not seem to excite your solicitude to the same degree : I refer to the political institutions of the Grand-Duchy. Do not forget that the object of the Government of the Republic in that country has been to assist in putting down anarchy, but not in destroying liberty. We can in no way lend our hand to an anti-liberal restoration. The Constitutional Monarchy felt the need to create or maintain free States around France. The Republic is still more obliged to do so. The Government therefore asks and imperiously insists that each of its agents shall faithfully conform to these necessities of our situation. See the Grand Duke, and give him to understand what are the wishes of France. We shall certainly never allow either a Prussian province or an absolute government to be established on our frontier instead of an independent and constitutional monarchy."

After some time, the executions ceased. The Grand Duke protested his attachment to constitutional forms, and his resolution to maintain them. This was for the moment all he was able to do, for he reigned only in name. The Prussians were the real masters.

was an army always ready to fall upon the neighbouring States. All the Cabinets were alarmed at it.

Austria and especially Prussia, which had already had reason to complain of the Confederation, and even Russia, which was in no way concerned, spoke of invading Swiss territory with armed forces and acting as a police in the name of all the governments threatened. This we could not allow.

I first endeavoured to make the Swiss listen to reason, and to persuade them not to wait till they were threatened, but themselves to expel from their territory, as the Law of Nations required them to do, all the principal ringleaders who openly threatened neighbouring nations.

" If you in this way anticipate what they have the right to ask of you," I incessantly repeated to the representative in Paris of the Swiss Confederation, " you can rely upon France to defend you against any unjust or exaggerated pretensions put forward by the Courts. We will rather risk war than permit them to oppress or humiliate you. But if you refuse to bring reason on your side, you must only rely upon yourselves, and you will have to defend yourselves against all Europe."

This language had little effect, for there is nothing to equal the pride and conceit of the Swiss. Not one of those peasants but believes that his country is able to defy all the princes and all the nations of the earth. I then set to work in another way, which was more successful. This was to advise the foreign Governments (who were only too disposed to agree) to refuse for a certain period all amnesty to those of their subjects who had taken refuge in Switzerland, and to deny all of them, whatever their degree of guilt, the right to return to their country. On our side, we closed our frontiers to all those who, after taking refuge in Switzerland, wished to cross France in order to go to England or America, including the inoffensive refugees as well as the ringleaders. Every outlet being thus closed, Switzerland remained encumbered with those ten or twelve thousand adventurers, the most turbulent and disorderly people in all Europe. It was necessary to feed, lodge, and even pay them, lest they should levy contributions on the country. This suddenly enlightened the Swiss as to the drawbacks attendant upon the right of asylum. They could have made arrangements to have kept the illustrious chiefs for an indefinite period, in spite of the danger with which these menaced their neighbours ; but the revolutionary army was a great nuisance to them. The more radical cantons were the first to raise a loud clamour and to ask to be rid of these inconvenient and expensive visitors. And as it was impossible to persuade the foreign Governments to open their territory to the crowd of inoffensive refugees who were able and willing to leave Switzerland, without first driving out the leaders who would have liked to stay, they ended by expelling these. After almost bringing all Europe down upon them rather than remove these men from their territory, the Swiss ended by driving them out of their own accord in order to avoid a temporary inconvenience and a trifling expense. No better example was ever given of the nature of democracies, which as a rule, have only very confused or very erroneous ideas on external affairs, and generally solve outside questions only by internal reasons.

While these things were happening in Switzerland, the general aspect of affairs in Germany underwent a change. The struggles of the nations against the Governments were followed by quarrels of the princes among themselves. I followed this new phase of the Revolution with a very attentive gaze and a very perplexed mind.

The Revolution in Germany had not proceeded from a simple cause, as in the rest of Europe. It was produced at once by the general spirit of the time and by the unitarian ideas peculiar to the Germans. The democracy was now beaten, but the idea of German unity was not destroyed ; the needs, the memories, the passions that had inspired it survived. The King of Prussia had undertaken to appropriate it and make use of it. This Prince, a man of intelligence but of very little sense, had been wavering for a year between his fear of the Revolution and his desire to turn it to account. He struggled as much as he could against the liberal and democratic spirit of the age ; yet he favoured the German unitarian spirit, a blundering game in which, if he had dared to go to the length of his desires, he would have risked his Crown and his life. For, in order to overcome the resistance which existing institutions and the interests of the Princes were bound to oppose to the establishment of a central power, he would have had to summon the revolutionary passions of the peoples to his aid, and of these Frederic William could not have made use without soon being destroyed by them himself.

As long as the Frankfort Parliament retained its *prestige* and its power, the King of Prussia entreated it kindly and strove to get himself placed by it at the head of the new Empire. When the Parliament fell into discredit and powerlessness, the King changed his behaviour without changing his plans. He endeavoured to obtain the legacy of this Assembly and to combat the Revolution by realizing the chimera of German unity, of which the democrats had made use to shake every throne. With this intention, he invited all the German Princes to come to an understanding with him to form a new Confederation, which should be closer than that of 1815, and to give him the government of it. In return he undertook to establish and strengthen them in their States. These Princes, who detested Prussia, but who trembled before the Revolution, for the most part accepted the usurious bargain proposed to them. Austria, which the success of this proposal would have driven out of Germany, protested, being not yet in a position to do more. The two principal monarchies of the South, Bavaria and Wurtemberg, followed its example, but all North and Central Germany entered into this ephemeral Confederation, which was concluded on the 26th of May, 1849 and is known in history by the name of the Union of the Three Kings.

Prussia then suddenly became the dominating power in a vast stretch of country, reaching from Memel to Basle, and at one time saw twenty-six or twenty-seven million Germans marching under its orders. All this was completed shortly after my arrival in office.

I confess that, at the sight of this singular spectacle, my mind was crossed with strange ideas, and I was for a moment tempted to believe that the President was not so mad in his foreign policy as I had at first thought him. That union of the great Courts of the North, which had so long weighed heavily upon us, was broken. Two of the great Continental monarchies, Prussia and Austria, were quarrelling and almost at war. Had not the moment come for us to contact one of those intimate and powerful alliances which we had been compelled to forego for sixty years, and perhaps in a measure to repair our losses of 1815 ? France, by platonically assisting Frederic William in his enterprises which England did not oppose, could divide Europe and bring on one of those great crises which entail a redistribution of territory.

The time seemed so well to lend itself to these ideas that they filled the imagination of many of the German Princes themselves. The more powerful among them dreamt of nothing but changes of frontier and accessions of power at the expense of their neighbours. The revolutionary malady of the nations seemed to have attacked the governments.

" There is no Confederation possible with thirty-eight States ", said the Bavarian Foreign Minister, Baron von der Pfordten, to our Envoy. " It will be necessary to mediatize a large number of them. How, for instance, can we ever hope to re-establish order in a country like Baden, unless we divide it among sovereigns strong enough to make themselves obeyed ? In that case", he added, " the Neckar Valley would naturally fall to our share."[1]

For my part, I soon dispelled from my mind, as mere visions, all thoughts of this kind.

I quickly realized that Prussia was neither able nor willing to give us anything worth having in exchange for our good offices ; that its power over the other German States was very precarious, and was likely to be ephemeral ; that no reliance was to be placed in its King, who at the first obstacle would have failed us and failed himself ; and, above all, that such extensive and ambitious designs were not suited to so ill-established a state of society and to such troubled and dangerous times as ours, nor to transient powers such as that which chance had placed in my hands.

I put a more serious question to myself, and it was this—I recall it here because it is bound constantly to crop up again : Is it to the interest of France that the bonds which hold together the German Confederation should be strengthened or relaxed ? In other words, ought we to desire that Germany should in a certain sense become a single nation, or that it should remain an ill-joined conglomeration of disunited peoples and princes ? There is an old tradition in our diplomacy that we should strive to keep Germany divided among a large number of independent powers ; and this in fact, was self-evident at the time when there was nothing behind Germany except Poland and a semi-savage Russia ; but is the case the same in our days ? The reply to this question depends upon the reply to another : What is

[1] Dispatch of the 7th of September, 1849.

really the peril with which in our days Russia threatens the independence of Europe ? For my part, believing as I do that our West is threatened sooner or later to fall under the yoke, or at least under the direct and irresistible influence of the Tsars, I think that our first object should be to favour the union of all the German races in order to oppose it to that influence. The conditions of the world are new ; we must change our old maxims and not fear to strengthen our neighbours, so that they may one day be in a condition with us to repel the common enemy.

The Emperor of Russia, on his side, saw how great an obstacle a United Germany would prove in his way. Lamoricière, in one of his private letters, informed me that the Emperor had said to him with his ordinary candour and arrogance ;

" If the unity of Germany, which doubtless you wish for no more than I do, ever becomes a fact, there will be needed, in order to manage it, a man capable of what Napoleon himself was not able to do ; and if this man were found, if that armed mass developed into a menace, it would then become your affair and mine."

But when I put these questions to myself, the time had not come to solve them nor even to discuss them, for Germany was of its own accord irresistibly returning to its old constitution and to the old anarchy of its powers. The Frankfort Parliament's attempt in favour of unity had fallen through. That made by the King of Prussia was destined to meet with the same fate.

It was the dread of the Revolution which alone had driven the German Princes into Frederic William's arms. In the measure that, thanks to the efforts of the Prussians, the Revolution was on all sides suppressed and ceased to make itself feared, the allies (one might almost say the new subjects) of Prussia aimed at recovering their independence. The King of Prussia's enterprise was of that unfortunate kind in which success itself interferes

with triumph, and to compare large things with smaller,
I would say that his history was not unlike ours, and that,
like ourselves, he was doomed to strike upon a rock as
soon as, and for the reason that, he had re-established
order. The princes who had adhered to what was known
as the Prussian hegemony seized the first opportunity
to renounce it. Austria supplied this opportunity, when,
after defeating the Hungarians, she was able to re-appear
upon the scene of German affairs with her material
power and that of the memories which attached to her
name. This is what happened in the course of September
1849. When the King of Prussia found himself face to
face with that powerful rival, behind whom he caught
sight of Russia, his courage suddenly failed him, as I
expected, and he returned to his old part. The German
Constitution of 1815 resumed its empire, the Diet its
sittings ; and soon, of all that great movement of 1848,
there remained but two traces visible in Germany : a
greater dependence of the small States upon the great
monarchies, and an irreparable blow struck at all that
remains of feudal institutions : their ruin, consummated
by the nations, was sanctioned by the Princes. From one
end of Germany to the other, the perpetuity of ground-
rents, baronial tithes, forced labour, rights of mutation,
of hunting, of justice, which constituted a great part of
the riches of the nobility, remained abolished.[1] The
Kings were restored, but the aristocracies did not recover
from the blow that had been struck them.[2]

[1] Private letter from Beaumont at Vienna, 10 October, 1849.—
Dispatch from M. Lefèbre at Munich, 23 July, 1849.
[2] I had foreseen from the commencement that Austria and Prussia
would soon return to their former sphere and fall back in each case
within the influence of Russia. I find this provision set forth in the
instructions which I gave to one of our ambassadors to Germany
on the 24th of July, before the events which I have described had
taken place. These instructions are drawn up in my own hand, as
were all my more important dispatches. I read as follows :

Convinced at an early date that we had no part to play in this internal crisis in Germany, I only applied myself to living on good terms with the several contending parties. I especially kept up friendly relations with Austria, whose concurrence was necessary to us, as I will explain later, in the Roman business. I first strove to bring to a happy conclusion the negotiations which had long been pending between Austria and Piedmont ; I put the more care into this because I was persuaded that, as long as no lasting peace was established on that side, Europe would remain unsettled and liable at any moment to be thrown into great danger.

Piedmont had been negotiating to no purpose since the battle of Novara. Austria at first tried to lay down unacceptable conditions. Piedmont, on her side, kept up pretensions which the state of her fortunes did not authorize. The negotiations, several times interrupted, had been resumed before I took office. We had many very strong reasons to desire that this peace should be concluded without delay. At any moment, a general war might break out in this little corner of the Continent. Piedmont, moreover, was too near to us to permit us to

---

" I know that the malady which is ravaging all the old European society is incurable, that in changing its symptoms it does not change in character, and that all the old powers are, to a greater or lesser extent, threatened with modification or destruction. But I am inclined to believe that the next event will be the strengthening of authority throughout Europe. It would not be impossible that, under the pressure of a common instinct of defence or under the common influence of recent occurrences, Russia should be willing and able to bring about harmony between North and South Germany and to reconcile Austria and Prussia, and that all this great movement should merely resolve itself into a new alliance of principle between the three monarchies at the expense of the secondary governments and the liberty of the citizens. Consider the situation from this point of view, and give me an account of your observations."

allow that she should lose either her independence, which separated her from Austria, or her newly-acquired constitutional institutions, which brought her closer to us : two advantages which would be seriously jeopardized if recourse were had to arms.

I therefore interposed very eagerly, in the name of France, between the two parties, addressing to both of them the language which I thought most likely to convince them.

I observed to Austria how urgent it was that the general peace of Europe should be assured by this particular peace, and I exerted myself to point out to her what was excessive in her demands.

To Piedmont I indicated the points on which it seemed to me that honour and interest would permit her to give way, I applied myself especially to giving her Government in advance clear and precise ideas as to what it might expect from us, so that it should have no excuse to entertain, or to pretend to have entertained, any dangerous illusions.[1] I will not go into details of the condi-

---

[1] Dispatch of the 4th of July, 1849 to M. de Boislecomte :

" The conditions laid down for Piedmont by His Majesty the Emperor of Austria are no doubt severe ; but, nevertheless, they do not affect the integrity of the territory of the Kingdom nor her honour. They neither take away the strength which she should preserve, nor the just influence which she is called upon to exercise over the general policy of Europe and in particular over the affairs of Italy. The treaty which she is asked to sign is a vexatious one, no doubt ; but it is not a disastrous one ; and, after the fate of arms has been decided, it does not exceed what was naturally to be feared.

" France has not neglected, and will not neglect, any effort to obtain a mitigation of this proposal ; she will persist in her endeavours to obtain from the Austrian Government the modifications which she considers in keeping not only with the interests of Piedmont but with the easy and lasting maintenance of the general peace ; and to attain this result, she will employ all the means supplied to diplomacy : but she will not go beyond this. She does

tions under discussion, which are without interest to-day ; I will content myself with saying that at the end they seemed prepared to come to an understanding, and that any further delay was due merely to a question of money. This was the condition of affairs, and Austria assured us through her Ambassador in Paris of her con-ciliatory dispositions ; I already looked upon peace as concluded, when I unexpectedly learned that the Austrian Plenipotentiary had suddenly changed his atti-tude and his language, had delivered on the 19th of July a very serious ultimatum, couched in exceedingly harsh terms, and had only given four days in which to reply to it. At the end of these four days the armistice was to be raised and the war resumed. Already Marshal Radetzky was concentrating his army and preparing to enter upon a fresh campaign. This news, so contrary to the pacific

---

not think that, within the limits of the question and the degree to which the interests of Piedmont are involved, it would be opportune to do more. Holding this firm and deliberate opinion, she does not hesitate to give utterance to it. To allow, even by her silence, a belief to gain ground in extreme resolutions that have not been taken ; to suggest hopes that we are not certain of wishing to realize; to urge indirectly by words to a line of action which we should not think ourselves justified in supporting by our acts ; in a word, to engage others without engaging ourselves, or unconsciously to engage ourselves more deeply than we think or than we mean : that would be, on the part of either the Government or of private in-dividuals, a line of conduct which seems to me neither prudent nor honourable.

" You can rely, Sir, that as long as I occupy the post in which the President's confidence has placed me, the Government of the Republic shall incur no such reproach ; it will announce nothing that it will not be prepared to carry out ; it will make no promises that it is not resolved to keep ; and it will consider it as much a point of honour to declare beforehand what it is not ready to do as to execute promptly and with vigour that which it has said it would do.

"You will be good enough to read this despatch to M. d'Azeglio."

assurances which we had received, was to me a great source of surprise and indignation. Demands so exorbitant, delivered in such arrogant and violent terms, seemed to announce that peace was not Austria's only object, but that she aimed rather at the independence of Piedmont and perhaps at her representative institutions ; for as long as liberty shows itself in the smallest fraction of Italy, Austria feels ill at ease in all the rest.

I at once came to the conclusion that we must at no price allow so near a neighbour to be oppressed, deliver a territory which touched our frontiers to the Austrian armies, or permit political liberty to be abolished in the only country in which, since 1848, it had showed itself moderate. I thought, moreover, that Austria's mode of procedure towards us showed either an intention to deceive us or else a desire to try how far our toleration would go, or, as is commonly said, to sound us.

I saw that this was one of those extreme circumstances, which I had faced beforehand, where it became my duty to risk not only my portfolio (which, to tell the truth, was not risking much) but the fortunes of France. I proceeded to the Council and explained the state of affairs.

The President and all my colleagues were unanimous in thinking that one ought to act. Orders were immediately telegraphed to concentrate the Army of Lyons at the foot of the Alps, and as soon as I returned home, I myself wrote (for the flaccid style of diplomacy was not suited to the circumstances) the following letter :[1]

" Should the Austrian Government persist in the unreasonable demands mentioned in your telegram of yesterday, and, abandoning the limits of diplomatic discussion, throw up the armistice and undertake, as it says it will, to go and dictate peace at Turin, Piedmont can be assured that we should not desert her. The situation

[1] Letter to M. de Boislecomte, 25 July, 1849.

would no longer be the same as that in which she placed herself before the battle of Novara, when she spontaneously resumed her arms and renewed the war against our advice. This time it would be Austria which would herself take the initiative unprovoked ; the nature of her demands and the violence of her proceedings would give us reason to believe that she is not acting solely with a view to peace, but that she is threatening the integrity of Piedmontese territory or, at the very least, the independence of the Sardinian Government.

" We will not allow such designs as these to be accomplished at our gates. If, under these conditions, Piedmont is attacked, we will defend her."

I moreover thought it my duty to send for the Austrian representative (a little diplomatist very like a fox in appearance as well as in nature), and, convinced that, in the attitude we were taking up, hastiness was identical with prudence, I took advantage of the fact that I could not as yet be expected to have become familiar with habits of diplomatic reserve, to express to him our surprise and our dissatisfaction in terms so rude that he since admitted to me that he had never been so received in his life.

Before the dispatch of which I have quoted a few lines had reached Turin, the two Powers had come to an agreement. They had come to terms on the question of money which was arranged practically on the conditions that had been previously suggested by ourselves. The Austrian Government had only desired to precipitate the negotiations by frightening the other side ; it made very little difficulty about the conditions.

Prince Schwarzenberg sent me all sorts of explanations and excuses, and peace was definitely signed on the 6th of August, a peace hardly hoped for by Piedmont after so many mistakes and misfortunes, since it assured her more advantages than she had at first ventured to demand.

This affair threw into great relief the habits of English, and particularly of Palmerstonian, diplomacy : the feature is worth quoting. Since the commencement of the negotiation, the British Government had never ceased to show great animosity against Austria, and loudly to encourage the Piedmontese not to submit to the conditions which she sought to force upon them. My first care, after taking the resolutions I have described, was to communicate them to England, and to endeavour to persuade her to take up the same line of conduct. I therefore sent a copy of my dispatch to Drouyn de Lhuys, who was then Ambassador in London, and instructed him to show it to Lord Palmerston, and to discover that minister's intentions. Drouyn de Lhuys replied :[1]

" While I was informing Lord Palmerston of your resolutions and of the instructions you had sent M. de Boislecomte, he listened with every sign of eager assent ; but when I said, ' You see, my lord, how far we wish to go ; can you tell me how far you will go yourself ? ' Lord Palmerston at once replied, ' The British Government, whose interest in this business is not equal to yours, will not lend the Piedmontese Government more than a diplomatic assistance and a moral support'."

Is not this characteristic ? England, protected against the revolutionary sickness of nations by the wisdom of her laws and the strength of her ancient customs, and against the anger of princes by her power and her isolation in the midst of us, is always pleased to play the part of the advocate of liberty and justice in the internal affairs of the Continent. She likes to censure and even to

[1] Dispatches of the 25th and 26th of June, 1849.

insult the strong, to justify and encourage the weak ; but it seems that she does not care to go further than to assume virtuous airs and discuss honourable theories. Should her *protégés* come to need her, she offers her moral support.

I add, in order to finish the subject, that these tactics succeeded remarkably well. The Piedmontese remained convinced that England alone had defended them, and that we had very nearly abandoned them. She remained very popular in Turin, and France very much suspected. For nations are like men, they love still more that which flatters their passions than that which serves their interests.

Hardly had we emerged from this bad pass, before we fell into a worse one. We had witnessed with fear and regret what was happening in Hungary. The misfortunes of this unlucky people excited our sympathies. The intervention of the Russians, which for a time subordinated Austria to the Tsar, and caused the hand of the latter to be more and more active in the management of the general affairs of Europe, was not calculated to please us. But all these events happened beyond our reach, and we were helpless.

" I need not tell you ", I wrote in the instructions I sent Lamoricière, " with what keen and melancholy interest we follow events in Hungary. Unfortunately, for the present, we can only take a passive part in this question. The letter and spirit of the treaties open out to us no right of intervention. Besides, our distance from the seat of war must impose upon us, in the present state of our affairs and of those of Europe, a certain reserve. Since we are not able to speak or act to good purpose, it is due to our dignity not to display, in respect to this question, any sterile excitement or impotent good-feeling. Our duty with regard to Hungarian events is to limit ourselves to observe carefully what happens and to seek to discover what is likely to take place."

Overwhelmed by numbers, the Hungarians were either conquered or surrendering, and their principal leaders, as well as a certain number of Polish generals who had joined their cause, crossed the Danube at the end of August, and threw themselves into the arms of the Turks at Widdin. From there, the two principal ones, Dembinski and Kossuth, wrote to our Ambassador in Constantinople.[1] The habits and peculiarities of mind of these two men were betrayed in their letters. The soldier's was short and simple; the lawyer-orator's long and ornate. I remember one of his phrases, among others, in which he said, " As a good Christian, I have chosen the unspeakable sorrow of exile rather than the peacefulness of death ". Both ended by asking for the protection of France.

While the outlaws were imploring our aid, the Austrian and Russian Ambassadors appeared before the Divan and asked that they might be given up. Austria based her demand upon the treaty of Belgrade, which in no way established her right; and Russia hers upon the treaty of Kaïnardji (10 July, 1774), of which the meaning, to say the least of it, was very obscure. But at bottom they neither of them appealed to an international right, but to a better known and more practical right, that of the strongest. This was made clear by their acts and their language. The two embassies declared from the commencement that it was a question of peace or war. Without consenting to discuss the matter, they insisted upon a reply of yes or no, and declared that if this reply was in the negative, they would at once cease all diplomatic relations with Turkey.

To this exhibition of violence, the Turkish ministers

[1] Letters of the 22nd and 24th of August, 1849.

replied, with gentleness, that Turkey was a neutral country ; that the law of nations forbade them to hand over outlaws who had taken refuge on their territory ; and that the Austrians and Russians had often quoted the same law against them when Mussulman rebels had sought an asylum in Hungary, Transylvania or Bessarabia. They modestly submitted that what was permitted on the left bank of the Danube seemed as though it should also be permitted on the right bank. They ended by protesting that what they were asked to do was opposed to their honour and their religion, that they would gladly undertake to keep the refugees under restraint and place them where they could do no mischief, but that they could never consent to deliver them to the executioner.

" The young Sultan ", our ambassador wrote to me, " replied yesterday to the Austrian Envoy that, while denouncing what the Hungarian rebels had done, he could now only regard them as unhappy men seeking to escape death, and that humanity forbade him to surrender them. Rechid Pasha, on his part, the Grand Vizier ", added our Minister, " said to me, ' I shall be proud if I am driven from power for this ' ; and he added, with an air of deep concern, ' In our religion, every man who asks for mercy is bound to obtain it '."

This was talking like civilized people and Christians. The Ambassadors were content to reply like real Turks, saying that they must give up the fugitives or undergo the consequences of a rupture which would probably lead to war. The Mussulman population itself took fire ; it approved of and supported its Government ; and the Mufti came to thank our Ambassador for the support he had given to the cause of humanity and good law.

From the commencement of the discussion, the Divan

had addressed itself to the Ambassadors of France and England. It appealed to public opinion in the two great countries which they represented, asked their advice, and besought their help in the event of the Northern Powers executing their threats. The Ambassadors at once replied that in their opinion Austria and Russia were exceeding their rights ; and they encouraged the Turkish Government in its resistance.

In the meanwhile, arrived at Constantinople an aide-de-camp of the Tsar. He brought a letter which that Prince had taken the pains to write to the Sultan with his own hand, asking for the extradition of the Poles who had served six months before in the Hungarian war against the Russian army. This step seems a very strange one when one does not see through the particular reasons which influenced the Tsar under the circumstance. The following extract from a letter of Lamoricière's describes them with great sagacity, and shows to what extent public opinion is dreaded at that end of Europe, where one would think that it was neither an organ nor a power :

" The Hungarian war, as you know ", he wrote,[1] " was embarked upon to sustain Austria, who is hated as a people and not respected as a government ; and it was very unpopular. It brought in nothing, and cost eighty-four millions of francs. The Russians hoped to bring back Bem, Dembinski, and the other Poles to Poland, as the price of the sacrifices of the campaign. Especially in the army, there reigned a veritable fury against these men. The people and soldiers were mad with longing for this satisfaction of their somewhat barbaric national pride. The Emperor, in spite of his omnipotence, is obliged to attach great value to the spirit of the masses upon whom he leans, and who constitute his

[1] Dispatches of the 11th and 25th of October, 1849.

real force. It is not simply a question of individual self-love : the national sentiment of the country and the army is at stake."

These were, no doubt, the considerations which prompted the Tsar to take the dangerous step I have mentioned. Prince Radziwill presented his letter, but obtained nothing. He left forthwith, haughtily refusing a second audience which was offered him, to take his leave ; and the Russian and Austrian Ambassadors officially declared that all diplomatic relations had ceased between their masters and the Divan.

The latter acted, in these critical circumstances, with a firmness and propriety of bearing which would have done honour to the most experienced cabinets of Europe. At the same time that the Sultan refused to comply with the demands, or rather the orders, of the two Emperors, he wrote to the Tsar to tell him that he would not discuss with him the question of right raised by the interpretation of the treaties, but that he appealed to his friendship and to his honour, begging him to take it in good part that the Turkish Government refused to take a measure which would ruin it in the eyes of the world. He offered, moreover, once more, himself to place the refugees in a position in which they should be harmless. Abdul Medjid sent one of the wisest and most clever men in his Empire, Fuad Effendi, to take this letter to St. Petersburg. A similar letter was written to Vienna, but this was to be handed to the Emperor of Austria by the Turkish Envoy at that Court, thus very visibly marking the difference in the value attached to the consent of the two Sovereigns. This news reached me at the end of September. My first care was to communicate it to England. At the same time[1] I wrote a private letter to our Ambassador, in which I said :

[1] Private letter, 1 October, 1849.

" The conduct of England, who is more interested in this affair than we are, and less exposed in the conflict that may arise from it, must have a great influence upon our own. The English Cabinet must be asked clearly and categorically to state *how far* it is prepared to go. I have not forgotten the Piedmont affair. If they want us to assist them, they must dot their i's. It is possible that, in that case, we shall be found to be very determined ; otherwise, not. It is also very important that you should ascertain the opinions produced by these events upon the Tories of all shades ; for with a government conducted on the parliamentary system, and consequently variable, the support of the party in power is not always a sufficient guarantee."

In spite of the gravity of the circumstances, the English ministers, who were at that moment dispersed on account of the parliamentary holidays, took a long time before meeting ; for in that country, the only country in the world where the aristocracy still carries on the government, the majority of the ministers are both great landed proprietors and, as a rule, great noblemen. They were at that time on their estates, relaxing from the fatigue and *ennui* of business ; and they showed no undue hurry to return to Town. During this interval, all the English press, without distinction of party, took fire.[1] It raged against the two Emperors, and inflamed public opinion in favour of Turkey. The British Government, thus stimulated, at once took up its position. This time it did not hesitate, for it was a question, as it said itself, not only of the Sultan, but of England's influence in the world.[2] It therefore decided, first, that representations

[1] Cf. *The Triumph of Lord Palmerston. A study of Public Opinion in England before the Crimean War* by Kingsley Martin, London 1924. (M.)
[2] Private letter from M. Drouyn de Lhuys, 2 October, 1849.

should be made to Russia and Austria ; secondly, that the British Mediterranean Squadron should proceed to the Dardanelles, to give confidence to the Sultan and, if necessary, defend Constantinople. We were invited to do the same, and to act in common. The same evening, the order was dispatched to the British Fleet to sail.

The news of these decisive resolutions threw me into great perplexity. I did not hesitate to think that we should approve the generous conduct of our Ambassador, and come to the aid of the Sultan ;[1] but as to a warlike attitude, I did not believe that it would as yet be wise to adopt it. The English invited us to do as they did ; but our position was very different from theirs. In defending Turkey, sword in hand, England risked her fleet ; we, our very existence. The English Ministers could rely that, in that extremity, Parliament and the nation would support them ; whereas we were almost certain to be abandoned by the Assembly, and even by the country, if things came so far as war. For our wretchedness and danger at home made people's minds at that moment insensible to everything else. I was convinced, moreover, that in this case threats, instead of serving to forward our designs, were calculated to frustrate them. If Russia, for it was really with her alone that we had to do, should chance to be disposed to open the question of the partition of the East by invading Turkey—a contingency that I found it difficult to believe in—the sending of our fleets would not prevent the crisis ; and if it was really only a question (as was probably the case) of taking revenge upon the Poles, it would aggravate it, by making it difficult for the Tsar to retract, and causing his vanity to join forces with his resentment.

I went to the meeting of the Council with these reflections. I at once saw that the President was already

[1] Private letters to Lamoricière and Beaumont, 5 and 9 October, 1849.

decided and even pledged, as he himself declared to us. This resolve on his part had been inspired by Lord Normanby, the British Ambassador, an eighteenth-century diplomatist, who had worked himself into a strong position in Louis Napoleon's good graces [by living and even allowing his wife to live in the company of Miss Howard, who was the President's mistress, or, to speak more correctly, his favourite mistress, for he had several mistresses at the same time]. The majority of my colleagues thought as he did, that we should without hesitation adopt the line of joint action to which the English invited us, and like them send our fleet to the Dardanelles.

Failing in my endeavour to have a measure which I considered premature postponed, I asked that at least, before it was carried out, they should consult Falloux, whose state of health had compelled him to leave Paris for a time and go to the country. Lanjuinais went down to him for this purpose, reported the affair to him, and came back and reported to us that Falloux had without hesitation given his opinion in favour of the dispatch of the fleet. The order was sent off at once. However, Falloux had acted without consulting the leaders of the majority or his friends, and even without due reflection as to the consequences of his action ; he had yielded to a movement of impulse, as sometimes happened to him, for nature had made him frivolous and light-headed before education and habit had rendered him calculating to the pitch of duplicity. It is probable that, after his conversation with Lanjuinais, he received advice, or himself made certain reflections, opposed to the opinion he had given. He therefore wrote me a very long and very involved letter,[1] in which he pretended to have misunderstood Lanjuinais (this was impossible, for Lanjuinais was the clearest and most lucid of men both in speech and action). He revoked his opinion and sought

[1] Letter from Falloux, 11 October, 1849.

to evade his responsibility ; and I replied at once with this note :

" My Dear Colleague,

"The Council has taken its resolution, and at this late hour there is nothing to be done but await events ; moreover, in this matter the responsibility of the whole Council is the same. There is no individual responsibility. I was not in favour of the measure ; but now that the measure is taken, I am prepared to defend it against all comers."[1]

While giving a lesson to Falloux, I was none the less anxious and embarrassed as to the part I was called upon to play. I cared little for what would happen at Vienna ; for in this business I credited Austria merely with the position of a satellite. But what would the Tsar do, who had involved himself so rashly and, apparently, so irrevocably in his relations towards the Sultan, and whose pride had been put to so severe a test by our threats ? Fortunately I had two able agents at St. Petersburg and Vienna, to whom I could explain myself without reserve.

"Take up the business very gently", I recommended them,[2] "be careful not to set our adversaries' self-esteem against us, avoid too great and too ostensible an intimacy with the English Ambassadors, whose Government is detested by the Court at which you are, although nevertheless maintaining good relations with those ambassadors. In order to attain success, adopt a friendly tone, and do not try to frighten people. Show our position as it is ; we do not want war ; we detest it ; we dread it ; but we cannot act dishonourably. We cannot

[1] Letter to Falloux, 12 October, 1849.
[2] Private letters to Lamoricière and Beaumont, 5 and 9 October, 1849.

advise the Porte, when it comes to us for our opinion, to commit an act of cowardice ; and should the courage which it has displayed, and which we have approved of, bring it into danger, we cannot, either, refuse it the assistance it asks of us. A way must therefore be found out of the difficulty. Is Kossuth's skin worth a general war ? Is it to the interest of the Powers that the Eastern Question should be opened at this moment and in this fashion ? Cannot a way be found by which everybody's honour will be saved ? What do they want, after all ? Do they only want to have a few poor devils handed over to them ? That is assuredly not worth so great a quarrel ; but if it were a pretext, if at the bottom of this business lurked the desire, as a matter of fact, to lay hands upon the Ottoman Empire, then it would certainly be a general war that they wanted ; for ultra-pacific though we are, we should never allow Constantinople to fall without striking a blow."

The affair was happily over by the time these instructions reached St. Petersburg. Lamoricière had conformed to them before he received them. He had acted in this circumstance with an amount of prudence and discretion which surprised those who did not know him, but which did not astonish me in the least. I knew that he was impetuous by temperament, but that his mind, formed in the school of Arabian diplomacy, the wisest of all diplomacies, was circumspect and acute to the pitch of artifice.

Lamoricière, as soon as he had heard rumours of the quarrel directly from Russia, hastened to express, very vividly, though in an amicable tone, that he disapproved of what had happened at Constantinople ; but he took care to make no official and, above all, no threatening representations. Although acting in concert with the British Minister, he carefully avoided compromising himself with him in any joint steps ; and when Fuad Effendi, bearing Abdul Medjid's letter, arrived, he let him know secretly that he would not go to see him, in order not to imperil the success of the negotiation, but that Turkey could rely upon France.

He was admirably assisted by this envoy from the Grand Seignior, who concealed a very quick and cunning intelligence beneath his Turkish skin. Although the Sultan had appealed for the support of France and England, Fuad, on arriving at St. Petersburg, showed no inclination even to call upon the representatives of these two Powers. He refused to see anybody before his audience of the Tsar, to whose free will alone, he said, he looked for the success of his mission.

The Emperor must have experienced a feeling of bitter displeasure on observing the want of success attending his threats, and the unexpected turn that things had taken ; but he had the strength to restrain himself. In his heart he was not desirous to open the Eastern Question, even though, not long before, he had gone so far as to say, " The Ottoman Empire is dead ; we have only to arrange for its funeral ".

To go to war in order to force the Sultan to violate the Law of Nations was a very difficult matter. He would have been aided in this by the barbaric passions of his people, but reproved by the opinion of the whole civilized world. He knew what was happening in England and France. He resolved to yield before he was threatened. The great Emperor therefore drew back, to the immeasurable surprise of his subjects and even of foreigners. He received Fuad in audience, and withdrew the demand he had made upon the Sultan. Austria hastened to follow his example. When Lord Palmerston's note arrived at St. Petersburg, all was over. The best would have been to say nothing ; but while we, in this business, had only aimed at success, the British Cabinet had also sought for noise. It required it to make a response to the irritation of the country. Lord Bloomfield, the British

Minister, presented himself at Count Nesselrode's the day after the Emperor's decision became known ; and was very coldly received.[1] He read him the note in which Lord Palmerston asked, in polite but peremptory phrases, that the Sultan should not be forced to hand over the refugees. The Russian replied that he neither understood the aim nor the object of this demand ; that the affair to which he doubtless referred was arranged ; and that, in any case, England had nothing to say in the matter. Lord Bloomfield asked how things stood. Count Nesselrode haughtily refused to give him any explanation ; it would be equivalent, he said, to recognizing England's right to interfere in an affair that did not concern her. And when the British Envoy insisted upon at any rate leaving a copy of the note in Count Nesselrode's hands, the latter, after first refusing, at last accepted the document with an ill grace and dismissed his visitor, saying carelessly that he would reply to the note, that it was a terribly long one, and that it would be very tiresome. "France", added the Chancellor, " has already made me say the same thing ; but she made me say it earlier and better."

At this moment when we learnt the end of the dangerous quarrel, the Cabinet, after thus witnessing a happy conclusion to the two great pieces of foreign business that still kept the peace of the world in suspense, the Piedmont War and the Hungarian War—at that moment, the Cabinet fell.

[1] Letter from Lamoricière, 19 October, 1849.

APPENDICES

APPENDICES

I have recently discovered these four notes in the charter-room at Tocqueville, where my grandfather had carefully deposited, by the side of our most precious family archives, all the manuscripts of his brother that came into his possession. They seemed to me to throw some light upon the Revolution of February and the question of the revision of the Constitution in 1851, and to merit publication together with the Recollections.

COMTE DE TOCQUEVILLE.
(Editor of the first French Edition.)

I.

Gustave de Beaumont's version of the 24th of February.

I HAVE to-day (24 October, 1850) had a conversation with Beaumont which is worth noting. This is what he told me :

" On the 24th of February, at seven o'clock in the morning, Jules Lasteyrie and another (I have forgotten the name which Beaumont mentioned) came to fetch me to take me to M. Thiers, where Barrot, Duvergier, and several others were expected."

I asked him if he knew what had passed during the night between Thiers and the King. He replied :

" I was told by Thiers, and especially by Duvergier, who had at once taken a note of Thiers' narrative, that Thiers had been summoned at about one o'clock ; that he had found the King in an undecided frame of mind ; that he had at once told him that he could only come in with Barrot and Duvergier ; that the King, after raising many objections, had appeared to yield ; that he had put off Thiers till the morning ; that nevertheless, as he showed him to the door, he had told him that as yet no one was bound one way or the other."

Evidently the King reserved the right of attempting to form another combination before the morning.

" I must here," continued Beaumont, " tell you a curious anecdote. Do you know how Bugeaud was occupied during that decisive night, at the Tuileries itself, where he had just received the command-in-chief ? Listen : Bugeaud's hope and ambition was to become Minister of War when Thiers should come into power. Things were so turning out, as he clearly saw, as to make this appointment impossible : but what preoccupied him was to assure his preponderance at the War Office even if he was not at the head of it. Consequently, on the night of the 24th of February, or rather in the early morning, Bugeaud with his own hand wrote to Thiers from the Tuileries a letter of four pages, of which the substance was :

" ' I understand the difficulties which prevent you from making me your Minister of War ; nevertheless I have always liked you, and I am sure that we shall one day govern together. However, I understand the present reasons, and I give way before them ; but I beg you, at least, to give M. Magne, who is my friend, the place of Under-Secretary of State at the War Office.' "

Resuming his general narrative, Beaumont continued :

" When I arrived at the Place Saint-Georges, Thiers and his friends had already left for the Tuileries. I hastily followed them, and arrived at the same time as they did. The appearance of Paris was already formidable ; however, the King received us as usual, with the same copious language and the same mannerisms that you know of. Before being shown in to him (at least, I believe it was here that Beaumont placed this incident), we talked about affairs among ourselves. I insisted urgently upon Bugeaud's dismissal. ' If you want to oppose force to the popular movement,' I said, ' by all means make use of Bugeaud's name and audacity ; but if you wish to attempt conciliation and you suspend hostilities [1] . . . then Bugeaud's name is a contradiction.' The others seconded me, and Thiers reluctantly and with hesitation gave way. They compromised the matter as you know : Bugeaud nominally retained the command-in-chief, and Lamoricière was placed at the head of the National Guard. Thiers and Barrot entered the King's closet, and I do not know what happened there. The order had been given to the troops everywhere to cease firing, and to fall back upon the Palace and make way for the National Guard. I myself with Rémusat, hurriedly drew up the proclamation informing the people of these orders and explaining them. At nine o'clock it was agreed that Thiers and Barrot should personally attempt to make an appeal to the people ; Thiers was stopped on the staircase and induced to turn back, but with difficulty, I am bound to admit. Barrot set out alone, and I followed him."

Here Beaumont's account is identical with Barrot's.

" Barrot was wonderful throughout this expedition," said Beaumont. " I had difficulty in making him turn back, although when we had once arrived at the barricade at the Porte Saint-Denis, it would have been impossible to go further. Our return made the situation worse : we brought in our wake, by effecting a passage for it, a crowd more hostile than that which we had traversed in going ; by the time we arrived at the Place Vendôme, Barrot feared lest he should take the Tuileries by assault, in spite of himself, with the multitude which followed him ; he slipped away and returned home. I came back to the Château. The situation seemed to me very serious but far from desperate, and I was filled with surprise on perceiving the disorder that had gained all minds during my absence, and the terrible confusion that already reigned at the Tuileries. I was not quite able to understand what had happened, or to learn what news they received to turn everything topsy-turvy in this fashion. I was dying of hunger and fatigue ; I went up to a table and hurriedly took some food. Ten times, during this meal of

[1] This clearly shows independently of what Beaumont told me positively, how absolutely the new Cabinet had made up its mind to yield.

three or four minutes, an aide-de-camp of the King or of one of the
Princes came to look for me, spoke to me in confused language, and
left me without properly understanding my reply. I quickly joined
Thiers, Rémusat, Duvergier, and one or two others who were to
compose the new Cabinet. We went together to the King's closet :
this was the only Council at which I was present. Thiers spoke, and
started a long homily on the duties of the King and the paterfami-
lias. ' That is to say, you advise me to abdicate,' said the King, who
was but indifferently affected by the touching part of the speech
and came straight to the point. Thiers assented, and gave his reasons.
Duvergier supported him with great vivacity. Knowing nothing of
what had happened, I displayed my astonishment and exclaimed
that all was not lost. Thiers seemed much annoyed at my outburst,
and I could not prevent myself from believing that the secret aim
of Thiers and Duvergier had, from the first, been to get rid of the
King, on whom they could no longer rely, and to govern in the
name of the Duc de Nemours or the Duchesse d'Orléans, after
forcing the King to abdicate. The King, who had struck me as very
firm up to a certain moment, seemed towards the end to surrender
himself entirely."

Here there is a void in my memory in Beaumont's account, which
I will fill up from another conversation. I come to the scene of the
abdiction, which followed :

" During the interval, events and news growing worse and the
panic increasing, Thiers had declared that already he was no longer
possible (which was perhaps true), and that Barrot was scarcely so.
He then disappeared—at least, I did not see him again during the
last moments—which was very wrong of him, for although he
declined the Ministry, he ought not, at so critical a juncture, to have
abandoned the Princes, and he should have remained to advise
them, although no longer their Minister. I was present at the final
scene of the abdication. The Duc de Montpensier begged his father
to write and urged him so eagerly that the King stopped and said,
' But look here, I can't write faster.' The Queen was heroical and
desperate : knowing that I had appeared opposed to the abdication
at the Council, she took my hands and told me that such a piece of
cowardice must not be allowed to be consummated, that we should
defend ourselves, that she would let herself be killed, before the
King's eyes, before they could reach him. The abdication was signed
nevertheless, and the Duc de Nemours begged me to run and tell
Marshal Gérard, who was at the further end of the Carrousel, that
I had seen the King sign, so that he might announce officially to the
people that the King had abdicated. I hastened there, and returned ;

all the rooms were empty. I went from room to room without meeting a soul. I went down into the garden ; I there met Barrot, who had come over from the Ministry of the Interior, and was indulging in the same useless quest. The King had escaped by the main avenue : the Duchesse d'Orléans seemed to have gone by the underground passage to the water-side. No necessity had compelled them to leave the Château, which was then in perfect safety, and which was not invaded by the people until an hour after it had been abandoned. Barrot was determined at all costs to assist the Duchess. He hurriedly had horses prepared for her, the young Prince and ourselves, and wanted us to throw ourselves all together into the midst of the people—the only chance in fact, and a feeble one at that, that remained to us. Unable to rejoin the Duchess, we left for the Ministry of the Interior. You met us on the road ; you know the rest."

2.

Barrot's version of the 24th of February

(10 *October,* 1850)

" I believe that M. Molé only refused the Ministry after the firing had commenced on the Boulevard. Thiers told me that he had been sent for at one in the morning ; that he had asked the King to appoint me as the necessary man ; that the King had at first resisted and then yielded ; and that at last he had adjourned our meeting to nine o'clock in the morning at the Palace.

" At five o'clock Thiers came to my house to awake me ; we talked : he went home, and I called for him at eight. I found him quietly shaving. It is a great pity that the King and M. Thiers thus wasted the time that elapsed between one and eight o'clock. When he had finished shaving, we went to the Château ; the population already was greatly excited ; barricades were being built, and even a few shots had already been fired from houses near the Tuileries. However, we found the King still very calm and retaining his usual manner. He addressed me with the commonplaces which you can imagine for yourself. At that hour, Bugeaud was still general-in-chief. I strongly persuaded Thiers not to take office under the colour of that name, and at least to modify it by giving the command of the National Guard to Lamoricière, who was there. Thiers accepted this arrangement, which was agreed to by the King and Bugeaud himself.

" I next proposed to the King that he should dissolve the Chamber of Deputies. ' Never, never ! ' he said ; he lost his temper and left the room, slamming the door in the faces of Thiers and me. It was quite clear that he only consented to give us office in order to save the first moment, and that he intended, after compromising us with the people, to throw us over with the assistance of Parliament. Of course, at any ordinary time, I should at once have withdrawn ; but the gravity of the situation made me stay, and I proposed to present myself to the people, myself to apprise them of the formation of the new Cabinet, and to calm them. In the impossibility of our having anything printed and posted up in time, I looked upon myself as a walking placard. I must do Thiers the justice to say that he wished to accompany me, and that it was I who refused, as I dreaded the bad impression his presence might make.

" I therefore set out ; I went up to each barricade unarmed ; the muskets were lowered, the barricades opened ; there were cries of ' Reform for ever ! long live Barrot ! ' We thus went to the Porte Saint-Denis, where we found a barricade two stories high and defended by men who made no sign of concurrence in my words and betrayed no intention of allowing us to pass the barricade. We were therefore compelled to retrace our steps. On returning, I found the people more excited than when I had come ; nevertheless, I heard not a single seditious cry, nor anything that announced an immediate revolution. The only word that I heard of grave import was from Étienne Arago. He came up to me and said, ' If the King does not abdicate, we shall have a revolution before eight o'clock tonight.' I thus came to the Place Vendôme ; thousands of men followed me, crying, ' To the Tuileries ! to the Tuileries ! ' I reflected what was the best thing to do. To go to the Tuileries at the head of that multitude was to make myself the absolute master of the situation, but by means of an act which might have seemed violent and revolutionary. Had I known what was happening at the moment in the Tuileries, I should not have hesitated ; but as yet I felt no anxiety. The attitude of the people did not yet seem decided. I knew that all the troops were falling back upon the Château ; that the Government was there, and the generals ; I could not therefore imagine the panic which, shortly afterwards, placed it in the hands of the mob. I turned to the right and returned home to take a moment's rest ; I had not eaten anything yet and was utterly exhausted. After a few minutes, Malleville sent word from the Ministry of the Interior that it was urgent that I should come and sign the telegrams to the departments. I went in my carriage, and was cheered by the people ; from there, I set out to walk to the Palace. I was still ignorant of all that had happened. When I reached the quay, opposite the garden, I saw a regiment of Dragoons returning to barracks ; the colonel said to me, ' The King has abdicated ; all the troops are withdrawing'. I hurried ; when I reached the wicket-gates, I had great difficulty in penetrating to the courtyard, as the troops were crowding out through every opening. At last I reached the yard, which I found almost empty ; the Duc de Nemours was there ; I entreated him to tell me where the Duchesse d'Orléans was ; he replied that he did not know, but that he believed that at that moment she was in the pavilion at the water-side, I hastened there ; I was told that the Duchess was not there. I forced the door and went through the rooms, which were, in fact, empty. I left the Tuileries, recommending Havin, whom I met, not to bring the Duchess, if he found her, to the Chamber, with which there was nothing to be done. My intention had been, if I had found the Duchess and her son, to put them on horseback and throw myself with them among the people : I had even had the horses got ready.

" Not finding the Princess, I returned to the Ministry of the Interior ; I met you on the road, you know what happened there. I was sent for in haste to go to the Chamber. I had scarcely arrived when the leaders of the Extreme Left surrounded me and dragged me almost by main force to the first office ; there, they begged me to propose to the Assembly the nomination of a Provisional Government, of which I was to be a member. I sent them about their business, and returned to the Chamber. You know the rest."

3.

Some Incidents of the 24th of February, 1848.

M. Dufaure's efforts to prevent the Revolution of February—Responsibility of M. Thiers, which renders them futile.

To-day (19 October, 1850), Rivet recalled and fixed with me the circumstances of an incident well worth remembering,

In the course of the week preceding that in which the Monarchy was overthrown, a certain number of Conservative deputies began to feel an anxiety which was not shared by the Ministers and their colleagues. They thought that it was more advisable to overthrow the Cabinet, provided that this could be done without violence, than to risk the adventure of the banquets. One of them, M. Sallandrouze, made the following proposal to M. Billault (the banquet was to take place on Tuesday the 22nd) that on the 21st M. Dufaure and his friends should move an urgent order of the day, drawn up in consultation with Sallandrouze and those in whose name he spoke, some forty in number. The order of the day should be voted by them on condition that, on its side, the Opposition should give up the banquet and restrain the people.

On Sunday, the 20th of February, we met at Rivet's to discuss this proposal. There were present, as far as I am able to remember, Dufaure, Billault, Lanjuinais, Corcelles, Ferdinand Barrot, Talabot, Rivet, and myself.

Sallandrouze's proposal was explained to us by Billault ; we accepted it at once, and drafted an order of the day in consequence. I myself drafted it, and this draft, with some modifications, was accepted by my friends. The terms in which it was couched (I no longer remember them) were very moderate, but the adoption of this order of the day would inevitably entail the resignation of the Cabinet.

There remained to be fulfilled the condition of the vote of the Conservatives, the withdrawal of the banquet. We had had nothing to do with this measure, and consequently we were not able to prevent it. It was agreed that one of us should at once go in search of Duvergier de Hauranne and Barrot, and propose that they should act according to the condition demanded. Rivet was selected for this negotiation, and we adjourned our meeting till the evening to know how he had succeeded.

In the evening he came and reported to us as follows :

Barrot had eagerly entered into the opening offered to him ; he effusively seized Rivet's hands, and declared that he was prepared to do all that he was asked in this sense ; he seemed relieved of a great weight on beholding the possibility of escaping from the responsibility of the banquet. But he added that he was not engaged in this enterprise alone, and that he must come to an understanding with his friends, without whom he could do nothing. How well we knew it !

Rivet went on to Duvergier's, and was told that he was at the Conservatoire of Music, but that he would return home before dinner. Rivet waited. Duvergier returned. Rivet told him of the proposal of the Conservatives and of our order of the day. Duvergier received this communication somewhat disdainfully ; they had gone too far, he said, to draw back : the Conservatives had repented too late ; he, Duvergier, and his friends could not, without losing their popularity and perhaps all their influence with the masses, undertake to make the latter give us the proposed demonstration. " However," he added, " I am only giving you my first and personal impression ; but I am going to dine with Thiers, and I will send you a note this evening to let you know our final decision."

This note came while we were there ; it said briefly that the opinion expressed by Duvergier before dinner was also that of Thiers, and that the idea which we had suggested must be abandoned. We broke up at once ; the die was cast !

I have no doubt that, among the reasons for Thiers' and Duvergier's refusal, the first place must be given to this, which was not expressed : that if the Ministry fell quietly, by the combined effect of a part of the Conservatives and ourselves, and upon an order of the day presented by us, we should come into power, and not those who had built up all this great machinery of the banquets in order to attain it.

Dufaure's conduct on the 24th of February, 1848.

Rivet told me to-day (19 October, 1850) that he had never talked with Dufaure of what happened to him on the 24th of February ; but that he had gathered the following from conversation with members of his family or of his immediate surroundings :

On the 23rd of February, at about a quarter past six, M. Molé, after concerting with M. de Montalivet, sent to beg Dufaure to come and see him. Dufaure, on his road to M. Molé's, called on Rivet and asked him to wait for him, because he intended to come back to Rivet on leaving M. Molé. Dufaure did not return, and Rivet did not see him till some time after, but he believed that, on arriving at Molé's, Dufaure had a rather long conversation with him, and then went away, declaring that he did not wish to join the new Cabinet, and that, in his opinion, circumstances called for the men who had brought about the movement, that is to say, Thiers and Barrot.

He returned greatly alarmed at the appearance of Paris, found his wife and mother-in-law still more alarmed, and at five o'clock in the morning of the 24th, set out with them and took them to Vanves. He himself came back ; I saw him at about eight or nine o'clock, and I do not remember that he told me he had taken this morning journey. I was calling on him with Lanjuinais and Corcelles ; but we soon separated, arranging to meet at twelve at the

Chamber of Deputies. Dufaure did not come ; it seems that he started to do so, and in fact arrived at the Palace of the Assembly, which had, doubtless, been just at that moment invaded. What is certain is that he went on and joined his family at Vanves.

4.

My conversation with Berryer, on the 21st of June, at an appointment which I had given him at my house. We were both members of the Committee for the Revision of the Constitution.

I thus opened the conversation :

" Let us leave appearances on one side, between you and me. You are not making a revisionist but an electoral campaign."

He replied, " That is true ; you are quite right."

" Very well," I replied ; " we shall see presently if you are well advised. What I must tell you at once is that I cannot join in a manoeuvre of which the sole object is to save a section only of the moderate party at the next elections, leaving out of the calculation many others, and notably that to which I belong. You must either give the moderate Republicans a valid reason for voting for the Revision, by giving it a republican character, or else expect us to do our best to spike your guns."

He agreed, but raised difficulties that originated with the passions and prejudices of his party. We discussed for some time what was to be done, and at last we came to the policy which he was following.

This is what I said to him on this subject, of which I particularly wish to retain the impression. I said :

" Berryer, you are dragging us all, in spite of ourselves, into a plight for which you will have to bear the sole responsibility, you may be quite sure of that. If the Legitimists had joined those who wished to fight against the President, the fight might still be possible. You have dragged your party, in spite of itself, in an opposite direction ; henceforth, we can no longer resist ; we cannot remain alone with the Montagnards ; we must give way since you give way ; but what will be the consequence ? I can see your thought, it is quite clear : you think that circumstances render the President's ascendancy irresistible and the movement which carries the country towards him insurmountable. Unable to fight against the current, you throw yourselves into it, at the risk of making it more violent still, but in the hope that it will land you and your friends in the next Assembly, in addition to various other sections of the party of order, which is not very sympathetic with the President. There alone you think that you will find a solid resting place from which to resist him, and you think that, by working his business to-day, you will be able to keep together, in the next Assembly, a group of men able to cope with him. To struggle against the tide which carries him at this moment is to make one's self unpopular and ineligible and to deliver the party to the Socialists and the Bonapartists, neither of whom you wish to see triumph : well and good ! Your plan has its plausible side, but it fails in one principal respect, which is this : I could understand you if the election were to take place to-morrow, and if you were at once to gather the fruits of your manoeuvre, as at the December election ; but there is nearly a year between now and the next elections. You will not succeed in having them held in the spring, if you succeed in having them held at all. Between now and then, do you imagine that the Bonapartist movement, aided, precipitated by you, will cease ? Do you not see that, after asking you for a Revision of the Constitution, public opinion, stirred up by all the agents of the Executive and led by our own weakness, will ask us for something more, and then for something more still, until we are driven openly to favour the illegal re-election of the President and purely and simply to work his business for him ? Can you go as far as that ? Would your party be willing to, if you are ? No ! You will therefore come to a moment when you will have to stop short, to stand firm on your ground, to resist the combined effort of the nation and the Executive Power ; in other words, on the one hand to become unpopular, and on the other to lose that support, or at least that electoral neutrality, of the Government which you desire. You will have enslaved yourselves, you will have immensely strengthened the forces opposed to you, and that is all. I tell you this: either you will pass completely and for ever under the President's yoke, or you will lose, just when it is ripe for gathering, all the fruit of your manoeuvre, and you will simply have taken upon yourself, in your own eyes and the country's, the responsibility of having contributed to raise this Power, which will perhaps, in spite of the mediocrity of the man, and thanks to the extraordinary power of circumstances, become the heir of the Revolution and our master."

Berryer seemed to me to rest tongue-tied, and the time having come to part, we parted.

5.

SPEECH BY M. DE TOCQUEVILLE

on the Roman Expedition delivered in the Legislative National Assembly on October 18th, 1849.

M. DE TOCQUEVILLE, Minister for Foreign Affairs.

Gentlemen, the Government thought that before opening this debate it might be of advantage for the discussion and agreeable to the Assembly that they should inform it of the progress and purpose of the negotiations which are to be the subject of the debate. This, Gentlemen, is the task I am here to fulfil. I do not intend to discuss the matter, discussion will come later. All I intend to do for the moment is to state the facts, and the only credit to which I mean to lay claim is that my exposition will be made with the utmost candour and absolute accuracy. Moreover, after every one of my statements I shall ask the Assembly's leave to read to them the relevant documents. To tell the truth, Gentlemen, the history of these negotiations should only begin with the taking of Rome.

Believe me, I have no intention of going into the past history of the debates that took place before that date. I would merely observe that when I reflect as to what was the desire of all—I repeat all—those who voted for the Rome expedition, I think I am justified in stating that they all desired the restoration of Pius IX.

ON THE LEFT : No ! No !

ON THE RIGHT ! You, you voted against it.

M. BERTHOLON : M. de Lamoricière protested against it. (Objections on the right.)

M. LATRADE : And M. Jules Favre, the Rapporteur.

M. HEECKEREN : M. Jules Favre did not vote on the findings of his own report. He abstained.

(Excited comments.)

THE PRESIDENT : Do you wish this to be a debate or a wrangle ? Which do you want, one or the other ? (Applause on the right, protests on the left.)

Here are the names of the members inscribed to speak for and against the findings of the Commission.

Against : MM. MATHIEU (la Drôme), Victor HUGO, Emmanuel ARAGO, SAVATIER-LAROCHE, MAUGUIN, Emile BARRAULT, JOLY, Edgar QUINET, Francisque BOUVET, CAVAIGNAC.

M. LATRADE : Does this answer the question ? (Noise on the left.)

THE PRESIDENT : And now here are the names of the speakers for the findings : MM. THIRIOT DE LA ROSIERE, de MONTALEMBERT, d'OLIVIER, FABVIER, de MONTIGNY, de la MOSKOWA.

All speakers on both sides will use parliamentary language and will refrain from noisy interruptions against which I protest from the outset. (Hear ! Hear !)

THE MINISTER FOR FOREIGN AFFAIRS : Gentlemen, I would observe for the benefit of those who interrupt me before I have been able even to finish my sentence or to make my idea clear that I am not speaking of those who have voted for this expedition (renewed interruptions from the left) and I say that in the beginning if not all—then almost all, if you like—of those. . . .

VOICE ON THE LEFT : You know nothing about it.

MANY VOICES ON THE RIGHT AND IN THE CENTRE : Do not interrupt. Order ! Order !

THE PRESIDENT, turning to the left:

We must at least know whether you mean to permit us to have a free discussion in this Assembly.

VOICE ON THE RIGHT : Call to order !

GENERAL TARTAS : We call for the strict application of the orders.

THE PRESIDENT : I do not know who the interrupters are. I hear them but I do not see them. Continue, Monsieur le Ministre.

THE MINISTER FOR FOREIGN AFFAIRS : What I say, even at the risk of being interrupted a third time, is that nearly all if not all those who voted for the Rome expedition might have differed as to the conditions under which Pius IX was to be re-established, but that all were in favour of this restoration.

This is what I say.

On the other hand I assert that on all sides it was recognized that this restoration must be both liberal and lenient. This was the view expressed by the Government and by the various speakers and not a voice was raised against it. It was said not only here, but was repeated officially beyond the mountains and there also nobody protested.

I am justified, therefore, in saying that according to France's original views and wishes our Rome expedition was to end in the restoration of Pius IX, but this restoration was to be liberal and lenient.

Well, Gentlemen, this is the point of view which has governed my own and the whole Government's negotiations and actions.

No sooner had Rome been taken than we encouraged—we exercised no pressure—we encouraged to the best of our ability the restoration of Pius IX. We did this all the more readily since we were then convinced—a conviction which has since been confirmed—that the restoration of Pius IX was in accordance with the wishes of the vast majority of the inhabitants of the Roman States although it might present different aspects according to the principles held. (Noise and protest on the left, applause on the right.)

SEVERAL MEMBERS ON THE LEFT : How do you know ? Ask them !

M. DUFAURE, MINISTER FOR HOME AFFAIRS : It is indisputable.

M. CHARLES ABBATUCCI : Except for the Roman citizens here. (Laughter.)

THE MINISTER FOR FOREIGN AFFAIRS : That was our conviction and this conviction was further strengthened by subsequent events. As I said before, I am not arguing, I am merely giving an account of the actions of the French Government. They will be discussed and judged later. It is no use interrupting me now, you will have plenty of time to speak later on.

Once Pius IX was re-established, what was our attitude toward him ?

Some reproached us with having attempted to coerce the Pope, others accused us of the contrary.

I may state here and now, most categorically, that never has it entered the French Government's mind to use the force in its hands to coerce the Holy Father. (Hear ! Hear !)

We would never have dreamt of doing so for two reasons : Firstly, because here we were dealing not only with a Prince but with a Sovereign Pontiff, and that Pontiff is the head of the Catholic religion, and a Government which represents a nation that is essentially Catholic could not contemplate using violence against a Prince who is at the same time the Supreme Head of that religion. (Hear ! Hear !) Our second reason, if we need give a reason for such actions, was that the Pontifical Power is a power immaterial, incompressible, intangible (Noise on the left, approval on the right and in the Centre) which at all times has worn down the greatest material powers on earth and against which they will never prevail. (Dissent and approval as before.) The only means by which this Catholic Government could—I will not say coerce, Heaven forbid that I should use such a term—the Pontifical Power, but exercise over it a legitimate and powerful influence, is to require of it things that are fair, wise and equitable, in conformity with the interests of the Catholic peoples, of the populations under its sway and in accordance with reason, good sense and justice ; to demand these things on behalf of all enlightened Catholics in the world, to demand them respectfully, but straightforwardly and publicly before the whole world. (Hear ! Hear !)

This we did, and this we are doing to this day.

What was it then that we asked for ? I will state plainly at the outset that in our negotiations with the Pope we did not press for the grant of institutions which might immediately establish great political liberty. We refrained from doing so because recent history and our own experiences had taught us that in the state in which the Roman people are at present faced as they are with a moderate liberal party disorganized and terrified, an anarchical party full of folly and fury and an inert mass, it would have been unwise to ask the Holy Father too insistently to restore the institutions which had already led to his overthrow. Therefore we did not press, I say again, for institutions conferring great political liberty. What we did ask for were institutions which would immediately ensure the welfare and civil liberty of the Roman States and at the same time would prepare them for political liberty as well within a reasonable time. That is what we asked for.

Now, Gentlemen, in order to leave these generalities and to come to particulars, I cannot do better than read to you the dispatches which bear out what I have had the honour to explain to you.

The dispatch or rather the note which I propose to read to the Assembly is by MM. de Corcelles and de Rayneval. It is dated August 19th and addressed to Cardinal Antonelli. The first part of this note is only a repetition of one of my dispatches of August 4th. The second part is the work, more particularly, of M. de Corcelles. Although very seriously ill he nevertheless in his ardent patriotism and zeal, found the necessary strength to write, as it were, with a dying hand the lines I am about to read to you. (Ironical laughter on some of the benches of the left.)

A VOICE FROM THE RIGHT : Very good, gentlemen, we know you respect nothing.

THE MINISTER FOR FOREIGN AFFAIRS : The note concludes with the following words :

" The Government of the Republic submit to the Holy Father the following demands which they consider it their right and their duty to persist in advancing. . . ."

(You see that these demands had been presented before.)

" 1) that several of the general principles set forth in Article 1 of the Statute of March 17th, 1848, be formally recognized, in particular those which guarantee personal liberty, sanction the public debt and safeguard the inviolability of private property.

" These are conservative principles common to all civilized societies whatever political form they may adopt.

" 2) that a new organization of the Courts of Law should afford real legal safeguards to the citizens.

" 3) that civil laws be promulgated similar to those governing the status of persons and property in Upper Italy and the Kingdom of Naples, laws taken from our own Code of Civil Law.

" 4) that elected communal and provincial assemblies be set up.

" 5) that the public administration be secularized.

" 6) His Holiness intends to re-establish the Council of State which he had set up in 1847 to advise in legislative and financial questions. The Government of the Republic would prefer that the members of this Assembly should be elected by the local bodies and not selected from among a list drawn up by those bodies. They consider it desirable and important that this assembly should retain a deliberative vote in matters of taxation. Besides, it would be very easy to devise a new form borrowed from certain foreign laws, which would place spiritual sovereignty quite out of reach of the assaults of some persons, without however meaning to suggest that such sovereignty could be endangered by these concessions.

" These, then, are the demands which the Government of the Republic have for a long time instructed their representatives to submit to the Government of His Holiness. The Government of the Republic noted with profound regret and deep concern that according to the declarations of the Cardinal Pro-Secretary of State at the last Conference the Pontifical Government's intentions are not exactly in conformity with the French Cabinet's ideas. Since His Holiness has been good enough to defer his final decision until France had made her ideas perfectly clear the undersigned thought that the time had come to comply with the orders they had received should the contingency arise. They therefore repeat and formally lay down the demands of France. They do not abandon the hope that these demands will be accepted by Pius IX in his generosity and they take the liberty of urging these demands upon the Pontifical Government with the profoundest respect but with the insistence which France's consistent concern for the greatness and prosperity of the Church must justify. In conclusion, the undersigned would draw His Eminence's attention to considerations of a more general and a more lofty order. They will not remind His Eminence how anxious is France, in particular, in view of her faith and public morals, that the Church should not abandon the liberal attitude which in 1848 won for it the approbation of the whole world a short time before that great and salutary revolution which reconciled the faith with the spirit of the new institutions. Nor will they remind him to what extent the general trend at that time differed from what it has become since. In political discussions as well as in the vagaries of literature there was nothing but hatred and reaction against the faith.

" Pius IX appeared and at his first words the war against the faith subsided as by a miracle. How great was the joy of the French clergy who felt that this happy pacification restored them to their proper place in the minds of the peoples. And how great was the enthusiasm with which the hopes held out by the Holy See were greeted not only by Catholics but by the very people who up to then had been their bitter opponents.

" There can be no question that religion then won one of its greatest triumphs. (Cheers and dissenting shouts.)

" It must be admitted that the reforms introduced by Pius IX gave rise to deplorable incidents, but it nevertheless constituted a providential support for the Church as a whole, this strength born of the reforms and of the hopes which had aroused such ardent and generous response.

" Is France doomed again to witness a complete reversal in the policies of the Council of the Holy See, bringing in its train as complete a reversal in the moral tendencies of the peoples ? Such a renewed reaction against religion would become a serious danger. Would this danger remain confined to France alone, would it not arise also among all Catholic nations where free discussion is possible ? Would Italy remain immune from the infection ?

" The undersigned have no doubt that His Eminence's enlightened mind will duly weigh these lofty considerations and that His Holiness will not fail to realize their full import." (Cheers from a few benches.)

THE MINISTER FOR FOREIGN AFFAIRS : The demands contained in the document I have just read have not been expanded, they have merely been further defined and detailed in a subsequent dispatch which I will not read to the Assembly, but which I shall hand to the Monitor.

Gentlemen, you have heard the nature of the demands presented by the French Government to the Holy See. We have urged them from the first day and have continued to do so to the very end. I was bound to acquaint you with them before referring to a document which, although it is not a diplomatic note, nevertheless made a deep

impression, natural and legitimate enough considering its importance and its author. I am speaking of the letter written by the
President of the Republic to one of his aides-de-camp. (Show of
keen attention.)

I have only a few words to say.

We have been asked outside this Assembly and within the Commission it appointed whether the policy laid down in the President's
letter was ours, whether it was the policy we had put forward and
supported and for which we assumed responsibility. We replied—
and I am very glad of this opportunity of giving this reply publicly
here—that this policy was exactly the same as that followed in our
dispatches. (Murmurs of approval on several benches.) The Assembly has just had an opportunity to judge for itself.

When all is said and done, what does the note of MM. de Corcelles
and de Rayneval contain that is not to be found in substance in the
letter of the President of the Republic ? What are the demands contained in the letter that we had not already put forward as you have
just heard ? The letter of the President of the Republic may be regarded as a summary—a summary in familiar terms if you like—of
our policy, but it is a faithful rendering of this policy. He interprets
it in a generous and lofty spirit. We never have and never will disclaim it. (Sensation. Murmurs of approval and dissent.)

M. PASCAL DURAT : Are you against the findings of the Commission then ?

THE MINISTER FOR FOREIGN AFFAIRS : Gentlemen,
now that you are acquainted with the contents of our principal
diplomatic documents I must say a word regarding the *Motu
Proprio*[1] which concludes the series. (Hear ! Hear !) I will not conceal from you—indeed, how could I in view of the documents I have
just read to you ?—that the *Motu Proprio* has not fully realized our
expectations.

A MEMBER ON THE LEFT : And yet you accept it !

THE MINISTER FOR FOREIGN AFFAIRS : One thing
however, must be said which is not known here ;—this *Motu
Proprio* which does not fully and immediately fulfil all the wishes of
our diplomacy has aroused the most profound misgivings and lively
opposition among the party of the old régime in Rome. This party
saw in it—or affected to see in it—the first steps in the Holy Father's
descent down the slope of liberalism which brought him to the brink

---

[1] Cf. F. A. Simpson, op. cit., pp. 81 sq. *See* also *History of Modern France* : 1815–1913,
Vol. 1., 1815–1852 by Émile Bourgeois, Cambridge 1919. Pius IX, issued the
Motu Proprio on September 12th, 1849, in which he promised reforms without
specifying any in particular. (M.)

of the abyss—yes, yes, to the abyss. This is what we must bear in mind. On the other hand it is only fair to say that the Pope's *Motu Proprio* provides for the majority of the most essential reforms which we asked for, and that those which are not explicitly provided for are contained in it in the germ, as it were, in the hopes which it holds out.

VOICE ON THE LEFT : Come ! Come !

ON THE RIGHT : Hear ! Hear !

M. BELIN : This is really charming.

THE MINISTER FOR FOREIGN AFFAIRS : What surprises me, Gentlemen, is the disbelief with which my words are received.

I ask leave of the Assembly to enter for one moment into the debate. I had no intention of doing so, but your scepticism leaves me no choice.

What were our demands ? We asked for civil reforms, judicial reforms, the *Motu Proprio* promises them. (Ironical laughter on the left.) You may doubt His Holiness' word, but you cannot deny that he has promised these reforms. (Renewed interruptions from the left.)

I was saying that these gentlemen (indicating the left) may doubt the Holy Father's word, that is their affair—for my part, I do not doubt it—but they cannot deny that the *Motu Proprio* gives a definite undertaking in that sense. (Renewed noise on the left.) I resume then, and I say : We have demanded reforms of civil and criminal law, they have been promised. We demanded municipal and provincial liberties ; they have not only been promised, but actually granted on the most liberal scale. (Outcry on the left.)

M. ODILON BARROT, President of the Council : Yes, yes, and perhaps on a larger scale than you will get !

THE MINISTER FOR FOREIGN AFFAIRS : We demanded the Consulta ; it has been granted. I am therefore fully entitled to say that several of France's demands have been immediately and fully complied with by the *Motu Proprio* and that the fulfilment of the others has been announced and promised. (Dissentient murmurs on the left.) As soon as the French Government had learned the contents of the *Motu Proprio* with mixed feelings of regret and approval, they sent the following dispatch to their Minister in Rome.

" September 30th, 1849.

" Gentlemen,

" The Government have taken note of His Holiness' manifesto of the 12th of this month. They feel bound to inform you of their views on this document and of the conclusions it suggests to them.

" The Manifesto confirms the institution of the Council of

Ministers established by Pius IX ; it sets up a Council of State ; it institutes a deliberate chamber under the name of Consulta, the direct result of elections, which will discuss all financial questions, will examine the budget and will advise on the levying, basic rate and collection of taxes. It grants or maintains far-reaching communal and provincial liberties.

" In conclusion it announces the coming reform of civil law, of judicial institutions and the rules of criminal justice.

" The institutions promised by the manifesto seemed to us lacking in some respects ; you inform us that you have already entered reservations in this connection. I fully approve of your action ; at the same time we recognize that these institutions would to a large extent meet the demands put forward by France and would introduce very notable and desirable innovations in the administration of the Papal States if, as in duty bound, Pius IX sees that they are properly carried out. Your chief duty, Gentlemen, will be to expedite to the best of your ability by disinterested and urgent advice the prompt and effective realization of the principle of liberal institutions which is adopted in the Manifesto. . . . I ask the Assembly's leave to pause for a moment for I can hardly speak. . . .

THE MINISTER FOR FOREIGN AFFAIRS, after a few minutes' rest resumes as follows :

Gentlemen, I have little to add. I have spoken of the institutions, I must now say a few words regarding the principles.

In regard to the principles we thought it right to speak in more forceful and more pressing terms than in regard to the institutions themselves. In this case, indeed, our object was not to coerce the Sovereign Pontiff to grant institutions that might seem unwise to him or repugnant to his conscience, but to be saved ourselves from seeing acts committed under our very eyes and under our own hands as it were, which would be contrary to our principles and offend French generosity. (Hear ! Hear !)

Immediately after our entry into Rome we realized that we had a duty as well as rights. Our duty was to complete the rout of, or rather to master the demagogic faction which we had already defeated. . . (violent interruptions from the left, cheers on the right).

A VOICE ON THE LEFT : Republican !

THE MINISTER FOR FOREIGN AFFAIRS : . . . . the demagogic faction which we had already defeated, and to confer upon the country we were occupying a real and lasting peace. We immediately applied ourselves to this task as will be apparent from a brief dispatch which I ask your leave to read to you. It was written before we took Rome, on June 26th : it is couched in very few words but it is clear and precise : " I repeat, once we are in Rome this town must first of all be occupied administratively and militarily. Everybody must be disarmed ; all dangerous aliens must be deported or arrested, then a Roman municipality must be set up and efforts must be made to gather together and to form a moderate liberal party." (Laughter and ironical remarks on the left.)

What we had been enjoined to do, thank God was done. Aliens who were a disturbing element were expelled, those who resisted were arrested and thus real peace was restored in the town and the States we were occupying.

A VOICE ON THE LEFT : What about the Roman Constituent Assembly. You expelled its members !

THE MINISTER FOR FOREIGN AFFAIRS : We were not content with this measure to facilitate the removal of the dangerous men of whom I have just spoken. (Laughter and whispering on the left.) We took steps to have them deported to France or elsewhere. We offered them admittance to our territory as an exceptional measure and they were received there. We even went so far as to give them assistance while taking the necessary precautions. We had recourse to these measures in order, as I said just now, to master the demagogic party we had defeated.

VARIOUS VOICES ON THE EXTREME LEFT : Republican ! You can be strong enough against the weak.

THE MINISTER FOR FOREIGN AFFAIRS : While we were taking these steps, confident that we were discharging a duty, we were conscious that we had a right as well. That right was, as I said just now, to prevent acts of violence from being committed under our eyes and almost through our own hands against certain persons. Nevertheless, I am bound to admit that several of the men whom we were thus protecting were not particularly deserving of our good will. Many of them were among those who having overthrown liberty at home did not allow us to restore it. (Ironical laughter on the left.)

Several of them had fought against us with the utmost violence and often unfairly : many of them after their defeat pursued us with insults, calumnies and contumely. Their friends scattered throughout Europe even now continue to attack our nation and its army. (Interruption from the left.)

A MEMBER ON THE LEFT : It is only you they are attacking.

THE MINISTER FOR FOREIGN AFFAIRS : Why did we want to shield and save them ? For a reason which everybody will understand. Because France could not surrender those she had defeated even though they were unworthy of her clemency.

ON THE LEFT : You must not insult them.

M. ANTOINE THOURET : What have you done with the Constituent Assembly ?

THE PRESIDENT : I wish the Monitor to place these interruptions and their character on record.

THE MINISTER FOR FOREIGN AFFAIRS : Those who are interrupting me would doubtless think it more patriotic to applaud the insults scattered throughout the vile pamphlets to which I have referred.

A VOICE FROM THE LEFT : They are directed against you, not against the army.

THE PRESIDENT : M. Pierre LEROUX and M. Pascal DUPRAT. I request you by name to be silent. You will have an opportunity to speak if you wish to, but do not interrupt.

VOICE ON THE RIGHT : Recall them to order.

THE MINISTER FOR FOREIGN AFFAIRS : They would no doubt think it even more patriotic to go and hiss our flag and our soldiers in some theatre or other.

ON THE LEFT : It is not the flag that is being hissed, it's the policy, the Ministry.

THE MINISTER FOR FOREIGN AFFAIRS : Not only did we ask that the acts to which I have referred should not be committed, but as His Holiness was not in Rome and his intentions might be misinterpreted we took steps to prevent them. It is in this sense that this dispatch sent on August 19th last to the General commanding our armies must be understood. " So long as we remain in Rome we cannot allow political violence to be committed under the very shadow of our flag."

There can be no question that we had the right to prevent them and we are determined to prevent them. Violence perpetrated against persons is one of the things which must not be permitted at any price. (Hear ! Hear !)

Subsequently, when the Commission of Cardinals introduced limitations to the amnesty granted by the Holy Father, we considered that we should immediately submit the following observations.

" Paris, September 30th.

" The Minister for Foreign Affairs to the Counsellor in Rome.

" The Government have taken note with pained surprise of the notice relating to the amnesty which the Commission of Cardinals saw fit to publish on the 18th of this month.

" Had the Commission refused to apply the amnesty promised

by the Holy Father to certain men who were particularly dangerous to public order we should have understood and approved. We did expect, however, that such persons would be few and would be mentioned by name in advance so as not to cause the others unnecessary apprehensions as to their fate. We were far from expecting that such numerous and ill-defined categories would be excluded from this act of clemency and prudence.

" I shall be glad if you will be so good as to represent to the Government of the Holy Father that an amnesty of this nature cannot fail to cause keen apprehension, continued unrest, profound resentment and great dangers and that it could not lead to the appeasement of the public temper and a voluntary return to law and order.

" In the interest of the Pontifical Power and the welfare of the Church, entreat it to reconsider this measure and radically to modify its principle and effect.

" The Holy Father who, as he himself so truly says, is inclined to mercy in virtue of his pontificial office, did not wish his benevolent intentions to be so inadequately carried out. When he announced an amnesty of this kind, he had no intention of making a vain promise. We appeal against his Government's decision to him personally. Represent to His Holiness with the filial respect we owe him but also with the firmness which is our duty and our right that France could not agree to be associated either directly or indirectly with the severe measures which such numerous exceptions foreshadow. France considers that they are diametrically opposed to one of the principal aims which the Catholic Powers had set themselves, namely the conciliation of the parties and the true pacification of the country." (Hear ! Hear !)

These, Gentlemen, are the demands we have respectfully laid before the Holy Father. (Ironical laughter on the left.)

THE PRESIDENT : You do not want anything to be respected, do you ?

M. HEECKEREN : They cannot bear us to be polite even.

THE MINISTER FOR FOREIGN AFFAIRS : I hope that our requests will be granted. I cherish this hope because I have faith in the word and the character of Pius IX, because in heeding our appeal he will be carrying out his great design—referred to by M. de Corcelles—to reconcile liberty with religion and to continue to play the lofty part he has so gloriously begun (ironical laughter on the left), this great part which has aroused so much enthusiasm and won him such noble support when at his first steps the whole of Europe acclaimed his efforts and on all sides, on this very tribune, eloquent

voices called out to him : " Courage, Holy Father, Courage."
(Shouts on the left.)

A MEMBER : That is M. Thiers.

MANY VOICES : Yes ! Yes ! Hear ! Hear !

THE MINISTER FOR FOREIGN AFFAIRS : I believe, there-
fore, that our plea will be heard. Some of the limitations introduced
in the amnesty have already been removed or modified in a sense
that is extremely favourable to those to whom it applies. In any case,
so far as it is possible to tell at present this Roman revolution which
began with violence and murder . . . (commotion on the left, shouts
of : " No, no, that is a libel " ;—on the right : " Yes, yes, quite
true, hear ! Hear ! ")

THE MINISTER FOR FOREIGN AFFAIRS : . . . which began
with violence and murder. (Renewed clamour and interpolations
on the left.)

M. TESTELIN : You lie ! (Oh ! Oh !)

MANY VOICES : Order ! Order ! (Continued commotion).

THE PRESIDENT : M. Testelin (Renewed shouts of Order !
Order !) Wait, Gentlemen, please.—(Then turning to the extreme
left.) M. Testelin, I have heard many interruptions from this side,
but they were simultaneous and I was waiting for the moment when
I should be able to recognize an individual voice saying things that
deserved censure. The word you have used is an insult and I call
you to order.

M. TESTELIN : I submit.

(On the right and in the Centre : Order ! Order !)

THE PRESIDENT : Instead of submitting you go on. For the
second time I call you to order, the fact to be entered in the ver-
batim record.

ON THE RIGHT : Hear ! Hear ! Censure !

On the left excited shouts and turbulence.

M. PASCAL DUPRAT rises and addresses the President, but in
the midst of the uproar it is impossible to hear what he says. Several
members of the extreme left appear for a moment on the point of
leaving the Chamber.

THE PRESIDENT : M. Duprat, you are not called upon to speak.
Please sit down and be silent. (M. Pascal Duprat sits down and calm
is restored.)

THE MINISTER FOR FOREIGN AFFAIRS : I have the most
profound contempt for such insults and I repeat that one thing is certain up to the present and that is that this revolution which began
with violence and bloodshed. . . . (Renewed shouts on the left : It
is not true.)

MANY VOICES : It is true. Hear ! Hear !

THE MINISTER FOR FOREIGN AFFAIRS : . . . which continued in the midst of violence and folly, has up to the present cost no man his liberty, his goods or his life for political reasons. That is the truth. When I remember—without wishing to allude to any particular incident—the more or less tragic events to which the restoration of former powers has given raise in recent times in Italy and elsewhere in Europe, when I think of all this I feel justified in declaring here and now that those whom we have defeated should thank Heaven. . . . (outcry on the left. On the right : Why, obviously !) . . . . I say that those we have defeated must thank Heaven that it was the arm of France that struck them and not that of another. (Lively applause on the right and in the centre.)

Gentlemen, I have said all I had to say. I have explained in the midst of interruptions which were, to say the least, uncalled for and certainly improper, the ideas and actions of French diplomacy. France and the Assembly will be the judges.

ON THE LEFT : Yes ! Yes !

ON THE RIGHT : Hear ! Hear !

(Lively applause from many sides.)

INDEX

A

ABDUL MEDJID, Sultan of Turkey (1823–1861), on question of Hungarian refugees, 295 sq.

d'Adel sward, in the National Assembly, 129

Ampère, Jean Jacques (1800–1864), character of, 69 sq.

Andrayne, in the Chamber of Deputies, 58.

Arago, Étienne, on the barricades, 305.

Austria, her relations with Hungary and Russia, 265.

—— Tsar's views on, 266.

Austrians, in Italy, 263.

—— submits to the influence of Russia, 279 (*foot-note*).

—— and Piedmont, 280.

—— demands Hungarian refugees from Turkey, 287.

B

BADEN, revolution put down in, 271.

—— Tocqueville interferes on behalf of the rebels (*foot-note*), 271 sq.

Banquets, the affair of, 16.

Banquet in Paris, forbidden by Government, 23 sq.

—— Rivet's statement in regard to, 306.

Barbès, Armand (1810–1870), in the National Assembly, 130 sq.

—— goes to the Hôtel de Ville, 134.

—— impeached by the Assembly, 138.

Barricades, the construction of, 38.

Barrot, Camille Hyacinthe Odilon (1791–1873), alliance of, with Thiers, 16 sq.

—— replies to Hébert in Chamber of Deputies, 23 sq.

—— recoils from Banquet in Paris, 25.

—— sent for by Louis-Philippe, 37.

—— on the Revolution, 47.

—— and the barricades, 59.

—— in Committee of Constitution, 193, 196, 199, 203.

—— tries to form a new Cabinet, 212 sq.

—— succeeds, 219.

—— with Beaumont, etc., 301.

—— his version of the abdication of Louis-Philippe, 304 sqq.

Bastide, gets the Assembly to appoint Cavaignac Military Dictator, 163.

Beaumont, Gustave de la Bonninière de (1802–1866), Tocqueville's conversation with, 33.

—— is sent for by Louis-Philippe, 36 sq.

—— tells Tocqueville of abdiction of Louis-Philippe, 46.

—— meets Tocqueville, 59.

—— sits with Tocqueville in National Assembly, 115.

—— in Committee of the Constitution, 201.

—— his interview with Tocqueville and political friends, 212.

—— sent as Ambassador to Vienna, 255.

—— letter of Tocqueville to, on the Hungarian refugees, 294 sq.

—— his account of the abdication of Louis-Philippe, 301 sqq.

Beaumont, Madame de, 33 sq.

Bedeau, General Marie Alphonse (1804–1863), 42.

—— character of 42.

—— nearly killed in Insurrection, 194.

—— his interview with Tocqueville and his political friends, 212.

Berryer, Pierre Antoine (1790–1868), his discussion with Tocqueville on the proposed Constitution, 309 sqq.

Billault, Auguste Adolphe Marie (1805–1863), in the Chamber of Deputies 59.

—— and banquets, 307.

Blanc, Jean Joseph Louis (1811–1882), in the National Assembly, 132 sq.

Blanqui, Louis Auguste (1805–1881), in the National Assembly, 130 sq.

Blanqui, Adolphe Jérôme (1798–1854), anecdote of, 157 sq.

Bloomfield, John Arthur Douglas Bloomfield, Lord (1802–1879), British Minister at St. Petersburg, 296.

—— snubbed by Nesselrode, *idem.*

325

INDEX

L

INDEX

—— his reflections on the course of history, 63 sq.
—— spends the evening with Ampère, 69 sq.
—— goes to inquire about his nephews on the 25th February, 72 sq.
—— walks about Paris in the afternoon, 73 sq.
—— reflections on what he sees, 74 sq.
—— keeps in retirement for some days, 82.
—— further reflections on the Revolution, 82 sqq.
—— his own individual feelings and intentions, 86 sqq.
—— resolves to seek re-election, 92.
—— visits the Department of la Manche, 93.
—— makes Valognes his headquarters, 95 sq.
—— his address to the electors, 96 sq.
—— meets the electors at Valognes, 97 sq.
—— addresses workmen at Cherbourg, 99.
—— goes to Saint-Lô to the General Council, 101.
—— his reflections on a visit to Tocqueville, 102 sq.
—— returns to Paris and finds himself elected, 105.
—— his view of the state of politics and of Paris, 105 sq.
—— National Assembly meets, 108 sq.
—— his opinion of the Montagnards, 111 sq.
—— his estimate of the Assembly, 114.
—— his estimate of the character of Lamartine, 117 sq.
—— his intercourse with Champeaux, 119 sq.
—— his observation of the popular mind, 128 sq.
—— his interview with Trétat, 134.
—— at the Feast of Concord, 141.
—— conversation with Carnot, 142 sq.
—— anticipations of the Insurrection of June, 147.
—— conversation with Madame Sand, 147 sq.
—— sees barricades of the Insurrection, 153.
—— interview with Lamorcière, 154 sq.

—— goes about Paris in time of insurrection, 156 sq.
—— describes the Assembly, 158 sq.
—— writes to his wife, 162.
—— protest against Paris being declared in a state of siege, 163 sq.
—— elected a Commissioner for Paris, 165.
—— as such, walks through Paris, 167 sqq.
—— his scene with his porter, 172 sq.
—— his scene with his man-servant, 174 sq.
—— in the streets in the Insurrection, 175 sq.
—— on his way to the Hôtel de Ville, 180.
—— appointed on the Committee of the Constitution, 186.
—— his narrative of its proceedings, 187 sqq.
—— on the duality of the Chambers, 193 sqq.
—— on the conditions of the Presidency 197 sq.
—— on principle of the irremovability of the judges, 202 sq.
—— re-elected for La Manche, 209.
—— leaves his wife ill at Bonn, 210.
—— his opinion of the new Assembly, 210 sq.
—— his interview with Dufaure, etc., 212.
—— ought he to enter the Ministry? 213.
—— accepts the Foreign Office, 217 sq.
—— intimacy with Lanjuinais, 217 sq.
—— his opinion of his colleagues, 221 sqq.
—— his opinion of France and the Republic, 224 sq.
—— his opinion of Louis Napoleon, 226 sqq.
—— speech in Assembly on the Roman expedition, 233.
—— his letters to and from Considérant 237 sq.
—— his view of affairs after the Insurrection, 239.
—— sends Lamoricière to Russia, 241.
—— his difficulties with Falloux and Dufaure, 243 sq.
—— his advice to Louis Napoleon, 251 sq.

331

INDEX

ALEXIS DE TOCQUEVILLE

Alexis Charles Henri Maurice Clérel de Tocqueville was born in Paris on July 29, 1805.

He entered government service, and in 1831 traveled to America to study the penal system. On his return he wrote DEMOCRACY IN AMERICA, *which was published in 1835 and immediately recognized as a masterpiece.*

He was active in politics, serving as Minister of Foreign Affairs in the government established after the Revolution of 1848. He retired from public life after the accession to power of Louis Napoleon, devoting his time to his RECOLLECTIONS *and to a study of the French Revolution, of which he completed only the first volume,* THE OLD REGIME AND THE FRENCH REVOLUTION.

Alexis de Tocqueville died in Cannes on April 16, 1859.

J. P. Mayer, the editor of this volume, is also editor-in-chief of the French edition of Tocqueville's collected works. He is the author of a number of books in politics and sociology.

MERIDIAN BOOKS

Social Sciences, Psychology, and Anthropology

MERIDIAN BOOKS

History

Meridian Documents of American History

Meridian Books are published by The World Publishing Company, Cleveland and New York. For a free Meridian catalogue write to Dept. AM, Meridian Books, 119 West 57th Street, N.Y.

MERIDIAN BOOKS

Philosophy

Meridian Books are published by The World Publishing Company, Cleveland and New York. For a free Meridian catalogue write to Dept. AM, Meridian Books, 119 West 57th Street, N.Y.

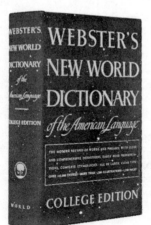